DELAYING THE REAL WORLD

BY COLLEEN KINDER

RUNNING PRESS
PHILADELPHIA · LONDON

9   8   7   6   5   4
Digit on the right indicates the number of this printing

Library of Congress Control Number: 2004095065

ISBN-13 978-0-7624-2189-3
ISBN-10 0-7624-2189-4

Cover and interior design by Dustin Summers
Edited by Jennifer Kasius
Typography: Gotham and Knockout

This book may be ordered by mail from the publisher.
Please include $2.50 for postage and handling.
But try your bookstore first!

Running Press Book Publishers
125 South Twenty-second Street
Philadelphia, Pennsylvania 19103-4399

Visit us on the web!
www.runningpress.com

CONTENTS

INTRODUCTION

You've got this pearl of a decade in front of you: THE TWENTIES. This is the prime of your life! You've been on a straight educational path since you learned to tie your shoes, and now suddenly you've got a diploma, enough energy to run the length of the globe, and all of the freedom in the world. So how are you going to spend the glorious days of your independent youth?

In a cubicle, perhaps? Filing papers, or maybe crunching numbers? How about answering phones and scheduling meetings?

WRONG! Now is the time to do exactly what *you* want to do and fulfill your wildest dreams. Don't be in such a rush to become boring! Let the early years be more unconventional and experimental. Try things you might never have the chance to do again. When else in life will you have such freedom? If you wait for retirement, the experience won't be nearly as cool. A thousand fleeting opportunities are waiting for you, and there is nothing holding you back from taking your pick. A year of teaching in Brazil? How about working on a vineyard in New Zealand? Or maybe biking across the U.S. strikes your fancy. From event planning at a Las Vegas resort to counseling at a wilderness camp for homeless children, you have such a rich variety of options you won't know where to start. Fortunately, you did the right thing and bought this little book. It's the perfect tool for beginning your hunt.

Every chapter has a handful of stories from young people who have done wildly inspiring things and lived to tell about them. So if it seems like *everyone* around you is doing the same 9-5 routine, let the spirited tales of these adventurers knock your socks off and give you a taste of what you too could do with a leap of faith. Pick one of the delicious options on the pages ahead and you'll be the envy of all your suit-wearing friends.

The coolest thing about any adventure you choose is that it will be a valuable experience and may even catapult you into a future career. You can never go wrong in doing what you love, because it will only lead you further into your passion. Anyone who says doing the Peace Corps in Botswana or acting in a Shakespeare festival is a waste of time needs to crawl back into their office space. Every experience in this book has the potential to be enriching, useful, and even life-altering. To ease any doubts you may have, the "Keeping it Real" sections at the end of each chapter highlight ways that your chosen post-college adventure will be constructive for your future.

So read on, dream big, be gutsy, and make your twenties the sweetest decade of your life.

TEN PILLARS OF DELAYING THE REAL WORLD
(ACCORDING TO SUCCESSFUL DISCIPLES)

Throughout this book you'll come across quotes and anecdotes from twentysomethings who have played their independence the right way and taken off running down the road less traveled. The tales and tips of these wise young folks echo one another and all point to a few crucial bits of advice. Follow these great pillars and you'll be off to an impeccable start in life.

1. THOU SHALL NOT RUSH IN VAIN.

This is a crucial truth to get through your antsy little mind. Repeat after me: THERE IS NO RUSH! Many of the young adventurers who contributed to this book mentioned how they were initially nervous about "taking a year off" while peers dove into the real world. They later saw that they hadn't missed a beat and could pick right back up in Normalville (if they wanted to, that is).

In the meantime, while everyone else had mastered PowerPoint, they'd gained invaluable experience out in the wide world that helped them sort out their goals. Considering you will likely retire in your late sixties, isn't rushing into a monotonous grind a bit silly?

2. REMEMBER WHAT YEAR YOU'RE LIVING IN AND KEEP IT HOLY.

In order to make a good decision today you don't have to know what you want to do twenty years from now. Throw the question "What should I do with my life?" to the dogs and just handle your next step as a twentysomething. Take a minute to imagine a situation in which you might thrive, rise to challenges, and feel satisfied every day that you work. Sound easier than charting your entire professional career? Just a bit.

3. THOU SHALL NOT COVET THY NEIGHBOR'S SALARY.

Trust me, it's not worth envying. Most people who get high paying jobs right out of college end up giving up their lives in exchange for money that they don't have time to spend. Don't emulate your peers unless you admire them. My first year out of college, it was plainly clear that the big money makers were exhausted and miserable while those scraping by to do something satisfying were much happier. Be willing to live on less and you'll buy yourself priceless freedom.

4. VARY, VARY, NOT THE CONTRARY!

Don't think everything you do has to be neatly related to your background and future goals. Having a diverse array of experiences can be even more impressive than a perfectly coordinated resume. The earlier you diversify and dabble in a number of areas and jobs, the quicker you will find your way to what you really love. Once there, your previous stints will come in handy. You might bring to the table expertise that no one else in your venue can provide. Never hesitate to vary.

5. BLESSED ARE THE ADVENTUROUS, THEY WILL STAY THAT WAY
(AND THEN INHERIT THE EARTH!)

Don't underestimate the power of momentum. One pattern I've noticed among peers is that people who start off their twenties doing interesting things usually keep right on doing them, and likewise, the straight and narrow typically (and tragically) remain straight and narrow. The odds get worse with every passing year, poor folks. My theory was confirmed when I emailed young adventurers to gather tips and anecdotes. My token Alaskan wilderness tour guide was now finishing a novel and planning a volunteer vacation in Belarus (and by the way, did she mention she was in the Peace Corps and hitchhiked across Ireland?). My poster child for around-the-world travel was currently job hunting in Boston, but P.S.-Ed that he would be in Havana (where I was, delaying the real world myself) for an educational trip next week and might I want to meet up for a mojito? Let the serial adventurers of this book illuminate the power of momentum for you. Do yourself a favor this year and it may just last for life. Most people who have interesting jobs got them by doing interesting things first.

6. **"A JOURNEY OF A THOUSAND MILES BEGINS WITH A SINGLE GOOGLE SEARCH,"** said one insightful contributor to this book, and she couldn't be more right. You can access millions of opportunities and acquaint yourself with just about any organization or potential employer through the Internet. In fact, your real challenge will not be finding enough information, but sifting through the excess of it. The best approach is to copy and paste all of the information that appeals to you onto one word document. Once you are through web browsing, you can format the document to your liking and compare all of the options you have amassed. For example, a global volunteer program that was the first link on your web search might have a $6,000 program fee. A similar organization listed a few pages later in your search results might actually pay *you* a monthly stipend. Laying all of the information out on one printable document will also gather all phone numbers and contact details in one place. Once you start eliminating some possibilities and focusing in on others, you can easily highlight and write notes in the margins of your printed record (i.e. "Called and spoke to director. Said to call back Tuesday.") Make things easy for yourself from the beginning.

7. IF IT SEEMS LIKE A LONG SHOT, THEN DEFINITELY SHOOT LONG.

One of the most remarkable things about the success stories in this book is that many of them came about through a move that seemed impossibly ambitious at first, then all too easy when it actually worked. Take Arianne, for example. She was web browsing late one night and came across an English-language newspaper in Cambodia that piqued her interest. While others might have assumed the publication was large (since the website was fancy) and that the editors would think she was a little American punk if she contacted them without reason (like a job posting), Arianne decided she had nothing to lose. The publication might have been a three-man operation for all she knew! She shot the editor a carefully crafted email and he got back to her in minutes with an eager reply: We'd love to have you! Remember, people don't always publicize their needs. If you cold-call or email someone and display your passion for their line of work, they are likely to be impressed by you. Pay attention to how many of the contributors to this book made their plans a reality by taking a step that most other people wouldn't even consider. Always reach farther than you think you can.

8. IF MONEY IS STANDING IN YOUR WAY, PLOW IT DOWN.

You will notice that many of the young dreamers featured in the pages ahead faced serious financial difficulties. If you are like most young'ns and don't have a penny to your name, you'll just have to search a bit harder, send out a dozen more applications or resumes, and log in more hours of grunt work before making your grand plans a reality. There is no adventure listed in this book, perhaps with the exception of the pricey trek up Mount Everest, that could not be financed through some hard core minimum wage work or temping. There are also plenty of cool jobs, internships, and volunteer programs that offer loan deferment and financial aid. Don't let money be your excuse to be lame; take it as a challenge.

9. JUST...DO IT.

Could that sound any simpler? Yet it's by far the hardest step: actually carrying out those plans that seem too good to be true. This book can inspire your pants off, but in the end, it's up to you to score... *[ahem]*, the mind-blowing job,

I mean. The stories ahead illustrate how things have a tendency to fall in place once you take the first leap of faith. Moving abroad, for example, seems like such a drastic life decision that we want to have everything perfectly in place before buying the ticket. However, many young adventurers said it didn't so much matter what they set up, but that they went ahead and made the move. Once in a foreign country, you can navigate through the opportunities much more easily and countless doors open. Of course it's a good idea to do your homework, but don't let the logistics keep you from committing to what you really want to do. Make a promise to yourself first—write it down if you think it will help—*then* dive into the practical questions of how you are going to make it happen. Be ready to act before you know exactly what you are getting yourself into.

10. REDEFINE REAL

In one way or another, every contributor to this book expressed that their adventures exposed them to a world more real than any fluorescent-lighted cubicle could have. They all swear by the value of what they pursued and insist they are fuller, more knowledgeable, worldlier people for doing something "a little different" than their peers. And lastly—the best test of a good decision—none of them have a regret to speak of. Neither will you.

CHAPTER ONE: HOME IS WHERE THE HIGH LIFE IS

I F YOU ARE LOOKING FOR A NEW and challenging experience, situating yourself in the right place is a key first step. The real estate mantra doesn't lie—location *is* everything! The right atmosphere and living situation are crucial ingredients to crafting your ideal experience. By plopping yourself down in a fabulous hotspot, you will guarantee that your every waking minute is a blast. It may be a leap of faith to pick up and move to whatever place is calling your name, but if you accompany the leap with some thoughtful planning and creative resourcefulness, things will fall into place just fine.

When college comes to a close, people tend to fall victim to the isolating mentality that *everyone* is doing such-and-such a thing or *everyone* will be in so-and-so City (as if it were really possible that a nation full of young people in pinstripe suits could descend on St. Louis for accounting jobs). It's important not to let this idea mislead you. First of all, people scatter and diversify more than you expect. It just happens that while boring commitments are lined up months in advance, you don't hear about brave moves and wild pursuits until they're underway, if ever at all. Besides, even if everyone and their mother became traveling salesmen, why should that make you doubt your alternative interests for a millisecond?

There will never be a better time to pick up and go. You are young, curious, and have loads of energy to pour into the place of your choice. Not to mention the fact that you are kidless, jobless, and totally autonomous—you may never again be this portable! So don't be afraid to let your thoughts creep beyond city or state boundaries and flirt with the idea of moving to a distant corner of this enormous country. Is there a place that makes your eyebrows jump every time you hear mention of its lifestyle or read of its distinct charm? With vibrant cities and enchanting towns of all locales and sizes to choose from, you will have no trouble finding a destination that fits your young heart's desires.

WHETTING YOUR APPETITE . . .

• Road trip to southern California, settle down where the sun always shines and get a job at the San Diego Zoo leading children's educational camps.

• Work at a comedy club, cozy café, or for an up-and-coming magazine in New York City.

• Do a year-long teaching fellowship at a high school in Hawaii.

• Lead outdoor adventure trips for a retreat center in the Ozarks.

• Score an internship at your dream organization or for your ideal employer.

• Plan events for a hotel in Las Vegas, putting together social events for the city's diverse conventions.

• Do a year-long fellowship on hunger and poverty in Jackson, Mississippi.

• Work as a safari driver for Alaska Wildland Adventures and navigate through trails of pristine national parks, or be a radio DJ for a local station in Nome, Alaska.

HELPFUL WEBSITES:

Craig's List: *(www.craigslist.org)* Listings of everything from apartments, room-mates, jobs, classifieds, and community events from Honolulu to London.

Cost of living calculator: *(www.cityrating.com/costofliving.asp)* Compare the cost of living in different U.S. cities.

City Search: *(www.citysearch.com)* In-depth information by city and neighborhood (entertainment, restaurants, careers, personals, "best of the city," real estate, shopping).

AOL City Guide: *(www.digitalcity.com)* Information on restaurants, entertainment, events and more.

Monstertrak: *(www.monstertrak.com)* A helpful employment finder.

URBAN LIVING: FINDING THAT CITY THAT NEVER SLEEPS

Cities can be paradise for recent college graduates because of their high concentration of twentysomethings, the energetic feel of their bustling streets, and the sheer quantity of diversions they provide to keep you constantly stimulated and on the go. The metropolis of your choice will place you in the heart of all the action and offer you all of the necessary elements to create your lifestyle of choice.

A KICKIN' CROWD:

If you are not ready to say goodbye to the dating pool and nightlife options of your college years, you're in luck. We young people make things very easy by flocking to the same areas. There are a handful of thriving U.S. cities that have become meccas for the young and the restless. Cities like Atlanta and Chicago have been known to draw hordes of twentysomethings.

" I always thought I knew what I wanted to do after college: move back home and settle into the place where I wanted to spend the rest of my life. Little did I know, this was basically saying, 'Nah, I'd rather not enjoy the years of my life when I'm young, in good health, and still without the responsibilities of serious relationships or kids. Can't I just move onto my early thirties?' Thank goodness Jesuit Volunteer Corps had something else in mind for me.

JVC placed me in San Francisco, a city that I previously had little to no interest in. They assigned me to work at a public interest law firm where I coordinated their free legal clinic for low-income and homeless people. The JVC package also included 'communal living,' which meant sharing a three-bedroom house with seven strangers who were all doing similar jobs. Did I mention I was paid $85 a month? You would be surprised how creative and resourceful eight twentysomethings can be when they are down to their last $10.

Being thrown into an unfamiliar situation with no money forced me get out and search the city. Though San Francisco has a high cost of living and my income did limit me in some ways, there is a strong grassroots subculture that allows those who are short on cash to still experience all it has to offer. There are free plays, concerts, rallies, and operas. Most take place in amazing outdoor parks.

San Francisco is the most liberal place I have ever been to. Despite a more conservative background, I found myself marching in rallies, signing up to campaign for my favorite candidate and attending informational sessions on workers' rights. Two years later, I'm still living here, and my passionate, yet slightly eccentric side has not worn off. Moving away from home at a time when I was most vulnerable was also the time I was most willing to learn about new things. "

And it's the type of young crowd a city draws that ultimately shapes the character of the nightlife. Once you have figured out what type of person resides in your prospective city, it won't be hard to get an idea for what the social style of the city is. Seattle has its pull on the environmentally-conscious coffee shop lover, while gentrified Boston brings in yuppie business types who enjoy a good Irish pub-crawl. Liberality and diversity are distinguishing factors in a city's young population as well. Minneapolis has a large gay population and New York City has representatives from nearly every ethnic group on the planet. Do a little neighborhood hunting to find your niche within the big city. You are bound to find the youthful flavor that suits you.

"Take advantage of this commitment-free time to start identifying your passions and your dislikes, to use your brain in ways untouched by academics, and as cliché as it sounds, to make the world your classroom. Go see the world. Bypass the rush of college graduates that scurry into the job market with unchecked enthusiasm and desire for stability and income. Going your own way will put you on a valuable path that will enhance your knowledge of yourself, test your skills, further refine your interests and undoubtedly, increase your marketability in the work world (should you choose to enter it!)."

—Alejandra Lopez-Fernandini, 25

TOP TEN CITIES FOR YOUNG PEOPLE:

1. Austin
2. Boston
3. San Francisco
4. Chicago
5. Washington, D.C.
6. New York City
7. Seattle
8. Charlotte
9. Denver-Boulder
10. Minneapolis

CHARM: Let's be honest, some places just have it. Whether it's with a breathtaking waterfront, a bustling Chinatown, or a historic baseball stadium, there are a number of U.S. cities that can allure you at first glance. Who could help but leave their heart in San Francisco after trucking up Lombard Street? Or not be wowed by ol' New Orleans after experiencing the madness of Mardi Gras? Once you get past the steaming sewers and packed street life of the Big Apple you'll find a lot to love in New York City's energy and diversity. Whether you prefer the aesthetic of skyscrapers or cobblestone alleys, there is a match out there for you.

"I highly recommend moving to a random city, especially if you are taking one year before graduate school or some other big change. I think that you end up meeting more people and doing more crazy things when you have the mentality that you're only in a place for one year and you're trying to make the most of it. I have gone on dates with the most random people. Dating is actually a great way to get to know different parts of a city. When you go out with someone who is from the area, he or she will probably share local secrets and hotspots with you while trying to impress."

—Brigid Boland, 22

NATURAL ATTRACTIONS: While living in a cool metropolis can provide enough around-the-clock diversions for any young adventurer, an urban location could also serve as a springboard to the great outdoors. Boulder, Colorado offers its inhabitants not only a view of Rocky Mountain ridges from just about anywhere in town, but also accessible terrain for hiking and a load of other adventure sports. You can trek through the foothills at 6 AM and be at work by 9 AM, not to mention the fact that ski slopes are just a car ride away. So all you outdoorsy types, look closely and you may be surprised to discover what natural jewels lie in a city's own backyard. Since not all of us have wheels, a sizable park within the city limits is a huge bonus.

ARTS & ENTERTAINMENT: If a beer and a bar stool aren't enough to hold you, a thriving cultural scene may be the essential ingredient in making your city stay rich and unforgettable. Washington, D.C. is rife with free museums and historical monuments, Santa Fe draws artisans by the dozens to its vibrant bohemian atmosphere and you can't throw a stone in New York City without hitting a tattooed artist or musical denizen of one of the city's many subcultures. So check it out, and keep in mind that ethnic and cultural diversity are key components in any city's art scene. Furthermore, just as universities bring bars, they also bring theater, conferences, speakers, readings, and other cultural and educational events.

"I didn't really delay the real world (unless you count the two months after college that I worked at a grocery store—nothing like a college degree to do price checks on detergent and make your parents really proud!). Instead, I started working for a major news magazine right out of school. Had I known what it was going to be like, though, I definitely would have done something sort of different—like volunteering or traveling. I still toy with the idea of taking off to another country, but even seriously thinking about moving to another city seems impossible. Whether you make $25,000 or $125,000 a year, you become very set in your ways and it is so much scarier to part from that consistent paycheck. Three years ago I wouldn't have thought about it twice. Actually, the week before I got the magazine job I was all set to move to Boston—no job, no money—but then I got the offer and thought it was the best thing for my career. While it was definitely good, I sort of regret not taking that adventure. I think it is really important to feel independent at this point in your life—financially, emotionally, in whatever way you need."

—Emily Cerow, 24

LOCALE: Your hometown or city is probably the most comfortable place in the world for you, but you never know how much more exciting things can get until you take a little risk. The United States is rich with regional flavors to chose from: the easy-going West Coast spirit, sun-belt conservatism, or East Coast intensity. America is big enough to give you a case of culture shock within its borders! A Southern belle in Vermont, a New Yorker in North Dakota, an Iowa farm boy turned San Diego surfer—mixing it up could be a quite a kick (for both you and all those lucky souls who stumble upon you!).

"If you have the opportunity, live somewhere outside the state or region where you grew up and don't be wedded to a particular location. I'm kind of a wanderer myself, but the chance to learn about a different place and different kinds of people is valuable for anyone. And don't worry if you aren't living where you dreamed about. I really had my sights set on New York City but ended up in D.C. I'm having a great time and I'd be happy to live here for at least a few more years."

—Nathan Littlefield, 22

WHY THE BURBS CAN WAIT:

"I would definitely nominate Madison, Wisconsin for a "cool place to live." Madison is a liberal enclave in the otherwise traditional Midwest. It is politically active, culturally rich, down-to-earth, and friendly. The city itself is situated on an isthmus between two beautiful lakes, the Mendota and Monona. Its waterfront location is ideal for outdoor activities, and its size (not too big but not too small) is conducive to lots of funky coffee shops, independent theaters and bookstores, and every variety of bar imaginable. Madison also has a very thriving youth culture, consisting of everyone from students to hippies, young professionals to musicians. I moved here knowing no one, and three years later I'm very hesitant to leave!"
—Susan Gloss, 25

"Charleston, SC is an amazing place to live or visit. It's full of history, very socially active, and has a lot of southern hospitality. Charleston offers great weather, proximity to the beach, lots of young people and diversity. The nightlife is lively, as are the festivals. Don't forget world class golf (Ryder Cup), art and great architecture. There is also a huge teaching hospital and many graduate programs."
—Justin Bagby, 25

"There aren't very many places in the world where you'll see twentysomething women walking around malls with small dogs in their purses. Los Angeles is one of them. Leaving the house in your pajama pants or, for that matter, a pair of old jeans and a T-shirt is a fashion faux pax. In spite of the superficiality of the place, I have to say that it feels oh-so-good to wear flip-flops year-round after bundling up on the East Coast. The California (and southern California, at that) sun never fails to shine. And California's people are of a more laid back variety than the frenzied folks of the East."
—Ruchika Budhraja, 22

"The people who are drawn to work in D.C. come to pursue their passion about a cause—something bigger than themselves. I'm surrounded by people with interesting jobs. Virtually no one can summarize their position with a one word title like 'banker.' Most peoples' response to 'So what do you do?' entails three paragraphs, a description of some interesting issue or cause, and a glimpse of their idealism. And it usually leads to a lively conversation!"

—Molly Kinder, 24

"I don't really think you can beat NYC. It's expensive, but there's a reason. It's a totally amazing place to live. It's such a fun time, especially before you're married and want a family."

—Sarah Smith, 22

"San Diego is a mecca for young people who love the outdoors and the beach: surfers, roller bladers, skaters, beach volleyball players. There are huge strips of beach front that are completely inhabited by young people."

—Libby Salloway, 34

"Austin is a thriving college town, spewing a ridiculous amount of unique cultural and social activities on its residents. For fresh college graduates, Austin offers something for nearly every personality. For me, the adventurous, do-all-I-possibly-can-while-I'm-here type, the eight months I spent in Austin were all about trying new restaurants, hitting up as many bars as I could, trying as many outdoor activities as possible, and embracing the eclectic cultural vibe that resonates from Congress Ave to the Hill Country. Austin also has a claim on the title the 'Live Music Capital of the World.'"

—Brian O'Connor, 24

"Phoenix has no winters, period. Yeah, summers are hot, but you adapt quickly. It also offers great outdoor recreation such as hiking, camping and mountain biking, cool nightlife, tons of Indian casinos, major sports, and a pretty affordable cost of living."

—Mike Kroeger, 28

"Chicago has so much to offer young people. The fast and furious nature of the city (and the wind!) will knock you down, and the friendly Midwestern people will pick you right up. The beauty of the city lies in its ethnic neighborhoods. Meandering down the streets, you hear Polish and can snack on a pierogi or a Serbian sarma. The city's charm is also in the influential architecture and the giant public art, as well as the music festivals that run all summer long—jazz, blues, country and gospel."

—Raul Romo, 27

"So, you like to hike, bike, run trails, ski, fish, hunt, ride white water and play ultimate frisbee? Do mild winters (OK, relative to the rest of the state) and a proximity to Glacier and Yellowstone National Parks sound appealing? Missoula, Montana is your place. In return for this nice quality of life and warm, active community you could give something back by working or volunteering with the many social service organizations assisting the transient and struggling populations. You can also look for opportunities with the National Park Service, tourist companies for outdoor summer trips or nearby ski resorts."

—Alejandra Lopez-Fernandini, 26

COST OF LIVING: If you want to settle into the heart of everything, keep in mind that a price tag will be attached. Unfortunately, the most desirable cities in the U.S. tend to be the most expensive. Rent and food in New York City, for example, cost more than twice what they might in, say, Kansas City. If you think a city home is worth the steep bills, make sure to read over the tips in the next section about how to afford the urban high life. Of course, if your financial outlook is just too grim, don't fret. There are plenty of cities out there that won't suck every penny from your piggy bank. Louisville (KY), Indianapolis (IN), Baltimore (MD), Philadelphia (PA), Baton Rouge (LA), Portland (ME), Memphis (TN), and Cleveland (OH) are on the less expensive side.

"Don't let college loans ruin your life. You have no idea what the future will bring, and to bring the right future, you have to follow your heart. Spend a lot of time thinking about cost of living in different cities. You might be better off with a modest-paying job in Ohio than a higher salaried job in New York."

—Melissa Blakeley, 22

Practical Tip: When investigating your cosmopolitan pickings, pay special attention to exactly where people live in a given city. The young people in sprawled out cities like L.A. or Atlanta don't concentrate in a single downtown neighborhood, so you'll have to seek them out, and most likely, invest in an automobile.

MAKING IT HAPPEN

So you want it all. Late-night pubs, spicy ethnic restaurants and ocean side boardwalks are infiltrating your dreams and making your current place of residence look about as cool as a high school cafeteria. You've got your perfect city recipe and are ready to get cookin'. Great, but just hold up a sec. The instructions are still coming.

Residential Perks: If you are moving to a city where you don't have any friends to crash with and you haven't exactly scrounged up enough funds to pay a rent check, consider applying to be a resident advisor at a university summer program. Many colleges run programs from June through August and need help managing the young people and international students that descend on their campuses. Such jobs often provide free room and board and could buy you some time to get the apartment and job hunt underway. I almost accepted a counselor position in Columbia's summer program because it was the only way I could even consider moving to NYC without a job (and yes, the whole business of getting a broker and signing a lease just really intimidated me). Sometimes, the biggest moves are much easier to make when you allow yourself some baby steps. A friend of mine found a position as a resident advisor at an all-boys prep school just outside of Washington D.C. Not long after he moved into the dorm, he found a job in the city and now has his ideal set-up (free housing, proximity to job and city, non-stop video games).

If you don't have a job lined up in your urban dreamland, your mind may already be reeling with visions of sleeping on park benches and subway *a cappella* singing. Before you resign yourself to abject poverty, give a thought to delaying your move until you have a substantial nest egg to take with you. Though there is a lot to say for just taking a plunge, you might also want to consider spending a summer in your hometown doing your traditional job routine so that your savings can pile up. Take advantage of free rent on Mom and Dad, fewer costly nights on the town and the lucrative summer job market. Landscape by day, wait tables by night and before the leaves fall you will have a small fortune to get you on your way.

PLAYING IT PRACTICALLY

"Make sure you have health insurance. This is a must—even if you have to buy it yourself. I have a friend who didn't have insurance her first year out of school and she ended up paying to go to the emergency room for stomach problems. After tests, medications, and hospital care, she is paying a couple thousand dollars off to the hospital. Even just minimal insurance that covers emergency room visits is a good idea."
—Emily Wright, 22

"Acquire every newspaper you can get your hands on. This will give you information on housing and jobs. Call every place you can until you've found what you want. You may want to check and find out when exactly the online classifieds are updated. The main one in my city changed every Tuesday at 3 PM. If you waited until Wednesday to act, it was already too late to snag the best listings."
—Sean Ford, 25

"If you arrive in a new place and are just getting started, try to find out if your college has any sort of community of alumni there—whether it be a loose group of people or a formal club. Those that stay connected and involved in these groups are the ones most likely to help you out in making connections and figuring out where to live. If you belonged to a national fraternity or sorority this might be an even more cohesive and helpful network."
—Ryan Milkowsky, 26

"If anyone wants to move to a new area, Craig's List is the best resource around (*www.craigslist.org*). I know a couple of guys who drove out to California from the East Coast and found an apartment, furniture, and jobs all on Craig's List. I also bought a car off of the listings. Talk about a place to find everything."
—Emily Wright, 22

"If you don't plan on having a regular job for a few years, open an IRA and put a few hundred dollars in every year. Retirement may seem light years away, but you will lose out big (thousands of dollars) in the long run if you start putting aside funds at 26 instead of 22."

—Jonathan Singer, 29

WHAT SHALL WE DO?

Once you have arrived in the big city, take stock of your full range of occupational options—from your "reach" jobs to your "safeties." Perhaps your ideal employer is right there in the heart of the city center—a shiny skyscraper that twinkles at you every time you pass by on the highway. Maybe you've never been closer to that record label headquarters, avant-garde publication, legendary sports team, or renowned non-profit, but you can't even *dream* of being hired by them until you have two more decades of schooling, five doctorates, and three best-selling books. But hey, don't fret! They'd be glad to take you on as an unpaid intern! Honestly, this is how the system sometimes works. You offer your basic services and get to spend your days close to the action, breathing the same air as your gods, and gleaning wisdom from their example.

Some people don't have the patience for positions on the bottom of the professional totem pole. However, if it inspires you just to be a part of this organization's mission and work, and you can negotiate some sort of reasonable work arrangement (like half-days), then it may be worth logging in some salary-less hours. A few things could happen:

1. You get an inside peek into a world of creators and makers or movers and shakers and walk away with a solid idea of what you want to do, and just as importantly, what you *don't* want to do.

2. Your co-workers notice your meager brown bag lunches and take pity. The organization scrounges up some kind of "stipend" to lessen your financial burden, and thanks-be-to-Santa, health benefits come your way.

3. You get your foot in the door, your passion impresses the heck out of them, a dream job opens up, and voila! You're the first one that comes to mind. Work your magic.

4. You not only rub elbows with hotshots and personal heroes, but you find a clan of young entry-levelers and interns. Happy Hour is now the highlight of your week and you can't imagine life without these friends that share your passion. They form your network—both social and professional—in the years to come.

5. You bow out gracefully after a short stint but have a sure-fire conversation piece for future interviews about the time you alphabetized the photo collection of that genius, canvassed for that bright, young congressman, or fielded press phone calls for that controversial NGO.

Perhaps the most valuable thing about an internship is its brevity. You get to test out a work environment in a concentrated chunk of time without making a commitment to an organization or company. I did a short internship right after college that not only handed me valuable experience and contacts, but also gave me the chance to release all of my post-graduation nerves and to temper that irrational need for stability. By the end of June, I had already realized that there was no rush to pen myself up in an office. Practically all of my co-workers had dabbled in numerous jobs before ending up at our organization. I left for a year overseas more confident in my choice to do something unconventional.

"There's Only One Place I'd Work For Nothing . . ."

Read what these former interns have to say about their unpaid, but most impassioned labor. Monica Lewinsky couldn't be contacted, but we all know how that went.

"After five months of living with my parents and looking for work, I knew my sanity was at stake if the stagnant gray matter in my head didn't get a jump start—and soon. I finally settled for an internship in the Asia Division of Human Rights Watch in Washington, D.C. For almost six months I interned four days a week and was not only introduced to the world of human rights, but also to the wild world of advocacy in our nation's capital. I took on all sorts of tasks, from sweeping the daily news for relevant stories, to attending Congressional briefings alongside the likes of Colin Powell and Richard Gere. Granted, the gig assumed a less glamorous face on the evenings and weekends when I morphed into a waitress at the local diner (and never mind the countless hours in between searching for full-time employment!). All that said, the course I took was a blessing in disguise. I learned so much about the field of human rights, unabashedly collecting on my free labor by asking as many questions as possible. And had my supervisor, the Division's Associate, decided to leave her post, I was a top candidate to replace her. Instead, my internship helped land me my current job at Oxfam."

—Stephanie Linakis, 24

"When the *Village Voice* offered me an unpaid internship with one of their city/state editors, I couldn't help but accept. Though I had to dip into my funds to survive in dear old New York City, my internship at arguably the nation's best alternative newspaper has since repaid itself tenfold. My editor was straight out of the old school of New York journalists: belligerent, populist and casual in his dress. He was as loyal and passionate about the dreams of his young intern charges as he was about the city itself. I worked late hours poring through New York healthcare records obtained through the Freedom of Information Act. I followed hunches that led us to crooked healthcare companies hidden inside legit businesses. And I felt the thrill of success when the subject of our investigation called the office to run spin control. I left the summer very happy, with much improved writing and research skills, and excellent contacts among like-minded young journalists. Lastly, I walked away with the knowledge that New York and journalism—at least for me—might just be *it*."

—Chris Heaney, 22

"I got a summer internship at VH1 in New York City through my friend's older sister who worked for the company. On my first day in the notorious Times Square high rise, I proudly weeded my way through the screaming teens cheering for 98 Degrees (the pop group—not the Manhattan June sun)—who were appearing that day on Total Request Live and into the internship orientation. Although I did my fair share of filing and answering phones, I also had some unforgettable experiences that would make any film student salivate. I spent one morning with a scantily clad Mariah Carey in her dressing room at the *Today Show* for a *VH1 Save the Music* piece. After the summer ended, I was elated to receive a call informing me that an assistant position was opening up in the VH1 Los

Get out there and present yourself to your dream employer. It is safe to assume that every one is accessible to you as long as you present yourself well when contacting them. Think through every email you compose very carefully. We young kids tend to be more conversational in our emails (IM's curse), while older professionals expect email correspondence to be just as formal and flawless as letters. Proofread. Heed spell check's squiggly lines of caution! Make the effort to tailor your resume to each specific organization or line of work. Be creative when trying to make yourself stand out. Show them why you are an ideal fit for them. Go the extra mile, and then another. For example, send a thank-you note to an interviewer or spend an hour researching the organization you are smitten with. You may be surprised how eager even the most well-known and prestigious organizations are to scoop up an enthusiastic young person.

I'LL TAKE THE DELUXE INTERNSHIP,
SUPERSIZED STUDIO APARTMENT, AND A SIDE ORDER OF MANUAL LABOR TO AFFORD IT, PLEASE.

"WAIT!" you say. "So what if I'm a part of something I believe in? I am totally broke! I can't even afford a haircut!" Simmer down, simmer down. First of all, haircuts are overrated. Ask that artistic friend of yours for a quick favor and she'll have you all sheered in a snip. You'll even get compliments, I promise. Second of all, there are plenty of ways a young person with enough schedule flexibility, ingenuity, and energy to spare can make a living. If you are willing to put in time during evenings and weekends, the city's entertainment industry offers a bevy of jobs to choose from. So before you go joining the ranks of burger flippers just to make rent, consider finding a service job that is in some way connected to your interests, or will be at least stimulating.

Think about what makes your chosen city so fabulous; what bit of charm enticed you there? Once you have your finger on that, try to come up with a way to turn that cool thing into an employment opportunity. Bartend on Bourbon Street, care for the darling sea creatures at Monterey Bay Aquarium, ride a bicycle-taxi through downtown Orlando, or landscape the turf at Wrigley Field. Find a way to relish the flavor and ambiance of your city while making money off of it at the same time.

> "I am working as an organizer of the San Antonio New World Wine and Food Festival and truly could not imagine a better first job. Unlike a standard entry-level position at a bank or firm, I have a flexible schedule and a very independent role. It is also a very exciting job for me because I am passionate about the food and wine industry. I helped bring in famous chefs from Sante Fe, Scottsdale, all over Texas, Mexico, Australia, South Africa, New Zealand, and Chile. I would highly suggest that recent grads go for unconventional jobs. Compared to my friends who are in business, legal, or advertising positions, I feel like I am much more inspired by what I do."
> —Elizabeth Arno, 22

If you're working nights and weekends, you might as well work a little social activity in. Aim for employment that places you among your peers. You could rack up dates and tips at the same time! Coffee shops catering to the young crowd have cropped up right and left in recent years. In the struggle to stand apart from the generic model, many cafés offer more than just hot cocoa and comfy chairs. If you are trying to get started as an artist, musician, or writer—or even just want to find the artists' community of your new city—working at a café might be a savvy move. Many cafes have regular shows and some even display work of local artists. When I interviewed the young owner of an edgy "salon" for Chapter Seven, he joked, "I strongly believe that my brunch chef came to work here so he could post his artwork." Back in the gallery, the work of the multi-talented cook was on display for the month.

If the caffeine scene isn't your thing, there are plenty of other atypical options. Man the late-night shift of your favorite radio station. Wait tables at an Ethiopian, Brazilian, or Afghani restaurant and learn the basics of a cuisine totally foreign to you. Work the reception desk of a sports training center for professional athletes.

Tutor struggling students in the evening (you might even get home cooked meals as a perk!). Bartend at a high-class piano bar. Hostess at a dinner murder mystery theater. Book comedians for a stand-up comedy club.

> "I recently got a job as a cocktail waitress by simply going to a fancy restaurant in nice clothes, asking to speak with the manager and promising her I was a quick learner. I love running around and staying on my toes, chatting with various people, and working in a fun environment. Especially after a slow day at the laboratory (my full-time job), waiting tables can be a real treat, as can the extra tips. I would recommend this sort of job to anyone who moves to a new city. It's a great way to start seeing familiar faces initially (feeling like you know them even if you're only serving them) and to meet new people who work there or are regulars."
> —Brigid Boland, 22

People often tell you that you can't have it all when you're just out of college. You've probably been notified that you are at the bottom of the totem pole now, that no one cares to use your creative powers, and that it's time to pay your dues. Of course it's true that you have to work harder until you've proven yourself, but that doesn't mean you pass three years of your life in monotony and misery. Hunt until you find something stimulating, hope that it pays you money, and make ends meet if it doesn't. By marrying mental stimulation and manual labor, partnering daily inspiration with daily income, you've guaranteed the survival of mind, body, and soul. No small accomplishment! In fact, people struggle their whole lives to get that combination down pat. Find the balance that works for you.

The cliche "Do what you love!" is timeless for one reason: people keep neglecting to heed it. The human being has somehow not internalized this simple truth in his bazillion-year evolution: that in order to *be* happy, one has to *do* something that makes one happy. We need to hear the adage every generation, every time a life decision presents itself. We talk ourselves into moves motivated by security, pressure, and greed. And the story always ends the same way (disappointment! disillusion! depression!—all very bad d-words!). One thing every young person realizes not long after college is that your job takes up a *huge* chunk of your time—of your *life*. If you are not pleased with what you do every day, then nothing—not bonuses, not stock options, not even a perfect lover or cuddly kitten to come home to—will keep you happy.

> "I wish I would have thought more about the day-to-day implications of my job. It's a great overall experience, but can be absolute hell on a day-to-day basis. I have a little pie chart in Excel that calculates the time remaining on my contract. The F9 key updates it. Sometimes I open up that file and just hit F9 every few seconds. It seems very therapeutic, until I realize that I'm not only hitting F9 on my job, I'm also hitting F9 on my life!"
>
> —Melissa Blakeley, investment banker, 22

VOLUNTEERING YOUR SERVICES

For the socially conscious, a public service program can be a great opportunity to get involved in a city and afford living there. Cities tend to have just as many social ills as they do amenities and many organized service organizations place their volunteers right in the heart of urban centers. What better way to develop a more mature awareness of Detroit's realities and complexities than to work with the homeless community or teach in an inner city school? You might have to get by on a small stipend, but many find it's worth the budget struggle to be able to get so directly involved in the community and comprehend it from the inside. You probably won't be in the mood to go out to the trendiest club after a long day at the soup kitchen, anyway.

There is a whole slew of domestic volunteer programs listed in Chapter Five that will plant you in cities across the country, from Columbia, South Carolina, to Albuquerque, New Mexico, and every urban center in between. Flip on ahead if you want to survey your options. Also take a look at these organized fellowships that combine public service with some sort of defined work project or educational experience. A number of them have a special focus on the city in which they place volunteers.

"I'm about halfway through a nine-month fellowship through the New York City Urban Fellows Program. Because of my placement at the NYPD's office of community affairs, I have visited places, met people, had experiences and learned things that I wouldn't have in any other job. But I have also learned that working full-time for several months at a stretch (as opposed to a summer internship or an extra-curricular activity) can be challenging, exhausting, and difficult. My advice is to be careful choosing your first post-college experience."

—Rachel Berger, 22

NEW YORK CITY URBAN FELLOWS PROGRAM: A nine-month fellowship for graduating college seniors and recent graduates (up to two years out of college). Fellows work in mayoral offices and city agencies and learn about the issues facing the city government through an intensive seminar. The program provides a $21,000 stipend plus health insurance (www.nyc.gov/html/D.C.as/html/urbanfellows.html).

MICKEY LELAND HUNGER FELLOWS PROGRAM: A year-long fellowship that places about twenty fellows in two six-month assignments. For the first half of the year, fellows work in a community organization anywhere in the United States that is doing local anti-hunger and poverty work. Next, they work in Washington D.C. at a national organization involved in the anti-hunger and poverty movement. The program provides a $9,000 stipend equivalent to income below the poverty line. Benefits include health insurance, travel expenses, housing and a $2,500 end-of-service award (www.hungercenter.org).

UNITED WAY OF TRI-STATE FELLOWS PROGRAM: A six-month fellowship that awards recent college graduates the opportunity to work cooperatively between the corporate and non-profit sectors. Fellows must commit 30 hours a week from July through December. Monthly stipend provided (www.uwts.org/tsvo.asp).

COMMON GROUND FELLOWSHIP IN CREATIVE RESPONSES TO HOMELESSNESS: A ten-month fellowship for recent college graduates interested in creative approaches to homelessness. The fellowship provides a $10,116 stipend plus medical benefits and an education grant (ww.commonground.org/employment/fellowship/index.asp).

EVERETT PUBLIC SERVICE FELLOWSHIP: A ten-week internship in which participants work with one of 62 organizations dedicated to improving the world. Everett interns develop professional skills while learning about the impact of public service. Those in New York City and Washington, D.C. have weekly educational events and social gatherings that bring in leaders in the public sector (www.everettinternships.org).

> "To get the most out of the Mickey Leland Fellows Program, it helps to leave yourself completely open to any kind of field site placement. You could be in Hawaii or Milwaukee; you could be living in a luxury apartment or a six-by-ten-foot room at the YWCA. The opportunity to become familiar with a completely different American experience and to learn about the wacky slices of American life that the other fellows have dropped into will serve you for the rest of your life. The U.S. is a great big strange country. Get to know all the little pieces that you can."
>
> —Bridget Murphy, 23

Thrifty Tips to Afford Living It Up the Urban Way

• Choose between a cell phone and an apartment phone. You don't need both. If you go with the mobile and have free evening minutes, train yourself to stick to night chatting. Exceeding your minutes even a few times a year can set you back hundreds of dollars.

• Don't use more than one-third of your income for rent.

• If credit cards have gotten you into trouble in the past, switch to a debit card. Spending money that you actually *have* does make more sense, right? If you insist on hanging onto your magic plastic, DON'T bring it out with you to the bars! A cash limit will serve you well.

• Learn about all of your housing options before you sign a lease. Some cities have special housing arrangements like "group houses," which can be much more economical than studio apartments. Take your time, suspend that sense of security for a few weeks, and make sure you check out a number of places *in person* before you make a decision.

- Rally your friends for free concerts, theater festivals and happy hours (note: happy hours with appetizers can kill two birds with one stone: "nutritional" intake and a nice buzz, the former safely tempering the latter).

- The best free activity is physical activity. Beach volleyball, running clubs, roller-blading, and hiking never get boring and don't cost a thing. I have a friend who joined a kick-ball team in her city on a good-humored whim and absolutely loves her teammates and their weekly games and social gatherings.

- Cut out at least one disposable thing, like a magazine subscription or that grande latte you simply must have every morning ($3.41 per day = $102.30 per month=$1,227.60 a year). Sometimes the trick to committing yourself to a personal goal is to just start with a small effort, and if you can stick to that, building on it will come easily.

- Ditch the wheels, or at least think really hard about whether you *need* a car. Getting around most cities without one is very doable. If public transportation intimidates you or sounds like a pain, it's probably because you've never given it a fair shot. Riding a bus to work can become a pleasant part of your daily routine, giving you just enough time to read the paper or sip your coffee. And think of it this way, if you cut out the monthly cost of insurance, gas, and those evil parking tickets, you would have a couple hundred dollars more to put towards rent and could afford to live in a nicer, more central location. Bike-friendly cities like Portland and Washington D.C. may help on the cheap transportation front.

"If you have the opportunity, take risks and be part of something new when you enter the work world. Whether it be a fledgling organization or Internet company you start with friends, the learning curve will be much higher, your job tasks/title will be more fluid and subject to advancement, and each day at work will be more exciting."
—Ann Gillespie, 45

" Moving to Burlington, Vermont is the most random thing I've done in my life (so far). 'You're WHERE?' is the question I get from friends I've contacted since graduation. "Why??" They tell me I'm the last person they would guess would move to Vermont. I'm a Jersey girl who grew up 40 minutes away from New York City. Now I live 40 minutes from the border of Canada, in a state that has more cows than Asian people.

There really wasn't a specific reason to move to Vermont. At the end of the summer after graduation, I was deciding between two (unpaid) internships—one in D.C. and the other in Burlington. While the organization in Burlington was offering everything I was looking for, its location made me hesitant. I was scared of being alone and away from my friends who had flocked to the major cities after graduation. After agonizing over the decision for weeks, I finally said, 'What the heck. Why not?' It would be temporary and I figured that moving to a random place would be easier now while I'm young and without any ties. I knew that I would most likely end up living in a city, so why not try something new?

This totally unexpected move was, without a doubt, the best decision I ever made. Working for such a small organization acted in my benefit as our office rapidly became overloaded with work and I got hired three months ahead of schedule. I can honestly say that I love my job. Outside of work, I have taken part in new experiences that I wouldn't have done had I not moved here. I have snow-shoed across Lake Champlain (something I thought only Eskimos did), have taken up snowboarding, and can expertly drive through two feet of snow. I live in a huge house, with a backyard the size of a basketball court, and pay a fraction of the rent in a large city.

Some days, while skidding on black ice on foggy mountains roads, the question 'what the hell am I doing here?' still pops up. I just think to myself, hey, I'm here for two years. When I'm 80 years old and looking back on life, two years will be nothing. "

WHEN LESS IS MORE: THE PROMISE OF A QUAINTER CITY

If the sight of hurried cell phone talkers pounding the pavement towards you makes you shudder, or if you secretly fear that those capricious subway doors will one day close right on your shoulders, a big city may not be your thing. Fortunately there are plenty of smaller cities and other substantial population centers that offer much more tranquility and cleanliness, without sacrificing any of the amenities. Madison, Wisconsin has the charm of a quaint Midwest town, yet it's booming with young people who fill up the bar strip on a nightly basis. Missoula, Montana combines youthful vibrancy, breathtaking natural wonders, and a tinge of hippie flair. Santa Fe (NM), Asheville (NC), Stowe (VT), Annapolis (MD), Bend (OR) and Athens (GA) are a few more examples of smaller cities that hold much promise for the energetic and adventurous young person. The atmosphere and activity of these places can be much less overwhelming to someone accustomed to a slower, quieter life, not to mention the fact that they're much bigger than the biggies.

OFF THE BEATEN TRACK: TINY TOWN, USA.

For the road-less-traveled type—those who prefer a destination overlooked, a well-kept secret—your possibilities are endless. This country is filled to the brim with Podunk towns that no one but their inhabitants have ever heard of. Maybe you're just a small town guy or gal at heart and you prefer the relaxed pace of village living and the intimacy of knowing your neighbors. Or maybe there has always been a quirky corner of the country calling your attention—a place you want to experience from the inside. If you decide to go really small, and you're used to the festive college lifestyle just be forewarned: there *is* such a thing as a "dry town" in the U.S. (yes, outrageous, but true). You may want to check that your new barrio has a watering hole or two, or you might find yourself spending every Saturday night at the movie theater.

A young friend of mine recently moved to Normal, Illinois for a graduate program. Of course we all had a field day cracking jokes about her new home ("How's it going out there in . . . whatsitcalled? Mediocre, Michigan?"). How could a town with such a name be in the least bit exciting? As it turned out, she had a fantastic experience in Normal, found a great clan of grad students (that were actually more diverse than those in her New York college) and came to appreciate her little town. Be open to an underrated or peculiar part of the country and it might surprise you. And if you have a sense of humor, your small town life can get pretty off-the-wall.

Nome-an's Land. For more than thirty five years, volunteers have trekked out to remote Nome, Alaska for year-long volunteer gigs at the radio station, which broadcasts to dozens of Eskimo villages. Volunteer DJ's produce, work on documentary projects and act as news reporters—often flying to remote villages to cover traditional festivals. Because this project is an AmeriCorps program, housing, food, a monthly stipend and health insurance are provided. Transportation to Alaska is also included. If you're cool with living in a state with only one person per square mile (over 70 in rest of U.S.!), then head on up and join the Nome folk (www.knom.org).

MIGHT AS WELL STAY ENTERTAINED!

Whoever said all Americans do for kicks is watch cable television must never have gone on vacation. This country offers a phenomenal array of vacation experiences—from the tranquil to the bizarre. And with every resort center, living history museum, and tour company there are entertainment and hospitality jobs to be had. Take your pick:

• Witness the Vegas madness firsthand by working casino security, dealing blackjack, or better yet, handling the frenzied folks that hit the jackpot (*www.jobmonkey.com*).

• Work as a living artifact at Colonial Williamsburg—petticoat, knickers and all (*www.history.org*).

• Head north to the land of the Eskimos and meet the sojourners passing through by working at Alaska Wildland Adventures as a safari driver, housekeeper or raft guide (*www.awasummer.jobs.com*).

• Organize outdoor excursions for Phantom Ranch on the floor of the Grand Canyon, a Xanterra Park that emphasizes ecologically sensitive tourism (*www.xanterra.com*).

• Be a crew member for the Delta Queen Steamboat Company, the oldest passenger cruise line in the U.S. (*www.deltaqueen.com/company/employment.htm*).

- Work as a tourism marketing intern at Royal Palm Tours in southwest Florida and lead international guests through this subtropical area of the state (*www.royal-palmtours.com*).

- Join the ranks of the dudes and dudettes at Coulter Lake Guest Ranch in Colorado and work as a horseback riding guide (*www.guestranches.com/coulterlake*).

- Intern for the summer at the Maine State Music Theater among top musicians and spend the fall and winter months working at a lobster farm or on a whale-watching tour in Bar Harbor, Maine (*www.msmt.org*).

- Move in among the rich and famous in the ski town of Aspen and see the town's sunnier side while working as an organizer for the Aspen Summer Music Festival (*www.skiaspen.com*).

WORK WORLD DELIGHTS YOU WON'T MISS

- Timed Lunches
- Itchy nude stockings and stiff collared shirts
- 10 days of vacation per year
- 4 x 4 working space
- A coffee addiction
- "Did you get the memo?"
- A boss

SIZZLING SUMMER HOT SPOTS

If you only have the summer months to work with, think about creating your ideal adventure in one of this country's gorgeous summer getaways. You will not only be placing yourself where the weather is like a dream and where all of the social action is, but you will multiply your chances of getting a short-term job.

Take Nantucket for example. Long idealized as the most superb place to pass the summer months, Nantucket is complete with a gorgeous shoreline, a rich community of artists and intellectuals, succulent seafood, and the occasional breeze to cool off its patrons. The glaring "con" on the Nantucket chart is its cost of living. Housing is very pricey and hard to come by. Try to beat the rush of college students who arrive in the late spring. If you can't arrive early, then get your hands on a local newspaper or find housing listings online and start searching aggressively. Another approach is to seek out employers that provide subsidized housing, like summer camps or local hotels. If you have experience waiting tables, aim for a job at a top-end seafood restaurant. This will probably be your best bet at actually pulling a profit on the summer.

Other sunny getaways worth considering are Hilton Head, Lake George, Myrtle Beach, San Diego, Mackinaw Island, the Florida Keys, Cape Cod, Padre Island, Lake of the Ozarks, and Lake Tahoe. You might even try to crash in a cottage or cabin that a friend or relative isn't using. Establishing yourself as the vacation community's babysitter (make a flier and network among soccer moms) could be a great way to supplement your official work. And remember, relaxed vacationers tip well!

COMPLETING THE UNION

Before you move past the domestic samplings onto the international pickings of Chapter Two, don't forget our most arctic and tropical states—numbers 49 and 50, of course! Unconventional jobs abound in both Alaska and Hawaii, as they are both common destinations for people seeking a change of pace, new scenery and a bit of adventure. Whether you've got a thing for glaciers or volcanoes, read the tales of these two adventurers to see how you can have a totally foreign experience without ever leaving the country. And take note of the advice of both Eskimo Andrea and Aloha Katie: you really can just pick up and go.

" I spend my afternoons surfing, hiking, or biking by the ocean. Every Friday I hit the beach at 2 PM until night comes and it's time to go out. I consider jeans 'dressy' attire and I can't remember the last time I spotted someone in a suit and tie. We all live in flip-flops. Yes, I have a *job*. I just happen to be employed in Hawaii.

Hawaii is full of people who move here to live in a relaxed place with a gorgeous climate. Many come without plans and just make it work once they arrive. The friends I've met tend to have jobs like bartending, teaching surfing, lifeguarding, and even guiding bike trips up volcanoes on local islands. There are lots of teaching opportunities in Hawaii for recent graduates—like the unique teaching program I am doing at Punahou Academy—and you don't need a teaching certificate to work in private schools. I had no teaching experience when I applied but somehow got one of the six positions they offer each year. There are also many opportunities for those with any sort of biology interest or background (working on ships or in marine biology labs) and I have some friends who have found these types of jobs by simply looking through the phone book.

The main drawback to living in Hawaii is the expense of housing. Apartments tend to be almost as pricey as in New York City, although you can find cheap ones if you look hard enough. What I think helps to offset this expense, though, is that you don't have to spend much money to go out. Here, young people pass their weekends on the beach, surfing, having cookouts, or doing other unique and cheap activities. If you are interested in moving out to Hawaii, I'd say just go make it happen. Things will fall into place from there. "

" The boldest move I've ever made was leaving my parents' house in Arizona to take a summer bartending job at a fishing lodge in the Alaskan wilderness. There were no roads to Yes Bay Lodge. Everything—including guests, crew, luggage, and supplies—was shipped in by floatplane. When I wasn't working, I did things I'd never had the chance to do in the desert, like bear-watching, kayaking, and catching salmon.

When I decided I wanted to stay on in Alaska for a full year, I realized I had talked to so many locals at the bar and in the staff quarters that I had plenty of connections to set up my life there. I rented half of a duplex from a woman who offered me a good deal because I was willing to take care of her three cats while she went away for the winter. I took the first job I was offered—lifeguarding—and settled in the city of Ketchikan. When lifeguarding got old, I started to apply for every job that looked interesting, even though I was mostly unqualified. My resume was varied and colorful, and instead of letting that make me look flaky, I packaged it in such a way that it said, 'I've done so many things, I could surely learn to work for you!' My strategy landed me a job at a company that was planning summer helicopter tours in the wilderness.

When people say they wish they could go on the kind of adventures that I do, I always ask, why can't you? Unless they have kids or house payments, their excuses are usually pretty feeble—they're scared, they're shy, they don't know what they'd do for money. But I've been as scared, shy, and broke as anyone. What makes me different is a willingness to put myself in uncomfortable, confusing or unstable situations and make the best of them. I have hitchhiked in Ireland, joined and quit the Peace Corps, volunteered in Croatia, and most recently moved to Las Vegas for graduate school. If you are willing to risk failing and make a fool of yourself a few times, I think you can learn how to succeed and flourish in any culture or situation. "

Avoiding THE TRAP of the Early Twenties. If you catch yourself using the words, "I have to..." when rationalizing where you currently are in life, grill yourself a bit. Is there any good reason you should feel chained to a certain track or job position, particularly if you have already identified that it doesn't satisfy you? Many young people continue working less-than-ideal jobs under the assumption that it is necessary to stay in a job for at least a year to make it worthwhile and to have a presentable resume. Although there is something to be said for getting a full experience that will aid you in your next career move, there are no hard-and-fast rules. Breaking out of a truly negative experience quickly will get you on the right track sooner rather than later. During my first year out of college, I was amazed at the way miserable friends responded to my question, "So why don't you just quit?" Sleep-deprived and without a personal life to speak of, they insisted: "Oh no! It's such good work experience." But for what? Corporate slavery is generally most valuable for one thing: more corporate slavery. If your work environment is stifling you now, don't think you are locked into it just because you started. Always keep your options open, and remember you've got one boss and one boss only. Me. Just kidding— *you,* silly! You've entered a phase in which usage of the phrase "have to" should drop to a lifetime minimum. Recognize your freedom and use it wisely.

KEEPING IT REAL

So we've established that moving to a new, fascinating location will spice up your early twenties like cayenne pepper hot sauce. You're pumped, you're prepared, now how in the world are you going to convince yourself, your parents, and your future employers that such a move and whatever pursuits come along with it are valid?

There are dozens of ways in which location can serve as a springboard into your future. On the most basic level, trying out a different place to live will give you a solid idea of where you want to settle down in the future. You will learn countless things about what you need out of a home, an environment, and a community of people. And don't underestimate how many doors your new location could open up. You choose a place because of the things that interest you: the people, the culture, the sports teams, the political climate, and the natural wonders. You will come across loads of work and volunteer opportunities that involve these same things. And whether you make connections casually at a happy hour or strategically through a volunteer group or professional organization, you will make hordes of them. In two months time your wallet will be bursting with telephone numbers and business cards. There is a lot to say for being where the movers and shakers are.

I know someone who was waiting tables at a coffee shop in downtown Baltimore when one of her early-morning regulars struck up a conversation. There was a new job opening at a small, unique team-building organization. The woman thought that someone with my friend's people skills would be perfect for the job. She applied and now organizes trips and retreats all over the country and world. You never know what opportunity will pop up—perhaps some type of job or niche that you didn't know existed but are a perfect match for—until you plant yourself right in the heart of the people traffic and keep your ears perked.

Being surrounded by your peers—whether that means aspiring young professionals or pensive poets—can do wonders for your soul searching. If you place yourself in a hotspot, you will encounter people who are doing all sorts of interesting things. Listen to every bit of encouragement and complaint that you hear at the bar, on the bus, and in the bathroom line. People make both wonderful and lousy career moves right out of college and you can learn from them both. As you are asking yourself "What next?" it will be highly helpful to have real life examples all around you.

And perhaps most importantly, finding like-minded people reinforces everything you think you know about yourself and your passions, but aren't quite sure of yet. Maybe you need something concrete to prove it to you, or a similar spirit to draw it out of you. After college, an old friend of mine picked up and moved to a ski town, where she discovered a whole crew of inspiring young adventurers overnight. While her decision initially raised eyebrows, she surrounded herself with people who reminded her why youth is worth relishing and adventure worth pursuing. In fact, she told me that the only downside to her new community was its transience. Her new friends were all serial adventure-seekers and after a handful of months on the slopes they were onto the next experience, whether in the Florida Keys, Patagonia, or Vancouver. The point is that encountering an enclave of daring spirits really gave my friend a boost. After making her move, she talked like a new person—more passionate and self-assured than ever, with a much wider scope for the future and its possibilities.

Returning to the question of how you are going to convince the peanut gallery of the validity of your move, just start by convincing yourself. Let the parent's club say what they will. Have confidence in your plans and execute them as soon as the chance presents itself. Housing will happen, jobs will be found, subway routes will be learned, and new friends and dates will pop up like dandelions. You will soon move on to the next step of your life knowing where you should be heading and what you want out of it. The rest is history, and a fine one it'll be.

CHAPTER TWO: THIRSTING TO LIVE ABROAD

WHEN WAS THE LAST TIME YOU OVERHEARD, "I wish I hadn't lived on the French Riviera," or "That year I spent volunteering in Costa Rica was really a bore"? You hardly ever come across young people who regret embarking on overseas adventures. Moving abroad gets at the very essence of the word adventure: new flavors, faces, politics, accents, style, festivals, even beer—a world of difference in every piece of your surroundings.

There is something about living among people in a different country that changes you fundamentally. Anyone who has spent a substantial chunk of time on foreign soil will tell you this. It imparts a certain perspective and wisdom that you can't get in any other way—not through classes, jobs, books or even short-term travel. You realize how the world views your country. You feel how the pace of life could be different. You realize what you could do without, and what you will never take for granted again. You accustom yourself to oddities you never imagined—afternoon naps, toilets without lids, coffee in tiny tea party portions, and (if you are lucky) men that hiss at you in the street. Adjusting and actually living and passing each day within a foreign context can be trying, but it is the most elementary and profound education you can give yourself.

The crucial secret of going abroad is not putting it off. I always wonder at folks who talk about moving across the world in a few years' time. Do they really think it's likelier to happen down the road, or even likely at all? As soon as you begin working in the area of your interest, you also begin working your way up the career ladder. It's less than easy to walk away from a promotion, not to mention end the lease of your dream apartment or put that budding relationship on hold. There are some things that you can't project into the distant years of your life so easily. Changing countries is one of them. Don't give yourself the luxury of vaguely entertaining the idea for the future. Treat living abroad as if it were a now-or-never choice, because it often is. There will always be something tying you to your homeland—family, friends, and later, career, children, spouse, maybe a needy puppy named Spike—but chances are that there will never again be this little tying you down. Commit to giving yourself the foreign experience and put the plan into action as soon as you possibly can.

If you missed the study abroad train in college, you're ripe for a bit of culture shock. It's time to experience foreign life from the inside. And now that you are independent, the experience has even more to offer—minus the constraints of an organized program and a huge group of gringos. If you *did* have the opportunity to study abroad, you've likely only whet your appetite for this international stuff and know firsthand how enriching overseas living can be. Don't hesitate to head to the hinterlands again because you can do it in a completely different capacity and have a more intense immersion experience.

This chapter is filled with anecdotes from young globalists to illustrate the infinite ways you can craft your overseas agenda. And since moving abroad sometimes takes an extra shot of courage, the accounts of these bold characters will help give you that nudge. If they just up and did it, why can't you? In many ways, their stories show just how doable living overseas is—perhaps even less complicated than you think. Draw from these special sections in whatever way you can—pointers, ideas, or inspiration. They are truly impressive. As for the possibilities—delectable. Take a sneak peek at what this chapter holds.

WHETTING YOUR APPETITE . . .

• Work on ocean-side vineyards or sheer sheep in rural New Zealand (*www.wwoof.co.nz*).

- Teach at a bilingual school in the mountains of Costa Rica called Monteverde Friends School, promoting environmental awareness and teaching peace issues. Salary, health insurance, visa costs and housing in the beautiful mountain terrain are provided (*Mfschool@racsa.co.cr*).

- Work at a private firm in Finland through the American Scandinavian Foundation (*www.amscan.org/training.html*) or nanny for a family in Italy (*www.princeent.com*).

- Write and edit for the South China Morning Post, an English-language newspaper in Hong Kong that offers paid internships (*www.scmp.com*).

- Serve as a ground crew member of Bombard Balloon Adventures and retrieve hot air balloons in the French countryside (*www.bombardsociety.com*).

- Lead groups of volunteers on Cross-Cultural Solutions trips to Kosovo or Eastern Ghana (*www.crossculturalsolutions.org*).

- Lifeguard, teach tennis, or guide snorkeling groups on the beaches of Cairns, Australia or Punta Cana, Dominican Republic as a Club Med employee (*www.clubmed.com*).

- Work on a kibbutz in Israel through the Kibbutz Program Center (*www.kibbutz.org,il/eng*).

- Participate in Himalayan Explorers Connection and teach in a Sherpa school near Mt. Everest, while living with Sherpa families (*www.hec.org*).

- Intern as a costume director at the Greek Stages Theater in Athens (*www.grdance.org*).

- Teach English as a Second Language at a school in China through the China Teaching Program, which includes both training and placement (*www.wwu.edu/~ctp*).

HELPFUL WEBSITES:

If you are considering living overseas, the World Wide Web is your new best friend. You could spend days roaming through your mind-boggling array of options. To cut right to the best, here are some of the most reputable.

University of Michigan's International Center's Overseas Opportunities Office: *(www.umich.edu/~icenter/overseas)* Widely regarded as one of the best resources for young people interested in working, studying, volunteering, or interning overseas.

Transitions Abroad: *(www.transitionsabroad.com)* A veteran in providing extensive coverage of work abroad options. This website sprouted from a unique magazine called *Transitions Abroad*. You can also join their helpful Listserv called "TA news".

University of Minnesota's International Study and Travel Center: *(www.istc.umn.edu)* This site offers great search provisions for overseas options.

Go Abroad: *(www.goabroad.com)* Considered one of the best sites for those contemplating overseas moves. You can search by country or subject to access extensive listings. While you're at it, check out their newer creations: InternAbroad, VolunteerAbroad, and TeachAbroad.

Dave's ESL Café: *(www.eslcafe.com)* The original source of information on teaching and working overseas. This site is currently home to thousands of helpful links.

Institute for International Education: *(www.iiepassport.org)* A search engine for study and work abroad programs that lets you search by the characteristics you are interested in (language, location, etc.).

Volunteer International: *(www.volunteerinternational.org)* The website of the International Volunteer Programs Association, which has listings of volunteer abroad programs.

Any Work Anywhere: (*anyworkanywhere.com*) The name says it all. Current job openings all over the world.

Idealist: (*www.idealist.org*) A superb online resource created by Actions Without Borders that has links to over 37,000 non-profit organizations in 165 countries.

"Escape Artists" Overseas Jobs: (*www.escapeartist.com/jobs/overseas.htm*) A website that allows you to browse jobs by country or by job category. Includes teaching, volunteering, and working overseas opportunities.

WHERE IN THE WORLD?

So you think you might be up for changing country codes? Sweet. Let's start by figuring out where to go. You can't exactly play the spin-the-globe-and-stop-it-with-your-finger game that so fascinated you as a kid. Although that would be pretty awesome and bold of you, you might end up in the middle of a blue body of water, where there is no job to be had, let alone any civilization to share in. Your decision process in choosing an international destination will have to be a bit more pragmatic than it would for a U.S. location, since employment opportunities are narrower and conditions so varied.

Some of the criteria for choosing an American city, however, do apply to your overseas city hunt. For example, cost of living may be a huge factor in your decision process, because there is an enormous range in the world. With the six dollars you throw down for a rum and coke in London, you could buy a cross-country bus ticket in Jamaica. But there is a whole other set of criteria that you need to consider when moving overseas. As you read these over, keep in mind that this isn't a question of "better or worse," rather you should be figuring out what *type* of experience you are looking for and what regions you might consider to find it.

MSEHIORFHQWJFELKNJJIOWOQD. Didn't catch that? Unless you are sticking to England, Canada, Australia, or a handful of smaller countries, language is an important issue that you will have to consider. If you know a foreign language, even just a little, go ahead and choose a place where that language is spoken. With solid fundamental knowledge and full immersion, you'll be speaking like a native in no time and will return home with a useful and marketable skill. If you don't know a single verb of the language of the country that your heart is set on, don't let that discourage you. You'd be amazed how much higher the learning curve is when you're actually living in a country where the language is spoken. Yes, it will be tough and frustrating at first, but you'll make up for lost ground rapidly. One way to get your feet wet (for both the language and the new surroundings) is to start with an intensive language-training course. If you are planning to just fall back on your mother tongue, don't assume that you can get by everywhere. Be realistic and find out where English is a common second language (Germany, India) and where you will likely be a lost soul (China).

> "Once you've adjusted to the whole "right hand for eating, left hand for wiping" rule, you know you've stopped being a pampered American and might be one step closer to understanding the most foreign regions of the globe."
> —Emily Hurstak, 22, from Bombay, India

ME, SLEEP IN A MOSQUITO NET?! The classifications "developed" and "developing" may sound like vague terms thrown around in political dialogue, but they shape a resident's experience tremendously. If you choose a developing country, you will most likely experience a whole gamut of changes, challenges, and inconveniences like power outages, cold showers, and overcrowded buses (the expression "packed in like sardines" will come to have new meaning to you!). A developing country will demand greater personal adjustment, but it will offer you a reality that few Americans get the chance to experience firsthand. Understanding how the majority of the world lives is invaluable. A developed country, on the other hand, will provide you with many of the same daily amenities (drinkable water, high speed Internet, peanut butter!) you have in the U.S. The question is not "Can you hack it?" but rather where you want to be at this stage of your life.

"LOOK MOM! I'M ON CNN!" Another factor to consider when choosing your distant locale is political stability and safety. Civil unrest can cut short even the most well-planned overseas experience. Be sure to do your homework and read up on any turmoil in your country of choice. Women especially should talk to people who have lived in the area and inquire about street safety.

EMAIL ALL POTENTIAL BOSSES, AND CC THE WORLD

BY RYAN FLOYD, 23

" When I decided I wanted to work in India after college, I began by contacting all of my old bosses, bosses' friends, friends of friends, parents of friends, professors, professors' colleagues, and so on. As a friend of mine joked, I 'cc'ed the world.' I ended up with a handful of leads and pushed them all very hard.

A friend's father knew someone who worked at a company in India and he put us in touch. The Indian friend emailed me, confused as to why I would want to work for them and what I'd do. Having gotten to this point through persistence, the next step demanded some creativity. I went through the company's website and outlined four different jobs I could envision myself doing for them, each involving my work and study background and also demanding something a foreigner may have an advantage doing over a native Indian.

I am now working at a conglomerate of the Indian company, developing European export markets for Indian fruits and vegetables. The job itself is great, but even more exciting is the experience of living like a member of the growing middle class in India. I live in the north of Bombay in a small apartment. Just like any other employee at the company. I have to save money and think about whether to take the bus or get crushed in the quicker, but smellier and tighter Bombay train system to get to work. It's harder than the life I'd live in the U.S., but a fantastic experience. "

SOUVENIR CENTRAL. Many young people enjoy the ethnic diversity and vibrant nightlife of large international cities. But since you are going to be *living* in your chosen foreign destination, mass tourism is an important factor to consider. While a view of the Eiffel Tower from your apartment window would be divine, throngs of tourist groups asking how to get to the Louvre everyday wouldn't be so cool. Be careful not to underestimate the influx of foreigners in popular destinations, particularly if your heart is set on a capital city. You may find that the fewer tourists there are around, the easier it is to slip into the local culture and uncover the genuine essence of the place. If immersion is your goal, give a country's second biggest city a shot. It usually retains the pleasurable aspects of a main center, but with a quieter, quainter feel.

> "If you decide to live abroad with a friend, I strongly encourage that the two of you do different things. One of you could teach while the other would restore Buddhist Temples. If you lead the same lives, you don't come out of your shell as much as you would otherwise, and won't end up experiencing as much as you could."
> —Roger Loughney, 24

BEYOND THE COMFORT ZONE
BY JESS MORRISON, 24

" Having already travelled in Japan, urban China, Malaysia, Vietnam, Thailand, and India as a student, I was itching to get back to the enchantment of living abroad after graduation. I wanted another adventure beyond the comfort zone—but with a twist. I wanted an isolated setting that provided opportunities to explore and engage. I soon found myself teaching English at an under-funded university in Northeastern China.

In the city of Jilin, I was the first foreigner most of my new students had ever met. I passed my free time taking Mandarin lessons and walking the streets. Each classroom experience helped advance the students' English as much as it advanced my own understanding of my Chinese pupils (many of whom were only two years younger than me). While I cannot speak for the billion plus people in China, I had a reasonably good handle on the second-year English students of Jilin Chemical College classroom 208. Their ideas of global economic structures and where they saw themselves as people and as Chinese people became a beautiful balance for my "educated" North American concepts of the world we shared. And they taught me a thing or two about eating dog, frogs, scorpions, and what a friend can be. "

Note: *Jess has also worked at an orphanage in Chile and is currently a live-in counselor at a home for at-risk youth in Chicago. For the next phase of his adventurous saga, he is planning trips to India and back to China, presumably to meet the billion or so folk he didn't have the chance to share with in Jilin.*

ESCAPING THE GOLDEN ARCHES. Very few countries have not yet been permeated by U.S. culture. If you are looking to get away and escape your mother country for a bit, seek out the more remote and culturally distinct regions of the shrinking globe. As you contemplate this issue, give anti-American sentiment a thought. If you love talking to locals and appreciate a warm reception, think twice about going where your jeans won't brand you a cultural untouchable. On the other hand, if your goal is to broaden your perspective, a country far from America's reach will help you do that.

STEPPING OUT. The geographical position of the country you choose can facilitate or limit your travel opportunities immensely. If you are the type of person who likes to see everything, don't put yourself in Japan without the financial means to hop around by plane a bit. It's a long swim to the Great Wall of China. Positioning yourself smack in the middle of continental Europe would allow you to visit a different country every weekend. You may, however, need a whole year or more to reach every corner of one country. It's a matter of priorities and personal preference.

HOME COOKIN'. If tasting the local cuisine, sharing in holiday traditions, and conversing in the native language are your priorities, definitely consider living with a local family. In certain countries this option will be more readily available than others. Homestays are sometimes so much cheaper than independent living that they can make your abroad adventure financially feasible. If safety is a major concern, placing yourself among people who know what daily precautions should be taken (and who might be a bit protective of you until you learn to be) is another benefit. On the other hand, if moving abroad is a long-awaited declaration of independence and you put a premium on personal space, solitude, or wild late nights, stick to a bachelor or bachelorette pad. You might find some foreign students from different countries to share an apartment with. In Havana, I ended up living with two Germans, two Italians, two Dutch folk, a Mexican, and a Bolivian. Quite a bunch we were! It was an added treat to learn about European and other Latin American countries while absorbing the culture of Cuba, and now I have great connections for future world travel.

Now that you've gotten some ideas brewing and your global curiosity is nice and piqued, let's talk business. On top of getting a passport, there are a few formalities that you have to take care of before bouncing out of this country. The whole process is less intimidating than you might think. This section breaks down the necessary steps it takes to transplant yourself overseas.

Some Asian, African, and Latin American countries have immunization requirements, like yellow fever vaccinations, for all those entering the country. See the Center for Disease Control website *(www.cdc.gov/travel/index.htm)* for specifics. If you purchase an International Student ID Card for $22, you get *basic* health and accident insurance, which should supplement a more extensive medical coverage. Considering that the average cost of a medical evacuation overseas is over $50,000, comprehensive medical insurance that covers evacuation is crucial. Travel health insurance can be purchased through companies such as International Medical Group *(www.imglobal.com)* for reasonable prices. Make sure you ask exactly what they don't cover. Some policies don't include sports injuries or any injuries related to "terrorism" (a term you want to clarify). To find out about visa requirements for a long-term overseas stay, visit the State Department's website *(http://travel.state.gov/foreignentryreqs.html)*.

If you will be seeking employment in your newly-adopted nation, the tricky part is the work permit. The requirements to obtain one vary from country to country. Often your employer has to state that you are providing a service that no person in that country can provide. Make sure to get on the ball early so you have enough time to dedicate to the planning process and a few roadblocks or complexities won't discourage you. Working overseas is well worth a little extra homework.

If the paperwork is giving you a headache, however, there are ways to simplify. Make your arrangements through one of the following organizations. Their experts will hook you up with the necessary papers you need to work overseas, and may even help you secure a job, too.

Council International Educational Exchange (CIEE) obtains a work permit for you and provides services to help you find a three to six month job (many are seasonal service industry jobs). The program cost is between $350–$450 and is open to young people within six months of college graduation. Possible countries include Ireland, France, Germany, Australia, Canada, Costa Rica and New Zealand. CIEE also offers a Teach in China Program and a Teach in Thailand Program *(www.councilexchanges.org)*.

The British Universities North America Club (BUNAC) is the largest work abroad program with over 6,000 U.S. participants. It provides U.S. students with a "blue card" to work in Scotland, England, Wales, and Northern Ireland for up to six months. Application fee is $225 and orientation materials include a handbook, advice, and 50 pages of potential employers to get you off on your search. For a higher fee, you can also do a similar program in Australia for up to twelve months *(www.bunac.org)*.

InterExchange obtains work and resident permits for participants and lines up overseas jobs for a $400–$700 placement fee. Placements range from teaching and aupair positions (six months to a year), farm work (two to four months), and internships (summer to yearlong). Sites include Australia, the Netherlands, Belgium, Norway, Russia, Bulgaria, Costa Rica, Great Britain, France, Germany, Japan, Spain, and South Africa. Apply four months in advance *(www.interexchange.org)*.

Association for International Practical Training (AIPT) is an umbrella for a variety of programs. IAESTE (www.iaesteunitedstates.org) offers science and engineering internships in over 60 countries. The Work Permit Service/U.S. Reserved Offer Program provides work permits for students who secure their own internships. The U.S. Professionals provides work permits for those who set up their own work in Austria, Britain, Finland, France, Germany, Ireland, Japan, Malaysia, Mexico, Slovakia, Sweden and Switzerland. Program fee is $250 *(www.aipt.org)*.

AISEC (International Association for Students in Economics and Business Management). An international student-run organization that places students and recent graduates in 84 different countries for paid internships lasting eight weeks to eighteen months. Most positions are in the business, education, development and information technology sectors and the majority are concentrated in India, Turkey, Germany, Eastern Europe, and Latin America. You have to work through your college's AISEC chapter to apply and get program fee details *(www.aiesecus.org)*.

> " After college I spent two amazing years working as a paralegal in Paris for a U.S. law firm. I was lucky because I had applied to work in the States and the firm asked me if I would rather work in France. Transferring overseas taught me some valuable lessons on how Americans can work in Europe. Unfortunately, the process requires some time and patience. However, the rewards make it well worth your while.
>
> Unless you are content with working 'under the table' as a bartender or an aupair, do not expect to find a proper, paying job once you arrive. Americans cannot work legally without working papers. Because any EU citizen can work anywhere in the EU without working papers, few European employers will go out of their way to hire Americans. Fortunately, there are three ways to get around this.
>
> The easiest way is to prove that one of your relatives (a grandparent perhaps?) came from Ireland. If you can do this you can get dual Irish citizenship and the right to work anywhere in Europe (this is much harder to do with other EU countries). A good alternative is to contact an organization like the Council on International Educational Exchange which will get you the working papers, help you find an internship and even obtain housing. Unfortunately, this is only a short-term option because the internship and the working papers are only good for a couple of months.
>
> The final and traditional option is to find an employer willing to arrange and pay for working papers on your behalf. Overseas American firms typically need native English speakers to communicate with their U.S. headquarters. You can contact the European offices directly or try the U.S. headquarters. Either way, give yourself plenty of time because getting working papers can take several months. Moreover, you may be required to work in the States for six months or more before being officially 'transferred' to an overseas office—a technicality that makes things easier for the firm. This process can certainly take time but it will be well worth it when you have a well-paying and legal job in Europe. "
>
> *Visit Rick Steve's Graffiti Wall 'Living/Working Europe' for some useful information and advice on working across the pond:*
> *(www.ricksteves.com/graffiti/archives/living_working.htm).*

EU EXPANSION
BY VLAD DORJETS, 28

WHERE THE JOBS AT

If you are thirsting to live abroad and want a cool job experience that will finance your stay, you've got quite an array of possibilities. Here is a quick overview of the biggest job categories to get you thinking about how you want to pass your foreign stay in the most enjoyable and lucrative way.

ESL. One of your best possibilities is to teach English as a second language. ESL is a mainstay of young Americans working overseas. As many young teachers in Asia will tell you, demand is so high that you can find a job without having any experience or training. It is safe to head off to most countries in the Far East and count on getting a job. However, if you get licensed through a Teaching English as a Second Language (TESL) course, you will multiply your options. Some employers do request TESL training and others require it. You'll have to investigate the general requirements in the area of the world you are considering. TESL programs vary in cost (around $300), but there are enough out there that you should be able to find one that fits with your schedule and budget. Once you're all trained and ready to go, you will be blown away by your options. English teachers are in constant demand. There are plenty of websites that list job openings by country, spanning the entire globe. In searching, be thorough and compare your possibilities and all of their benefits. This is one employment niche where you can be a little picky.

ESL Websites:

Dave's ESL Café (*www.eslcafe.com*).

ESL/EFL job seekers (*www.TESall.com*).

Ohio University Employment Resources for Language Teachers (*www.ohiou.edu/esl/teacher/index.html*).

U.S. Department of State, Office of Overseas Schools (*www.state.gov/m/a/os*).

ESL Directory (*www.esldirectory.com*).

ESL Teachers Board (*www.eslteachersboard.com*).

ESL Data Bank and Spoken Languages (*www.elsdatabank.com*).

Teach Abroad (*www.teachabroad.com*).

Demand for English as a Second Language teachers varies greatly across the planet. Here are the hotspots to help get your job search underway.

The **Japanese** government facilitates foreigners living and teaching in Japan by issuing 4,000 visas to English teachers every year. Demand for English instruction is high and salaries reflect it. However, arranging housing in Japan will require a hefty security deposit (Tokyo is one of the most expensive cities in the world) and the work arrangements are not conducive to flitting around Asia in your spare time. As a teacher you are expected to be very professional and commit serious time (six months to a year) to your job position.

TEACH FOR THAILAND
BY KITTY LAWN, 25

"After graduation, I had to decide between spending a year teaching in Thailand or jumping into the real world and putting my English and Spanish degree to use. When I asked my older brother for advice, he told me that the real world could wait. He said I'd have the rest of my life to focus on a career, but the year (or few years) after college is when you can really explore the many opportunities, cultures, and experiences that are out there. I moved to Bangkok. He was right.

I did a teaching program in Thailand that Loyola offers for college graduates. The Loyola program covered airfare and accommodations in Bangkok, plus a salary of about $200 a month. This was a pretty decent package and most of the program's teachers went to Thailand with just a few hundred dollars for travel and activity costs. This particular teaching program is very lax, with very little supervision. They do not provide much class material or direction on lesson plans.

My advice to someone looking into a teaching position abroad would be to figure out how much direction you want with your classes and students. You should know if you want a program that has strict guidelines and methods, or if you'd prefer one that allows the teacher to make most decisions. Another characteristic to consider is direct immersion versus expatriate support. My university had a handful of teachers from all over the world: the U.S., Australia, India, Laos, China, and so on. I met and worked with a large group of people, which I really enjoyed. Other teaching programs might have just two or three other teachers, so your network is immediately smaller."

Note: *Kitty continues to be an exciting young person. She now works for MTV in New York City.*

While the wages you will earn in **South Korea** are comparable to Japanese wages, the cost of living is lower, allowing you to live better and save more. You can work at a "hagwan" (a special learning institution for both students and business people) for a decent salary and well-organized teaching assignment. Private lessons are extremely lucrative (you could pull in fifty dollars an hour) and teaching at a university might give you large chunks of vacation time to travel. South Korea, Japan, and **Taiwan** have the highest paying jobs but also the most demanding hiring criteria.

Indonesia offers a more laid-back work environment and a lower cost of living. Without teaching experience or certification, you'll have no trouble finding a job. It is safe to go there and begin your hunt in person. For a teaching stint in **China**, however, it is advisable to plan ahead due to government bureaucracy. Send applications to various schools well in advance. ESL training (as in all countries) will help your odds, but is not necessary.

Teaching opportunities abound in **Thailand**. You can get the employment scoop by scanning your Bangkok hostel's bulletin board or by asking around expatriate circles once you get there. You can also make job preparations ahead of time through one of the large English schools (ie. The English International Schools, Berlitz). Other countries where you will have your pick of English teaching jobs are **Malaysia, Singapore,** and **Vietnam.**

Jumping to the other side of the world, **Eastern Europe** is another promising ESL job market. Check out established English language schools, and count on a bounty of tutoring opportunities to supplement your income (though building up a clientele of students takes time and networking). Most hiring is done locally, so pack your bags with a good chunk of money and job search in person. Peak hiring times are at the end of the summer (for the school year) and late spring (for summer courses). The best positions can be found in **Poland, Hungary,** and the **Czech Republic. Russia** also has a considerable demand for English teachers.

Though most say that the working conditions are poor throughout **Latin America**, it is still a good job market, not to mention an interesting place to live. Opportunities exist throughout Central America. **Mexico** is the largest market and **Costa Rica** is known to offer the best working conditions.

Keep looking! Though openings may be more sparse, give **Egypt, Morocco, Nepal** and **Tunisia** a shot.

THE COMMON UNIQUE EXPERIENCE
BY BRENDAN LYNAUGH, 22

" I came to Prague the summer after graduating to take a TESL certification program and hopefully find a job teaching English. Having seen older friends graduate and move on to low paying, entry-level positions, I knew I wanted my life to be less ordinary; I wanted a challenge and an adventure.

Prague held the romantic allure of the café culture of the 'Paris of the Nineties' and I could just see myself sipping absinthe while discussing Kafka. As it turns out, Prague is saturated with Americans and most are twentysomethings passing through for six months to a year, whether spurred by graduation or a quarter life crisis. Having escaped from a deadening job or an ex-boyfriend, they simply want to enjoy the cheap beer.

Despite the disappointment of finding Prague less unique than I had imagined, I've had my share of moments that confirm the advantages of living an ocean away from my cubicle-enslaved counterparts. Here in Prague, your morning commute might take you past Wenceslas Square, where thousands of students protested during the last days of communism. In the evening, a quiet stroll might lead you to the Charles Bridge where you are treated to a fairy tale view of Prague Castle, lit up against a backdrop of stars.

As far as actually teaching goes, the hours are tough, the pay is low, but there is little I would trade the experience for. Three of my classes are at the Ministry of Agriculture, where I teach businessmen and women who are truly eager students. In my first week I discovered that a successful class is a great natural high.

As I make plans for the coming year, the transient nature of this city pushes me to move on. Friends appear and vanish like blips on a radar screen. But like most things in life, it is what you make of it. I'm taking advantage of every minute. "

Lost in Translation. Just like anything else, English language schools are a business. You have to exercise serious caution when committing yourself to a teaching position. Read your contract through carefully and clarify any vague terms. It would be terrible to tie yourself to a sub-standard situation when you intended to have a liberating enrichment experience. Here are some questions that you can ask to ensure that you know what you are getting into.

- How much will I be working each week? Will I have the opportunity to tutor outside of the school?

- How organized is the curriculum? Will I be given lesson plans or be expected to develop them myself? Will I be provided books and teaching materials? (If your school is a large chain, chances are that your curriculum will be highly organized. Conversely, smaller schools typically don't provide much structure).

- What is the history of your institution? When and why did it start? Does it normally recruit young Americans as teachers? Have any recent teachers left the school early due to dissatisfaction with working conditions? (You may want to ask for contact information of a current teacher to get their input).

- Will the school help me obtain the necessary work and resident visas? What other benefits are offered (health insurance, meals, paid vacation, loan deferment)?

- Will I be provided housing or assistance finding housing? What is housing and transportation in the area like? What does it normally cost?

- Will my job offer me any opportunities to travel (long vacation periods)?

Another option to consider is teaching at a private international or bilingual school overseas where native English speakers with teaching ability are in demand. This may also be your best shot at finding a job without the benefit of experience. Private schools usually pay well and they might also afford you the most opportunities for tutoring students privately for additional income.

" When I reached the end of college, I knew I wanted to live abroad. As I investigated my options, it became clear that teaching English is by far the easiest way for liberal arts majors to work their way around the globe. I applied for a job at Athens College through the Hellenic-American Educational Foundation Teaching Fellowship. Yes, it's a mouthful, but well worth looking into. They advertise on the career websites of a select few universities, but any recent college graduate with a bit of teaching experience is eligible for one of the six fellowships granted each year. I lived rent free on campus with five other young American teaching fellows, worked about 30 hours a week and pretty much got to design my own schedule. Knowing Greek is not important; it's your English skills that are in demand. With few hours, a flexible schedule, and a substantial cash flow (I gave private English lessons in my spare time), I was able to explore Greece in full, from its smoggy capital to the ancient Delphi to the mountains and orange groves of the Peloponnese. Fully foreign but only half tourist, I gained a much richer experience in Greece than I would have just passing through. "

ENGLISH-LANGUAGE PUBLICATIONS. If you just can't see yourself in front of a classroom, there are a number of other ways to capitalize on your English skills without teaching them. Overseas companies that do any sort of business or marketing in the U.S. need help drafting and perfecting advertisements, brochures, sales pitches, and basic correspondence. I never realized how valuable native English reading and writing skills are until I helped a Spanish-speaking friend correct a tourism brochure he had written in English. He spoke near perfect English but lacked that added ability to create smooth, appealing prose for advertising. If a company wants to choose the perfect words and produce impeccable sentences, it is almost always necessary to invest in a native speaker. Knowing this should convince you that you have a marketable skill in your back pocket. Put it to good use! You might end up with much more impressive and upper-level employment than you had planned.

If you are interested in working for an actual publication rather than just a company or organization, there are plenty of newspapers and magazines around the world that take on interns. The challenge is getting paid to work as a reporter, writer or editor. My senior year in college, I discovered quite a few intern-friendly publications by moseying around the Internet—*Tico Times* in Costa Rica *(www.ticotimes.net)*, *Buenos Aires Herald* in Argentina *(www.buenosairesherald.com)*, and *The Asahi Shimbun* in Tokyo, Japan *(www.asahi.com/english/english.html*—but no one willing to pay me—in any currency. It is still worth hunting for a salaried position, especially if you have impressive experience in print journalism. The most promising route, however, is to just earn a bundle of cash here in the old US of A and begin an overseas internship when you can support yourself. Another money-making opportunity will likely present itself once you arrive on foreign soil.

Capitalize On Those Foreign Looks! If you transplant yourself on the other side of the world to teach English, you may find yourself meddling in a dozen odd jobs that you never would have envisioned. The English tongue isn't the only hot commodity in the Far East—the non-Asian face is in demand as well. You might do a juice advertisement in Jakarta, represent a research institute in Seoul, hostess at an all-male bar in Taipei (yes, there are un-sketchy ways to do this), or model American sneakers in Bangkok. What could be a better souvenir of your overseas escapades than a dorky catalog picture of yourself!

THE MOTHER OF ALL TONGUES
BY ALEXIS SWERDLOFF, 21

❝ I arrived in Rome with one large suitcase, an unpaid writing internship with the Associated Press, and a very, very empty wallet. After a week of being a tourist, I had thrown my last Euro in the Trevi fountain and I came to the sad conclusion that I needed to get a paying job. I sat myself down in an Internet café, went through job websites, and came across this ad: 'TV Production company looking for touch typist. English mother tongue required.' Hmm, I thought. I can type. I have an English mother tongue—I think. I called them up and was at work the next day.

Thus began my job adventure as a production assistant at Brando-Quilici Productions. The small company, which makes science documentaries for the Discovery Channel, needed someone to log and transcribe 50 hours of volcano footage. So as I relished the sights and sounds of the great Italian capital (not to mention many pounds of gelato), I transcribed away and slowly became part of the editing process. I eventually got to work closely with the editor and made important editorial decisions. So while my friends at home were passing monotonous days in the office, I was earning a good chunk of money in an interesting job in one of the world's most enchanting cities. ❞

TOURISM/TRAVEL INDUSTRY. Because hotels, resorts, theme parks, and tourist sites will always be in need of English speaking employees, you can find entry-level tourism jobs in nearly every corner of the planet. To start you on your search, think of a popular travel destination for Americans. Let's take the Bahamas as an example. Then imagine what Americans would do on a getaway to the Bahamas (fry themselves on the beach) and you're on your way to investigating life guarding positions at all-inclusive resorts there. One of the most effective ways to conduct your search is to start with U.S. chains that have hotels in overseas locations, or a large resort company like Club Med that hires young people from all over the world *(www.clubmed.com)*.

AUPAIR. Don't let the fancy name for babysitter scare you away. Working as an aupair can be a wonderful way to finance your overseas living and also connect you with a local family. Many positions require a minimum time commitment, such as one year. Positions are most likely to begin in September. Make sure your potential employers lay out all working conditions and clearly define any terms like "light housekeeping." There are plenty of agencies that will link you with prospective families and may even screen them first so you don't end up in a house that makes the Osbournes look serene. However, the Internet is free and you may be able to find an employer and set good working conditions without a middleman. Poke around web classifieds first and pursue as many options as you can so that you have some comparative material (salaries, duties, free time, benefits, vacation). Give these websites a look to commence your search: Work Exchange Ideas *(www.workexchange.org)*, International Aupair Association *(www.iapa.org)*, Worldwide Aupair *(www.worldwideaupair-nanny.com)*.

AGRICULTURE. Whether you want to pick rhubarb on an organic farm in Finland or chase down disobedient cows in rural Spain, there are enough low-level farm positions that you could follow the seasons around Continental Europe. And won't Mom and Dad be thrilled to tell their friends that you have become a migrant farm worker! But seriously, the experience of farm work will give you invigorating daily workouts and also offer you invaluable insight into one of the most crucial and overlooked world industries. Check out the international farming programs listed in Chapter Four to see how you can work out the logistics of farm work overseas *(www.wwoof.org)*.

JUST MAKE IT HAPPEN
BY JEN BRANT, 28

" Deciding to go live abroad is without a doubt the best decision I ever made. Everyone thought I was crazy when I just took off to go live in Italy after graduating from UCLA. The key piece of advice for anyone who wants to live abroad is just to make it happen. I lived at home for two months and worked my tail off until I could buy a plane ticket to Milan. I used the rest of my savings (only about $1,400!) to live in Italy while I looked for work.

I ended up nannying for a horribly bratty six-year-old girl from Milan. I lived with her family by the sea near Genova for four months and then got lucky and found another job in Milan. I lived there for three years, then went off to work in Switzerland and then returned to Italy again. Right now I am in the States, but I am starting to get the abroad itch again! Once you get a taste of traveling and living outside the U.S., you have to keep fighting the urge to pick up and run! "

UNIVERSITY PROGRAMS. Work as a program coordinator or resident assistant of a study abroad program. These positions offer you the stability of a regular job, but with the bonus of residing in a foreign country, interacting with college students, and the possibility of leading travel groups. You might even have the chance to take some graduate-level classes while working full-time. These jobs are pretty hard to come by, but absolutely worth pursuing. If you studied abroad in college through a program with multiple sites, you have a better chance of obtaining a job. Call the director of your former program and ask how you might find out about any job openings. This will ensure that he or she keeps you in mind when news of a vacancy arrives.

"I was having coffee with a friend one day and we started talking about the COPA study abroad program we had both done in college. She had heard through the grapevine that they were hiring a young person to help with our program. The following day I made a phone call and two days later I had agreed to the position of assistant on-site program advisor in Cuba."
—Keli Lerdal, 24

" My year in Cambodia began with a late-night dorm room email to the editor of the *Cambodia Daily* newspaper. I looked up his email address online, introduced myself in a cover letter, asked for an internship, and attached my resume. I hoped he'd respond that month. Ten minutes later, my email dinged. He had responded—it was mid-afternoon in Asia—and said that I sounded like a good match for the newspaper. He gave me the email address of the deputy editor and told me to pick an arrival date.

English-language newspapers around the world host interns (usually unpaid) and offer a great way to get to know a country. After three months at the *Daily*, I was a quasi-expert on Cambodian politics, functional in the Khmer language, and knew my way around the country. The job did not last as long as I had hoped due to financial problems at the paper. However, if you are flexible and anticipate a bit of job fluctuation, finding alternate employment is usually not a problem. I had no difficulty finding a much more fulfilling teaching job at an organization that schools 4,000 street children.

There are many jobs for English speakers available in non-English speaking countries: English language teaching, corporate editing, administrative work, brochure writing, international school teaching. These jobs also allow flexibility, vacation time and a chance to travel. Some international organizations even pay Western salaries, or if you're really lucky, 25 percent extra for a 'hardship' posting. Though it is comforting to leave home with a job in hand, it is not necessary and much easier to negotiate once you are in your new country. For example, locating the expatriate community—mainly a matter of figuring out where Westerners socialize in the evenings—can bring you instant leads.

Many young expats begin with an easy-to-find two or three month teaching position, and use that time to search for preferable work. As long as you arrive with enough savings to cover a couple months of living expenses and adequate evacuation and medical insurance, you will be able to gain stability in your new country, and have a fantastic immersion experience. "

SERVICE. Service is a wonderful way to live abroad and do so in an affordable and altruistic way. Inserting you directly into the local community, volunteer programs offer just about the most authentic immersion experience you could ask for. Many of the organized programs also take care of the pain-in-the-neck logistics that come along with moving overseas: international health insurance, housing arrangements, travel expenses, and visas. Doing a service program might be the magic answer to the your question, "How in the world am I going to afford a year in the Philippines?" Many well-established service programs provide their participants with monthly stipends in addition to covering all major costs. Make sure to peruse the international section of Chapter Four to learn about all of the options you have as someone willing to offer your time and talents. If you are interested in one of the more costly international service programs but are unable to afford it, be smart and work the system. Apply to be a leader or counselor for such a program. Young college graduates are ideal applicants to lead student groups and "volunteer vacations."

YOUR HOMETOWN. Because actually making money overseas can be a challenge (and also since your biggest expenditure—plane fare—hits you before you even arrive), many young people opt to work at home and save money for as long as they need to and *then* move abroad. This may be your best bet if you have your eye on a third world country because finding a job will be more difficult (though not impossible—read on) and if you do find one, your wages will probably be lower than what you could potentially earn in the U.S. The almighty dollar goes far in most regions of the world.

PROGRAMMING YOUR MOVE:
ORGANIZED WORK, VOLUNTEER, AND INTERN ABROAD PROGRAMS

You could spend *days* web-browsing through the various overseas programs. There are hundreds of them, and more sprouting up each year. Don't let the quantity of options overwhelm you. Instead use the plethora to compare your possibilities very carefully. Many programs charge their participants substantial fees. Because you can't possibly know what it costs to arrange an internship for a foreigner in Turkey, it is hard to judge how reasonable the prices of every program really are. However, if you look long enough and paste all of your options onto one document, you will be able to quickly compare the full package each program offers and zone in on those with the best value and most promising all-around experience.

In gathering information for this book, I was originally discouraged by the high price tags attached to some quality overseas work, intern and volunteer programs. As I kept searching and web-browsing, however, I came across fantastic affordable options. For every ten enticing programs that will cost you an arm and a leg, there is at least one that has minimal fees and offers a comparable package. You just have to keep looking and comparing (make sure you go beyond just the first page of your web search results). The information in the coming sections is arranged in such a way as to show you that you don't have to break the bank to take part in exciting and valuable work overseas. The first listings are the most economical and the last, the priciest (note: this order does not reflect on the merit of the programs, but is instead a practical arrangement of information for young folks with serious budget constraints).

If you want to volunteer or work in an area of the world where the cost of living is low, try to find a local NGO (nongovernmental organization) that arranges work projects and home stays. They won't have the overhead fees that U.S. organizations do and will charge you a more reasonable price for what you are getting. Oftentimes what you are paying for when you mail in that $1,400 check is an intermediary with connections overseas to set up your experience for you. If you can cut out the middleman and invest some time taking care of the logistics yourself, you will save yourself some serious cash and probably learn a lot about what exactly you are getting yourself into before you leave. Take the Rajahat Institute, for example. A group of 36 government English schools in Thailand, this institute is one of the program sites that World Teach sends its participants to. By simply mailing a resume, letter, and transcript directly to the Institute, you can become a volunteer (or even employee if you are highly qualified) and receive a stipend and benefits. Voila. You've just saved yourself $4,000. Take a look at more examples of organizations run from the country of the project site.

- **FRENCH CULTURAL SERVICES & ENGLISH ASSISTANTSHIPS IN FRANCE:**
  A program run by the French Ministry of Education which places 1,500 Americans in French schools to assistant teach English. Knowledge of French is required. Program provides a monthly salary of about $900. Applying early (December) improves chances of acceptance (www.frenchculture.org/education/support/assistant/index.html).

- **JAPANESE EXCHANGE AND TEACHING PROGRAM** (JET): A Japanese government-sponsored program that hires American college graduates to work in local government organizations throughout Japan for one year (but renewable up to two additional years). While over ninety percent of the program's participants work as assistant language teachers, JET also offers positions as "coordinator of international relations" or "sports exchange advisor." The program includes orientation, round-trip airfare, and a salary of around $30,000 (remember: the cost of living is very high in Japan). TESL is not a requirement, but helpful. *(www.jetprograme.org/e/)*.

- **SIPAZ SERVICIO INTERNACIONAL PARA LA PAZ** : (SIPAZ) is an international observation organization created to monitor conflict in Chiapas, Mexico and work toward non-violent solutions. Yearlong volunteers work in human rights observation, peace observation, and inter-religious dialogue. Spanish fluency, conflict resolution skills and at least 23 years of age are required. Room, board, medical insurance, a modest stipend and transportation costs are covered. SIPAZ has no program fee *(www.sipaz.org)*.

- **ENGLISH PROGRAM IN KOREA**: A one-year teaching program sponsored by the Korean government that places English speakers in Korean schools. Teachers are provided airfare, housing, work permits, vacation, insurance, pensions and monthly salaries. Requirements include a bachelor's degree and a TOFEL/TOESL certificate *(http://epik.knue.ac.kr)*.

- **EDUCATION CENTRE FOR HELPLESS CHILDREN**: Volunteers offer services in the operation of an orphanage in Nepal and take part in other projects geared towards improving the opportunities of the children. $850 program fee covers all costs for five months *(www.echcnepal.org)*.

- **JOINT ASSISTANCE CENTRE**: This program places 2,000 short (at least one month) and long-term volunteers from around the world in volunteer positions across the Indian subcontinent. Short-term projects place volunteers in villages to work with NGOs on projects such as health, the environment, agriculture and literacy. Long-term placements are designed for the particular individual, and can be tailored according to your interests (i.e. teaching, working in a medical center, writing, etc). Program fee is $300 for short-term (includes one month room/board) and $600 for long-term, plus $150 for each additional month after three months *(www.jacusa.org).*

• **BURMA PROGRAM**: Volunteers teach English to Burmese refugees at the Thai-Burma border. The groups are usually involved with labor rights, social development, and women's issues. Minimum commitment is three and a half months. Volunteers live with other volunteers, and a small stipend is provided to cover food costs *(www.geocities.com/maesotesl).*

• **CHATTERIS EDUCATIONAL FOUNDATION**: Hires English Language Teaching Assistants for Hong Kong Schools and pays them a flat monthly allowance. Housing is provided *(www.chatteris.org.hk).*

If you would prefer to go through an established U.S. program that has a user-friendly website, representatives you can call and get information from, and all of the added advantages and conveniences that come with an office and staff on American soil, then you should definitely take stock of your options. Because arranging your situation and work assignment overseas through a reliable program may make the overseas jump smoother and easier to make, it may be worth earning the money required to participate in the program. While a few thousand dollars for a two-week volunteer stint is a lot (or, less kindly put, a rip off), it may be a decent value for twelve months of housing, food, insurance, and a pre-departure orientation trip. Use common sense: if you are providing a valuable service for a long period of time, you shouldn't go into debt to do it. Check up on your potential programs and find out how long they've been in operation, why they were started, and whether they are nonprofit organizations (the dot-org vs. dot-com designations should give you a heads-up). These three factors are very telling and should hint at whether your middlemen are pulling a profit on your work or whether they are dedicated to facilitating global interchanges.

" My 'plan' was to live in Japan and teach English for one year with the JET program (Japan Exchange Teacher Program), and return home to begin graduate school. I wanted to have my graduate degree completed before reaching 'a certain age.' Because of this self-imposed, arbitrary time boundary, I immediately answered no when asked if I wanted to stay in Japan another year. 'That's not the plan!' I thought. However, my culturally enriching experience could have continued if I just could have unencumbered myself from my life calendar! I had made great friends (whom I wasn't ready to say goodbye to), had traveled around half of Japan's beautiful countryside (which I wanted to see more of) and had visited Korea, but this was only the first on a list of East Asian countries I wanted to visit.

Why do we have these notions—that certain milestones should be reached at ideal times—be it graduate school, marriage, children, or home ownership? I'm somewhat regretful that it took returning from Japan and wishing that I had stayed to learn that if you are enjoying what you are doing, are learning, and having personally enriching experiences, you should continue until you are ready to move on. Plans *can* be changed, life calendars *can* be altered, and in the long run you will feel gratified for having done what made you happiest at that time. "

Here is a list of work and volunteer abroad programs that make overseas arrangements, offer great benefits, and don't charge a fortune.

• **YMCA'S OVERSEAS SERVICE CORPS PROGRAM** (OSCY): A program that places twenty-five to thirty teachers in local YMCA's throughout Taiwan. Requirements include a one-year commitment, a four-year college degree and interest in teaching and English language skills. Previous teaching and/or TESL experience is preferred. Benefits include housing, medical insurance, one-week paid vacation, contract completion bonus, visa, student loan deferment, orientation, training, and airfare to U.S. upon completion of contract *(www.ymca.net/yworld/taiwan/titlepg.htm)*.

- **THE AMERICAN-SCANDINAVIAN FOUNDATION**: This foundation arranges work on small farms or in schools for recent college graduates. There is a $50 application fee and participants earn about $350 for farm work and $900 for teaching per month depending on work. The foundation can also help you obtain a work permit if you arrange your own job in Scandinavia. Participants are responsible for rent which is usually around $250 per month. The program commitment ranges from two to ten months *(www.amscan.org/training/htm)*.

- **CONCERN AMERICA**: An international development organization that does work with refugee communities through the help of volunteers (ages 21 and up) with valuable professional experience. Volunteers assist impoverished communities in improving living conditions. Spanish is necessary for Latin America assignments and Portuguese for Mozambique assignments. Room and board, health insurance, round-trip transportation, and a small monthly stipend are provided *(www.concernamerica.org)*.

- **AMITY INSTITUTE**: A four-to-ten month English language teaching program in well-established schools and institutes in Latin American countries. Experience abroad and Spanish language skills are preferred. Home stay and small weekly stipend are provided. Program fee is $100 and paid upon placement *(www.amity.org)*.

- **WORLD TEACH**: A volunteer program that arranges overseas living and teaching arrangements for college graduates. The Poland, China, and Marshall Islands programs are the most economical options (they are all partially or fully funded), and the large price tags attached to the other teaching sites can be drastically lowered by fundraising as World Teach suggests. Also keep in mind that unlike most program fees, World Teach's includes round-trip airfare in addition to field support, training, and a small stipend. Teaching commitments are generally long-term, though an eight-week Summer Teaching Program in China exists, as does a six-month Mexico Nature Guide Training Program *(www.worldteach.org)*.

• **FULBRIGHT ENGLISH TEACHING ASSISTANTSHIPS**: Recent college graduates are selected to assistant teach English in Belgium/Luxembourg, France, Germany, Hungary, Korea, Taiwan, and Turkey *(www.iie.org/fulbright)*.

• **VOLUNTARY SERVICE OVERSEAS**: Two-year overseas service projects for Canadians and Americans in 39 developing countries. Requirements are a college degree and two-to-three years' working experience. Volunteers are placed according to their skills and interests. Applications are accepted on a rolling basis throughout the year. The program offers generous benefits including transportation, a pre-departure equipment grant, living allowance, health insurance, and a resettlement grant upon return *(www.vsocanada.ca)*.

• **VISIONS IN ACTION**: Skilled volunteers are placed in six-to-twelve month assignments with local non-governmental development organizations, health clinics, and community groups, working on issues such as community development, social work, health care, human rights, democratization, communications, and the environment. Sites include Uganda, Tanzania, Zimbabwe, South Africa, Burkina Faso, and Mexico. Volunteers are encouraged to find external funding to finance their experience *(www.visionsinaction.org)*.

• **PRINCETON IN ASIA**: A program that offers about 75 recent college graduates the chance to teach English throughout Asia for one or two years. ESL experience is expected. Participants must pay for transportation to their teaching sites and contribute $300 *(www.princeton.edu/~pia)*.

HOW I TOSSED MY JOB OFFER TO THE WINDS, AND LIVED TO TELL ABOUT IT

By MICHELLE LAPOINT, 24

"I left for Costa Rica three days after graduation for what was supposed to be a three-month internship to bridge the gap between college and an upcoming full-time job in New York City. I interned at Casa Alianza, a non-profit children's rights organization, through the generous assistance of my college, which funds a slate of public interest internships each summer. At some point in July, I realized that I did not want to go back to the States at the end of the summer as planned. Casa Alianza was happy to have me stay, but could not offer me a salary. So I turned back to my college and applied for financial support for a six-month stay in Costa Rica. To my surprise and delight, they agreed. I ended up leaving Costa Rica a full year later than I had originally planned.

The weeks following my decision to remain in Costa Rica were filled with self-doubt and a less-than-enthusiastic reaction from my parents. They assumed that I wanted an extended vacation, rather than an experience, which—while different than the path I had mapped out at graduation—nonetheless continues to define me intellectually, professionally, and personally. Giving up a job at the time the economy had begun to tank was a risky choice, but staying in Costa Rica turned out to be the best decision for me. I traveled to Nicaragua and Guatemala and worked with children who carved out an existence on the streets. On a personal level, I became more fully committed to working for social justice and developed a deeper understanding of the culture and politics of Latin America. By the time I did return to this country, I felt confident that my choice would open up more doors for me professionally, as it did indeed do. I now work at the Inter-American Dialogue, a center for Latin American policy analysis in Washington, D.C. Most importantly, I was grateful to have lived abroad and to have pursued the path that offered me the most personal fulfilment. "

International internship programs are an appealing option for those who want to live overseas while gaining solid professional experience that will pretty up their resumes for the future. Spend a few minutes browsing the web and you'll see there are plenty of folks out there who want to set up an overseas internship for you. The trick is to find a quality internship program that will facilitate your arrangements without subtracting all of your earnings and then some. Below are a few of the finest opportunities across the globe for eager little interns.

- **CDS INTERNATIONAL**: A multi-part program for young people with German language skills and a strong interest in living in Germany. The Work Authorization Program provides working papers for those who arrange an internship on their own. The placement program sets up internships in business, graphic design, marketing, multi-media, engineering, or hotel management. The Robert Bosch Foundation Fellowship Program provides work opportunities and includes round-trip transportation and health insurance. The Congress Bundestag Scholarship, which is awarded to sixty people, includes two months of intensive German, four months education at a technical school and a five-month internship. CDS also offers summer internship programs in Greece and Turkey. For all CDS programs there is a participation fee of $200–$400. All participants are paid salaries *(www.cdsintl.org)*.

- **INSTITUTE OF INTERNATIONAL EDUCATION—LATIN AMERICA**: Participants work in the Institute's Mexico office as student advisors, providing information about U.S. educational opportunities, editing publications, and representing at college fairs. Internships are typically for three-month periods and a monthly stipend of $300 is provided. Applicants must speak Spanish and have an interest in Latin America and international education *(www.iie.org/latinamerica)*.

- **FASCELL FELLOWSHIP**: A one to two-year fellowship through the State Department that places fellows in China, Eastern Europe, and the former USSR to support a diplomatic or consular mission. Duties include administrative, consular, or political and diplomatic duties. Applicants must be at least 21 and fluent in the language of the country. Preference is given to applicants with academic degrees pertaining to the region. Benefits include housing, travel, and transportation costs *(www.careers.state.gov/student/prog_fell.html)*.

- **UNITED NATIONS VOLUNTEERS**: One-year services projects around the world. There is no program fee. Room, board, transportation costs, and stipend are provided. Applicants must be 25 and have foreign language fluency and expertise in the area where they plan to provide services *(www.unv.org)*.

- **INTERNSHIPS INTERNATIONAL**: Places college graduates in internships in major international cities including Budapest, Cologne, Bangkok, Nairobi, Florence, Glasgow, London, Melbourne, Paris, Saigon and Santiago. Placements are available in a wide array of disciplines. Internships have a minimum duration of six-weeks and are unpaid. Placement fee is $700 *(www.rtpnet.org/~intintl)*.

- **INTERNATIONAL COOPERATIVE EDUCATION PROGRAM**: Two to three-month paid internships in Switzerland, Germany, Belgium, Japan and China for students and recent college graduates with foreign language skills. The range of job areas includes retail, hotel, engineering, teaching, banks, recreation, and hospitals. Application fee is $250 and placement fee is an added $700 *(www.icemenlo.com)*.

- **FOUNDATION FOR SUSTAINABLE DEVELOPMENT**: Eight-week internships for college students, graduate students, and professionals that provide the opportunity to gain hands-on experience with grassroots development in six South American and East African countries. Internships are eight weeks or longer and include home stays and orientation. Interns also gain experience with grant writing. Program fee is between $1,500 and $2,000 *(www.fsdinternational.org)*.

Putting Off Medical School for a Year or Two? Consider a program that will give you exposure to your field and make use of your knowledge and skills. Child Family Health International is an international health, service-learning program for medical, pre-medical and other health students. By sending students to work with their international partners, CFHI is able to provide free medical care around the world.

Okay, I'll stop being stubborn and discuss the pricier programs. They shouldn't be ruled out for a number of reasons. One, you may be an heiress and have the money to pay a steep program fee. Two, trust fund or not, a summer of dedicated labor and thrifty living will amass enough cash to afford almost any program. An established program that is highly organized and also accountable to you (should something go wrong) could be extremely valuable. By paying more, you could save yourself frustrating experiences with bureaucracy, inefficiency, and disorganization overseas. Also keep in mind that a high price doesn't necessarily mean a bad deal. The Institute for International Cooperation and Development, for example, provides six months worth of food and lodging *plus* transportation costs for your program fee of $3,300. When you consider all you receive for your money and also take into account cost of living, it's not such a bad deal. The third reason you should investigate these listings is that you might be able to finagle yourself a *job* at one of these programs (check out the employment section of their websites, or just give them a call) and thereby benefit from all of the perks while earning a salary. The fourth and final reason is that a fair number of these programs offer financial aid or "diversity funds" to enable broad participation. Here is a list of some of the biggies. Browse away.

- **Operations Crossroads Africa** *(www.oca.igc.org)*
- **Amizade** *(www.amizade.org)*
- **Cross-Cultural Solutions** *(www.crossculturalsolutions.org)*
- **Global Citizens Network** *(www.globalcitizens.org)*
- **Global Crossroad** *(www.globalcrossroad.com)*
- **Global Routes** *(www.globalroutes.org)*
- **Global Service Corps** *(www.globalservicecorps.org)*
- **Global Volunteers** *(www.globalvolunteers.org)*
- **Institute for International Cooperation and Development** *(www.iicd-volunteer.org)*
- **i-to-i** *(www.i-to-i.com)*

" My goal after graduating from college was to take a 'productive pause.' I was tired of school, had never been out of the United States and had become interested in international development. I really wanted to combine travel with career exploration. And while I wasn't looking to become rich, I didn't want to go into debt either.

I didn't know where to begin, so I met with a development economics professor that I knew from class and asked for advice about working abroad after graduation. A few weeks later she put me in touch with another professor who was looking for a research assistant in Kenya. The job entailed working with a local NGO, overseeing evaluations of their health, education, and agriculture projects. The pay was enough to live comfortably in Kenya (in other words, not very much!), and I also got a free trip to Africa, as well as health insurance, vaccines, and other benefits.

I loved my two years in Kenya. I got to see a side of Africa that few foreigners are exposed to. I also enjoyed taking time to be a tourist. I went on a safari, went whitewater rafting in Uganda, and explored historical sites in Ethiopia. Working for an economist, I realized pretty quickly that I didn't want to become one myself. But I also discovered that I was fascinated by political institution building and democratization in developing countries. I've continued working on development issues now that I'm back in the U.S., and draw from my time in Kenya in much of the work I'm doing now. "

ALL BY YOUR LONESOME:
FINANCING FOREIGN LIVING

Is there any good reason why you can't line up your experience overseas yourself? There is nothing standing in your way other than that idea in your head that foreign things are inherently more complicated and intimidating. If you have the time and energy to invest in some planning, you can arrange for anything and everything over the web or with a few phone calls. So if none of the above programs struck you as the perfect fit, but you are still bound and determined to live abroad, just start researching and planning away. The process may be time-consuming, but probably easier than you think. And remember, a journey of a thousand miles begins with a single Google search!

I was able to arrange for a full year of living and volunteering in Cuba by emailing every American NGO that worked there and asking for advice. About one fifth of them had time to help a young idealist who wanted to live and volunteer abroad. From these folks, I got invaluable advice, obtained names and phone numbers of community leaders, and set up my first work site in the Cuban countryside. Religious organizations were extremely helpful and some even offered me free housing and food in return for my volunteer work. The nice thing about working through religious organizations is that most are part of an international web. Call someone in Baltimore and they might be able to put you in touch with someone just back from two years in Tunisia, or better yet, a permanent resident overseas who is eager to help a new arrival get settled into the community and the make the best use of your talents.

I purchased a year of travel health insurance for a couple hundred dollars, arranged reasonably priced housing through email, and got on the plane with my fingers crossed. Licenses and visas were the toughest part of the process (and I often wondered why I had chosen the one country with an ironclad travel ban), but I was also able to get them on my own with some carefully crafted letters. My financial support came through the Samuel Huntington Fellowship, a fantastic resource that can be applied to public service anywhere in the world.

" If the thought of dragging around a backpack full of dirty clothes for a year makes you cringe, but you still want to go abroad, consider the alternative. Pick one place overseas and make it your new home for awhile. I may not have 35 stamps in my passport by the time I finally leave Taiwan, but I'll always know that in one neighborhood on the far side of the world, I'm a local.

The challenge of living overseas is finding a way to finance it. The easiest way I've found to fund a long-term stay is to create an academic or research project and apply for a fellowship. There are plenty of national fellowships open to students across the country, but many colleges have their own specific programs. I am currently in Kaohsiung, Taiwan, researching and writing on the migrant labor flows from Southeast to East Asia on a fellowship through my university. The fellowship money was even enough to buy a motorcycle—a necessity in Taiwan, and another personal lifetime goal accomplished.

The wonderful part about actually living abroad is that no matter what you came for, you'll find yourself faced with new, unexpected opportunities. On top of my migration project, I write a weekly column in a national bilingual paper (I sent a letter to the editor and he offered me the spot), teach at a university (it would be five more years and a PhD before I could do that at home), and play on a local cricket team. It's these opportunities more than anything else that let me forget I'm a foreigner. I may be delaying something—maybe owning a dog, buying a car, or joining a bowling league—but I'm quite sure it's no more deserving of the title 'real world' than what I'm living. **"**

GRANTS AND FELLOWSHIPS

Try applying for a grant or fellowship that will enable you to live abroad. Many fellowships will fund a year or two of study, work, or volunteering in a foreign country. These awards are competitive, but you should definitely give it a whirl and see what you come up with. Pay attention to early deadlines. For some fellowships, you will have to pass through first round selections at your college in the fall before moving ahead to the national competition in the winter and spring.

- **THE MITCHELL SCHOLARSHIPS**: Funds twelve Americans for one year of graduate study in Ireland. Open to college seniors and recent college graduates. Awards granted on basis of academic achievement, extra-curricular accomplishment, and integrity. *(www.us-irelandalliance.org/scholarships.html)*.

- **LUCE SCHOLARS**: Eighteen individuals are selected for one-year internships in the Far East. Internships vary greatly, from master gardening in Kyoto to banking in Tokyo. Award available to college seniors and recent graduates with a minimum GPA of 3.7 *(www.hluce.org/3scholfm.html)*.

- **THE MARSHALL SCHOLARSHIPS**: Up to forty individuals are chosen for two years of graduate study in the UK in any discipline. Committee looks for intellectual distinction and strong character *(www.marshallscholarship.org)*.

- **FULBRIGHT GRANTS**: The U.S. State Department awards 1,000 grants supporting study or research in over 140 countries with the aim of bettering global understanding and cooperation. Applicants must limit their proposal to one country only *(http://exchanges.state.gov/education/fulbright)*.

- **COLOMBIAN STUDY AND RESEARCH GRANTS**: Finances one year of study in a Colombian university including monthly stipend, health insurance, and airfare. For more information, contact the Institute of International Education at 809 United Nations Plaza, New York, NY 10017.

- **ROTARY FOUNDATION AMBASSADORIAL SCHOLARSHIPS**: Three types of scholarships available:
  Academic-Year Ambassadorial Scholarships—funding (up to $25,000) for one year of study overseas. Nearly 1,000 awards granted each year.
  Multi-Year Ambassadorial Scholarships—a flat grant of $12,500 for either two or three years of degree-oriented study in another country.
  Cultural Ambassadorial Scholarships—funding ($12,000–$19,000) for three or six months of intensive language study and cultural immersion in another country. Must apply well in advance (almost two years) and check with your local Rotary chapter about specific instructions, deadlines, and availability of awards *(www.rotary.org/foundation/educational/amb_scho/index.html)*.

- **SAMUEL HUNTINGTON PUBLIC SERVICE FELLOWSHIP**: A year-long public service project anywhere in the world. Applicants submit proposal of volunteer project to a committee, which selects one to two winners every spring. Open to graduating college seniors only. *(www.nationalgridus.com/masselectric/about_us/award.asp)*.

Other fundraising options are organizations like Rotary, Kiwanis, Optimist and religious organizations. The World Teach website *(www.worldteach.org)* also offers fundraising suggestions that you might not have thought of.

TRACKING THE FELLOWS:

"I'm studying in Vladivostok, Russia this year as a Rotary Foundation 'Ambassadorial Scholar.' I'm having an amazing time and would suggest the scholarship to anyone and everyone. The scholarship requires me to be an 'ambassador of good-will' and has enabled me to both dig deep into studies here and have time to volunteer with local NGOs."
—Leah Zimmerman, 24

"Taking this year off (or, as my father says, 'taking this year on!!!') before graduate school was definitely a good idea. I have a Fulbright Grant in Morocco and feel so lucky to be here—especially when I hear from my friends who are working 12-hour days or plowing through 40-page research papers! I know this is probably the last time I will have such flexibility in terms of what I want to research and see. While studying the local environmental movement of Morocco, I have driven through torrential rain in the Sahara, ridden a camel on the beach, and watched real-life snake charmers. In addition, the Fulbright has also given me the chance to live in Fez, the most remarkably beautiful city in the world, where you have to dodge donkeys laden with vegetables as you make your way through tangled, cobblestone streets."
—Sarah Izfar, 22

"As a Rotary Ambassadorial Scholar you not only receive a scholarship to pursue higher education in almost any foreign country (up to $25,000 USD), but are also given an open invitation to become part of the Rotary International family, a network of clubs and individuals all across this planet who all share in the ideals of 'service above self.' When I landed in Australia to begin my studies at the University of Melbourne, I was soon greeted at the airport by my assigned scholarship counselor who invited me into his home and made me more welcome than I ever could have imagined."
—Van Nguyen, 22

The Big Chill

Filled with giant icebergs and cold nothingness, Antarctica has never had a native population. Nevertheless, many people interested in polar exploration and untouched natural wonders have found their way to this isolated continent. Why would *you* ever want to? Well, you probably don't, unless you prefer the company of ice caps to humans, or are just the type whose ears perk up every time you hear a zany idea. If you have a background or interest in science and want to do some work that may give you experience for the future, the U.S. government sponsors a science program called the National Science Foundation Antarctic Program that employs about 700 people annually. While many positions are for experienced science professionals, there are also entry-level spots, like scientist's assistant. The work can be grueling, but earning a good salary while living abroad is no small feat. Bundle up and bring some good music. Sanity is key! *(www.nsf.gov)*

FOLLOWING YOUR GUT
By DAVID SCHACHT, 30

" Have you ever woken up nauseous because you hate your job? Two weeks after graduating college I was running as fast as I could in the rat race—as a financial analyst in prestigious investment banking firm. I was lucky to have a great job with a clear set of success hoops to jump through. However, that promise of a better future couldn't sugar-coat the bitter taste of the actual job—80 hours a week with the title 'slave.' Thankfully, my gut knew that my job was emotional food poisoning and I chose to listen to it.

I left that job and took a chance on a less lucrative, less demanding banking job in Paris despite many peers saying that it was a mistake and that I was selling myself short. After all, now was the time to work my tail off, right? Wrong. What was most important to me at age 21 was to live abroad, meet new people, and learn languages. France allowed me the time to experience the world and enrich my life. During my two years there, I learned very little about banking. But I grew more as a person in those amazing years than I ever would have 'sucking it up' in the dreary confines of the cubicle back home.

When I learned that a good friend had a free apartment in Chile, I left my job in France with the little money I had saved ($3,000) and moved to Santiago to enroll in

(continued)

language classes and become a bartender. This was not what a 'European banker' was supposed to do. Heck, I couldn't even find a job as a bartender! But the experience in Chile fostered my passion for history, politics, and Latin American economic development. Six years later, I have a Masters in Latin American studies and work in a field I love, supporting Latin American Foreign Ministries with their international trade negotiations.

Thank God I followed my gut and moved to France. Thank God I followed my gut and moved to Chile. Thank God I followed my gut and spent a summer studying coffee production in Central America and decided to learn Portuguese for fun. For each of us the story is different. For me it was traveling, languages, and culture. For you, it may be painting, or sports or theater. Think about where you want to be in ten years or twenty years and the types of stories you want to be able to tell about your life. Life is just too short to do anything other than create your own path. You may not know how all of the pieces will ultimately fit together. That is part of the fun. Just focus on following your gut and pursuing your dreams. 🙴

FOLLOWING YOUR GUT
By DAVID SCHACHT, 30

KEEPING IT REAL

Living overseas carries a number of added advantages that will make future employers drool over you. What organization or company *doesn't* prefer someone with a little foreign experience and expertise in this age of globalization? While many people travel, few people can claim to have *lived* overseas. Those future interviewers who've never resided outside of the U.S. will be wowed by your courage. Those who *have* will be even more impressed because they know all that it says for your character and maturity.

By becoming part of another country, you gain a much deeper understanding of its complexities and nuances than anyone passing through could hope to develop. Language proficiency is an invaluable skill that will put your resume a notch above the rest. Independent thinking is perhaps the most underrated life skill that comes with leaving your own shores. The business arena praises the ability to "think outside the box." Thinking outside of your borders just takes that capacity one step further. You are no longer someone that accepts the version of events that cable news feeds you; you think critically and draw on your own experiences to come to intelligent judgments. This mental adeptness carries over to all mental tasks you approach.

You can frame your overseas experience in a way that illustrates how much your skills were demanded and developed. Communication skills are a great example. Say you had to organize and carry out collaborative projects in a foreign language. This is the best crash-course in verbal and non-verbal communication imaginable. Having adjusted and survived in a foreign country also speaks to your adaptability and self-reliance. It shows that you put yourself in challenging situations and make the best of them. Regardless of whether you nanny for a Finnish family, intern at a video game company in South Korea, or lead volunteer vacations in Belize, you will absolutely return home with an experience of great value in both your personal life and professional pursuits.

CHAPTER THREE: TAKE IT OUTSIDE

YOU FEEL ALIVE WITH THE SUN ON YOUR NECK and grass between your toes. You thrive on physical activity and envy the animal world, where all of this "indoors" nonsense hasn't caught on. Why force yourself into a stuffy office space or rigid career path that doesn't fit your nature? If you aren't ready to retire your flip-flops and get suited up for the office, then Mother Nature beckons. Luckily, she's got more than just grass for you to graze on. There is an enormous amount of outdoor adventure jobs that are prime employment options for the young and tie-less. In addition to job ideas for those who want sustainable, longer-term outdoor activity, this chapter also contains physical challenge suggestions for those who want to brave the elements in one event or concentrated period of time. The possibilities are as diverse as this planet's terrain and climate, from tropical island bike tours to ski bumming stints, parasailing instructor positions to dude ranch wrangler jobs.

The coolest perk of your outdoor ventures—other than the year-long tan and the abs of steel—is that you will arrange a lifestyle that is healthy, holistic, and personally fulfilling. Such a set-up will raise the bar high for future years in terms of what ingredients you seek out for your work, living situation, and personal life. The community of co-workers or fellow athletes you encounter among the pine trees or white sands will prove a source of support and enthusiasm for all that you are passionate about (not to mention an attractive dating pool!). Even if you never pick up another oar after your year of sea kayaking or live far south of the ski slopes for the rest of your life, you've treated your mind and body to the most natural challenges and lifestyle possible.

The world is your playground, and a big one it is. Head for the hills, live by the sun instead of the clock, and relish every day of your free-spirited existence.

"I take issue with this notion that leaving the conventional path to follow some personal dreams and adventures is somehow a 'year off.' Doing something you've always wanted to do is actually a 'year on.' And I think many people who are brave enough to start doing it for a year, end up leading a 'life on' instead of a 'life off.' This is not 'delaying' the path. This is the path. This IS the real world."
—Cross-country biker Carl Shepherd, 25

WHETTING YOUR APPETITE . . .

- Lead groups of teens on adventure trips through the Rocky Mountain region (www.trailmark.com/staff).

- Monitor marine life in the northern Bohol, Philippines as a scuba diver for Project Seahorse (www.seahorse.fisheries.ubc.ca).

- Join the burly crew of a fishing boat in Alaska and pay off your college loans by way of salmon (www.AlaskaJobFinder.com).

- Intern on the nature preserve at Starr Ranch Sanctuary in Trabuco Canyon, California (www.starranch.org).

- Lead sea-kayaking trips through the picturesque San Juan Islands in Washington State (www.sanjuansafaris.com).

- Finance a year on the slopes of the finest ski resorts (www.jobmonkey.com).

HELPFUL WEBSITES:

Green Dream Jobs: *(www.sustainablebusiness.com/jobs/index.cfm)* A database of environmental jobs.

Job Monkey: *(www.jobmonkey.com)* A host of outdoor job resources and ideas.

Adventure Sports Online: *(www.adventuresports.com)* A comprehensive website of outdoor touring companies, adventure racing competitions, wilderness travel, climbing, mountaineering and more.

Gorp.com: *(www.gorp.away.com)* A website for adventure travel and outdoor recreation with information on destinations, national parks, outdoor gear, and hiking.

PHYSICAL CHALLENGES

Let's face it. By the time we reach our thirties, our bodies may very well be on their way to flabbiness. Now is the time to reach your pinnacle of fitness and take your body to the limits. Imagine biking across the country or reaching the peak of a famous mountain. People with no outdoor experience and minimal fitness have achieved both. It's just a matter of dedicating yourself to accomplishing that feat you'll one day boast to your grandchildren. This section describes a handful of physical challenges that can be short-term adventures or longer athletic experiences, depending on how many months and calories you've got to burn. Go ahead, set your sights on the impossible, grunt your way to the finish line and then sit back on your buns of steel, saying "Hell yeah I did that!" Completing a physical challenge makes you feel like you can accomplish anything, and that's not a bad feeling to have at this transitional point in your life.

BICYCLE BUILT FOR YOU. Imagine hopping on your bike in California, and cruising into Washington, D.C. two months later, having seen every type of landscape and the full garden variety of Podunk towns across the continental U.S. A bike tour combines an intense physical challenge with a totally authentic cultural and travel experience. If you join a group tour, you have the added bonus of team camaraderie, planned itineraries and a backup van to carry your luggage (and you on the rougher days!). However, these trips are pretty costly. You can cut your expenditures by 60 to 70 percent by self-guiding your trip.

Another option is a charity cycling trip sponsored by a nonprofit organization. Participants raise a few thousand dollars in donations by canvassing among neighbors, friends, and relatives, and then pedal their little hearts out, sometimes doing community service projects along the way. For example, the Habitat for Humanity summer bike tour includes house construction (*www.yale.edu/habitat/info/info.htm*). The Coast-to-Coast Community Challenge allows you to raise money and awareness for the charity of your choice. Bike Aid (www.bikeaid.org) cyclists raise one dollar for every mile of their cross-country journey. Bike and Build (www.bikeandbuild.org) raises money for affordable housing groups in the U.S. and Canada as bikers perform advocacy work and construct affordable homes en route.

Wanted: Leader of the Pack! Get paid to be the hot-shot on wheels. Guide groups of young and old bikers for a company like Sockeye Cycle *(www.cyclealaska.com)*, which will bring you through gorgeous Alaskan landscapes as you work—and work out!

Because your route possibilities are wide, you have the luxury of planning according to your geographical curiosities. Choose from national park tours (Yellowstone, Grand Canyon, Red Woods), bicycle camping vacations, cross-state tours, or mountain routes for the extra hardcore among you. If you are considering going overseas, try a coastal tour of any island. Bike among the volcanoes of Hawaii or along the shoreline of New Zealand. Most islands are small enough to cover in one trip, though the views will make it a challenge to keep your eyes on the road! Other organized international tours include a trip through the Gobi Desert in Mongolia, along the Danube River in Austria and in Portugal's Alentejo. Many people recommend continental Europe as the best place for cycling tours. Not only are most towns very close together, but the space between is filled with vineyards, quaint towns, ancient ruins, and flower fields. Some European tours have a cultural component as well, like wine tastings or evening performances. And you will have ample opportunity to savor the local cuisine, as your daily workout will demand the calorie consumption of an elephant.

SO I DECIDED TO BIKE ACROSS AMERICA

BY MIKE ZIMMER, 24

" Many of my classmates spent their senior years scrambling to fire off resumes, concoct cover letters, and interview for all types of 'jobs that paid money.' Early on, however, I had decided that the real world could wait for one more summer.

So I decided to bike across America. Not necessarily a logical leap, but I figured at the least I'd end up with a shapely backside. I joined the Habitat Bicycle Challenge and raised $3,500 for a local Habitat chapter. I departed from Connecticut with 30 other young people on a rainy morning and by lunchtime, I thought about calling it quits. But instead I kept pedaling, and pedaling, and then pedaling some more. For the next nine weeks, I saw America from a vantage point that few people get to experience. I stayed in community centers and churches in small towns, meeting diverse and interesting new people every night. I rode through some of the world's most beautiful terrain—the lush mountains of West Virginia, the rolling Bluegrass of Kentucky, the golden plains of Kansas, the stately Rocky Mountains, the unearthly landscapes of Bryce Canyon National Park, the majesty of Yosemite. All of that, plus enough road kill to fill up ten Olympic swimming pools. The Habitat Bicycle Challenge was not easy. But it paid me more in experience, adventure, and fun than any 'real' job could have ever offered. "

IN IT FOR THE LONG RUN: **The Marathon**. Even if you passed out after jogging a mile in gym class, you're not out of the running for making it through 26 of them. Yes, 26 miles. With a few months of training (three to five, depending on experience), multiple gallons of water, and a positive attitude, you'll be amazed how far your little feet can carry you. You could view your marathon as a one-time athletic pursuit for a summer or transition period between jobs or school, or as a commitment to fitness training for the entire following year or the rest of your life. Running is a fabulous sport for any young person, because it is cheap, you can do it anywhere and it is a great way to meet people. Local running clubs facilitate the social aspect of the sport. If 26 miles is definitely out of your league, split up the race between you and your buddies to make a relay. You can always do a half marathon, too—racing thirteen miles is no small accomplishment!

If you think crossing the marathon finish line would be amazing, imagine racing through a charming town or city's most historic streets while roaring crowds cheer you on. Cool marathon routes make every grueling mile worthwhile. There are the American classics, like Boston and New York City, for those who can meet qualifying standards, and some funky terrain courses, like the Snow Mountain Trail Marathon in Boulder and the Honolulu Marathon that starts in early morning darkness, bringing its runners through the Hawaiian sunrise. If you really want to reach your physical peak, give Pike's Peak a shot. This course goes all the way up the 11,000-foot famous American mountain. If you want to take your physical challenge overseas, or combine it with a traveling itinerary, you have some unbelievable courses to choose from. Run through the loud crowds of downtown Berlin, take part in the Thailand Temple run, or hop into Australia's Gold Coast Marathon. Don't miss out on the postrace parties to toast your athletic triumph. The alcohol flow at the Guinness Marathon party will knock you off your sore little feet. Check out *www.marathonguide.com* for a calendar.

If the price of airfare to these exotic locales makes you balk, consider a marathon training program organized by a nonprofit (such as the Leukemia Society). In exchange for raising money for a great cause, you'll score coaching and guidance, a weekly group of runners at your level, a ticket to a very cool location, and the best kind of motivation. Give *www.aidsmarathon.com* and *www.teamintraining.org* a look.

"The 'first marathon' is an experience you will only have once—make it memorable and have fun. Test your limits, learn more about yourself and earn more respect from your peers. The experience of crossing the finish line should be one filled with elation." —Vicki Mitchell, young professional runner

THE IRON MAN CAN
BY ANDY CHASIN, 28

" Some people join the army. Others scale mountains. I do triathlons. If you're looking for an invigorating challenge, then swimming, riding, and running your way to your goal (and a harder body) may be for you. Apart from the challenge, the best part of triathlons is the culture. I became hooked on the sport during my first race when I finally passed a guy who I had been trailing for almost the entire race. Instead of spitting at me or giving a grunt of indignation, he put his hands together and cheered me on.

My favorite race was the Santa Cruz Sentinel, which started with a Baywatch style mad beach dash into the ocean, a ride out along the breathtaking Pacific Coast Highway, and a run along the cliffs above the ocean. For a more social event, the Wildflower race is a weekend party, where racers camp out in the hills of northern California before a tough hilly course through a beautiful wild preserve. On the East Coast, the St. Anthony's race in Florida is early in the season and offers a sunny ocean swim as well as the chance to watch top professionals compete.

As triathlons become increasingly popular, especially among the twenty-to-thirty-year-old crowd, they are popping up all over. To get comfortable with crowded open-water swimming and transitions, you should start with a local sprint race—which is a .75k swim, 5k run, and 20k bike—then work up to an Olympic race, which is double those distances. An Ironman, which involves a grueling 2.5 mile swim, 100 mile ride, and 26 mile marathon, are for the truly insane and will suck up your life with training. But more power to you!

Gear for triathlons can get expensive, but it doesn't have to. Depending on where you race, you may need a wet suit for the swim, but you can probably rent one at a dive shop if you plan ahead. Good running shoes are a must for the knees, but any old bike will get you there. Triathletes reportedly have the highest per capita income of any organized recreational sport, so beware of lots of tricked-out yuppies on the latest carbon-fiber creations. But it will be all the more satisfying when you pass them on your old ten-speed. "

AIN'T NO MOUNTAIN HIGH ENOUGH. Looking for a giant challenge? One so huge the clouds hide it from your view? Mountain climbing is an intense experience that pits your body and will against the elements—the fiercest cold, steepest incline, and thinnest air. The world's highest peaks invite your challenge: Kilimanjaro in Kenya, Denali in Alaska, and Everest in Nepal. Just imagine the satisfaction of reaching the peak or that silly grin on your face on the way down. You can also trek through a mountainous region—such as Patagonia or the Mexican volcanoes—rather than marching up one killer incline.

For the larger peaks you will need to have general climbing skills and be able to handle high altitudes. Mountain treks, particularly the big ones, can be very expensive. A two-month trip up Everest could cost you $7,000! Ouch is right. So if you really want to go all out, you will have to dedicate some time to earning the money first. You can cut down the cost of your mountain trek dramatically by choosing a smaller peak and the cheapest outfitting company. Some peaks in the U.S. can be scaled in four days for $600. Most of the outfitters with websites are pretty costly, so if you have a chance to actually go to the area beforehand, try to find local guides who may lead your expedition for a discounted price. Just make sure you keep safety as much of a priority as savings.

> "One of my favorite hikes is the Chilkoot Trail in Southeast Alaska. It follows the historic path of Klondike gold rushers and is a fun trip and beautiful area."
> —Dave Pavlik, 26

HIKE IT. If a mountain trek adventure appeals to you, but the cost and intensity of the experience are a bit too much, hiking may be more your cup of tea. You don't have to hop on a plane or pay an exorbitant fee to explore nature. Nearly every corner of the world has a unique hiking route of its own and anyone can pick up this outdoor sport. Grab some friends, pack some treats, and chart your own course.

Start your preparations with a little research to find out which routes are doable in the season you plan to hike. And if you are going to be traveling overseas, consider incorporating a hiking adventure into the trip. In Peru, you can journey the Inca Trail to Macchu Picchu. In England, try the coast-to-coast walk through the pastoral highlands. Between Spain and France is the Pyrenean High Route and in the shadow of Mount Everest is the Nepalese Route.

"Hiking in Denali National Park was definitely the highlight of my year in Alaska. The park officials want to keep the human stain on the grounds to a minimum, so you can only have a specific number of hikers in one area at a time. We hiked in the middle of nowhere and there were absolutely no signs of human civilization. The landscape of Denali is amazing. Because it's the tundra, the ground itself looks very different than anywhere else in the Lower 48. We had to cross partially frozen creeks and found a ton of bear scat. Meanwhile we were darting through trees with heavy equipment and making sure to not follow in a line so we didn't ruin the tundra."
—Liz Hanpeter, 24

Extra Cool Hiking Routes:

- the Ozarks of Missouri
- Florida's Ocala National Forest
- the Grand Canyon in Arizona
- the John Muir Trail in California
- Vermont's Long Trail
- the West Coast Trail in British Columbia
- Alaska's Denali National Park
- the Appalachian Trail

Check out *www.backpacker.com* for more hiking route ideas and expert advice.

"I believe in doing what you want first and finding a way to pay for it second."
—Andrew Liverman, 24

CHOOSE YOUR OWN ADVENTURE. If you think your options end there, think again. With all of the diverse terrain covering the earth and with people constantly developing new challenges, an adventure seeker could never get bored on this planet. Every locale and season brings an exhilarating possibility.

- Cross-country ski or snowshoe in Alaska. For a cool spectator sport, go in time for a dogsledding competition.

- Sea kayak along the Southern California coastline.

- Embark on a river odyssey through the nation's heartland. Test your luck with fly-fishing while you're there.

- Take your pick from adventure racing, eco-challenge, or an iron man triathlon.

- Grab your cowboy hat and horseback ride in the Grand Canyon region. Yee-haw.

- Celebrate your youth with a spontaneous sky dive or bungee jump. Experience the most intense natural high money (and bravery) can buy.

For more wild ideas check out *Travels Along the Edge: 40 Ultimate Adventures for the Modern Nomad—From Crossing the Sahara to Bicycling Through Vietnam* by David Noland (Vintage, 1997).

WHISTLE WHILE YOU WORK:
OUTDOOR ADVENTURE JOBS

What if you could stretch out your mountain hike or river odyssey and turn it into a career? You would officially qualify as the luckiest person alive, surrounded by active young people and the fresh open air. Cubicle workers nationwide (and no, that's not a union, though perhaps it should be!) will look upon you with supreme envy. In this section you will find dozens of ways that you can construct such an ideal lifestyle by "working" in the great outdoors.

ADVENTURE SPORTS ASSISTANCE AND TOUR GUIDING All kinds of people are hungry for adventure—whether it's a quick weekend adrenaline rush or a vacation thrill for the whole family. Companies have sprouted up all over the U.S. and overseas, offering attractive options to adventure seekers. Lucky for you, these companies need employees. Here is a list of some of the job positions within the adventure sports industry:

- White-water rafting guide
- Bungee jumping attendant
- Kayaking instructor
- Hot air balloon attendant
- Rock climbing attendant
- Mountaineering guide
- Kite surfing instructor
- Cycling leader
- Hiking leader
- Caving instructor
- Parasailing instructor
- Scuba instructor
- Surfing instructor
- Sky diving instructor

Get Official. Many outdoor adventure companies have specific training requirements for their employees. The following is a list of common certifications employers demand. Read them over and consider enrolling in one or two certification classes to improve your chances of obtaining a job:

- CPR & First Aide Certification
- Wilderness first aide
- Water safety
- Lifeguard training
- Commercial driver's license
- U.S. Coast Guard Freshwater & River Guide License
- Professional Ski Instructors of America certification
- Snowboarding certification

"Talk to any 50-year-old about your dreams for adventure and he will tell you to 'Do it now; you can't do it later.' Speak with any of your peers and they will rant, 'I am so jealous. I wish I could be a river guide.' Guess what? They can, and so can you.

I decided that after college was the best time for embracing true passions. My passion is water. In particular whitewater. It was an easy decision to make. Granted, you don't get paid much money, but as I used to say, 'We get paid in adrenaline!' Rent is free because you live outdoors in a tent alongside people who share your same interests. Everyday I woke up for work excited about the day. That alone is worth a million bucks. It's very easy to get into the rafting world. You just have to be in good physical condition and be prepared for an extremely rigorous training program. As far as my career goes, it hasn't been hampered a bit.

After working on the river for a season, followed by stints at a cookie factory and a ski resort, I got a call from my former employer on the river about a job as a sales manager. They wanted a kayaker who was educated, had some personality, and had a good work ethic. I'm not sure which one of those won me the job, but here I am. I still live right near the river and have the best life imaginable for someone with a 'real' job. I ski, kayak, climb, or mountain bike after work and get to travel to cool places like Utah, Maine, Ottawa, and hopefully Japan and Europe in the near future. My advice? Follow your passion. And remember, raft naked! It adds color to your cheeks! "

How do you score one of these dream jobs that will place you outdoors in a picturesque location, offer you the good company of sporty young co-workers, and pay you to do what you would do anyway in your free time? Well, employers are often looking for physical fitness, strong people skills for dealing with guests and customers, leadership ability, capacity for teamwork, flexibility, tolerance for rough outdoor conditions, and sometimes experience teaching children. Past work experience and specific work skills may be preferred for some positions, but don't let this deter you from applying. Play up any of the above skills you possess and convey how enthusiastic you are at the prospect of being part of their team. Also be sure to complete as many of the certification courses as you can.

If you happen to have a good chunk of cash saved from your last job, or perhaps have a generous graduation gift coming your way, consider investing in an intense outdoor experience at National Outdoor Leadership School (*www.nols.edu*). Though there is a large price tag attached to this wilderness education program (as high as $3,500), it is a good investment if you are committed to working in the great outdoors. Completion of NOLS's challenging curriculum is widely recognized in the adventure sports industry as a mark of a seasoned outdoorsman and equips you with both leadership and technical skills. Choosing one of the nine schools that are spread all over the country and world (Kenya, Mexico, and Chile), you will participate in such activities as kayaking, backcountry skiing, mountaineering, and rafting. You have your choice of dedicating 10 or 30 days to NOLS training or opting for their semester-long course. Outward Bound offers similar outdoor education programs in over 26 countries(*www.outwardbound.org*). Regardless of which school you choose, you will have a valuable experience behind you that makes you more attractive to potential employers.

KUMBAYA: CAMPS

Picture your classic summer camp: tree-lined lake, narrow trails through the woods, and a toasty campfire for making gooey S'mores. Now imagine being able to enjoy all that without sleeping in bunk beds, wearing the heinous bathing suit your mom packed, or living in fear of daddy-long-legs. Fortunately, the camp experience as a counselor is much cooler than it is as an awkward teen. And today there are countless alternative camps that have unique philosophies, activities, locations, and groups of campers. You can work at a camp for disabled children, inner-city kids, or troubled youths. Some camps focus on one specific goal or program, such as a sport, environmental conservation, weight-loss, religion, or natural science.

Camp counseling may be your ideal job if you love to be outdoors, have the patience and desire to work with children, or possess certain athletic, craft, musical, or academic skills. Counseling could also be the perfect enjoyable moneymaker for the fleeting sunny months after graduation. But there are plenty of camps that function all year around as well, such as therapeutic camps, survival camps, retreat centers, and team-building camps for company employees. You will be amazed at the perks, amenities, and grounds of some of the newest camps when you find yourself trout fishing, climbing through ropes courses, and scuba diving. Enjoy the perks, the paychecks, and the second childhood.

LIONS AND TIGERS AND TEENS, OH MY.

BY BRITT HARTER, 22

“ If you love to be outside and have some backpacking experience, then I would recommend working in Wilderness Teen Adventures for the summer. You have to be pretty hardcore and have lots of experience to lead trips for National Outdoor Leadership School (NOLS) or Outward Bound, but other wilderness travel companies are slightly less rigorous (companies such as The Road Less Traveled, Adventures Cross Country, Wilderness Ventures, etc.). These companies offer summer experiences to teens that combine the beauty and disorientation of the wilderness with friendship and team-building activities. I got to spend the night amidst Anasazi potsherds on the red dirt of a Navajo family's backyard, hike breathtaking 13,000 foot New Mexican mountain ranges, learn to rock climb, and be a positive influence on young teenagers. And I got paid for every minute of it. My groups were an interesting mix of privileged and scholarship kids who both needed my interest and support in different but meaningful ways. The only thing you need besides a little experience and a love of kids is a Wilderness First Responder (WFR) certification, which is an eighty-hour course in wilderness medicine that takes two weeks and is well worth the time—if only for the practical medical skills you learn. ”

CAMP CAT MAN WHO?:

I was reading over a list of international programs for teens, turning green with envy and wondering when pimply kids stopped going to Camp Onawanda and started popping over to Kathmandu, when it dawned on me. All of these fancy shmancy programs need reliable role models to lead awkward hormone cases overseas, right? Well you're just the one to do it! That is, as long as you don't mind holding the hands of teens through a bout of culture shock and handling some uninvited crushes. The majority of these programs run in summer months and many provide room and board, weekly stipends, and travel expenses for their employees.

Take advantage of this opportunity to explore nature's worldwide treats without the burden of costly travel expenditures.

Blue Dorado Teenage Summer Adventures *(www.bluedoradoadventures.com)* Take ten teenagers on a three-week yacht trip in the Caribbean, teaching scuba diving, sailing, water-skiing, and more.

Adventure Teen Travel *(www.adventureteentravel.com)* Lead summer camps and travel tours for teenagers aged 12–18 in the Canadian Rockies, the Pacific Coast, Quebec, the Caribbean, and Europe.

Camp Counselors USA, Outbound Program *(www.ccusa.com)* Work as a counselor in Australia, New Zealand, Russia, Brazil, the UK, and the U.S.

Broadreach *(www.gobroadreach.com)*. Lead groups of teens on adventures in the Carribean, Australia, Honduras, the Sinai Peninsula, Fiji, or Baja..

American Adventures Venture Everywhere *(www.aave.com)* Lead adventure travel for teens in diverse places such as Alaska, the Galapagos, and Vietnam.

CAMPS FOR THE MIND, BODY, AND SPIRIT

If you are into self-exploration, spiritual growth, and alternative lifestyles, look into the many yoga institutes, holistic learning centers, and Zen centers that have popped up across the country. Many are located in beautiful remote wilderness areas and focus on meditation, crafts, communal work, bodywork, and healthy living. Some centers hire employees to serve visitors while others offer work-study programs. Check out Omega (www.eomega.org) and Kripalu Center for Yoga and Health (www.kripalushop.org).

PARK IT RIGHT HERE

If you love the outdoors, and also take natural conservation and maintenance very seriously, pick up an application for a position at one of our country's pristine national parks. Work on trail maintenance, serve as an interpretive naturalist, or keep vigilant watch for forest fires. One of the best ways to get your foot in the door in the National Park Service is through the Student Conservation Association. An internship at this conservation education association has become a rite of passage for national parks professionals. There are paid positions within the SCA and both seasonal and year-round assignments are available.

TAKE NOTE! If applying for a federal government job, it is important to meet their strict deadlines. Keep these dates in mind.

November 1st: First day that you can get an application for summer employment.

December 1st: Aim to send in your application on the first day possible—the first of December.

January 15th: Last day you can submit a summer application. Mark your calendar!

Another technicality to note is that you can apply to just one national forest and two national parks every year. The obvious precaution to take is to call the hiring officials at each forest or park and find out what your chances are of getting a job. Lastly, take the application process seriously and leave yourself adequate time to complete the tedious paperwork.

During your job hunt, keep in mind that the most famous national parks like Yellowstone will be the most competitive. If working within feet of Ol' Faithful is a lifelong dream, then go ahead and pursue a position. Otherwise, use the directory of the National Park Service to find names of less-known, but very interesting sites that have cool attractions like caverns, fossil beds, glaciers, mesas, sand dunes, or even flamingos! Because you'll be passing every waking (and possibly sleeping) minute outdoors, take the weather of the regions you consider into account, especially if the summer season brings severe conditions. Also remember that national parks aren't limited to the 50 U.S. states, but extend to Guam, Puerto Rico, and the Virgin Islands. Housing—which is typically provided or available for a small charge—could range from a floating cabin to a tent in the heart of the woods.

If you would prefer to work for a nonprofit devoted to the preservation of nature, there are plenty of conservation agencies, mountain clubs, and even hiking societies across the U.S. Non-government jobs typically require less paperwork from their applicants and have less strict hiring practices. For budding environmentalists there are nature centers, wildlife sanctuaries, naturalist societies, botanical gardens, environmental advocacy groups and environmental education centers. One good option is to work for a private contractor who is doing reforesting work on government lands (work is concentrated mainly in the Northwest). Check out *JobMiner.com* for employment leads.

HOW TO BE A HOTSHOT

BY ASHLEY FLORADAY, 21

"I had never even been camping until I went to college, so I certainly never considered becoming a 'hot-shot,' or a highly skilled wild land firefighter. A six-month internship with the Student Conservation Association at Hovenweep National Monument started me on this path. My job with the SCA enabled me to do really interesting things, ranging from trail rebuilding with the Sierra Club, teaching Navajo children science and archaeology, and getting government vehicles really muddy on park roads!

The Student Conservation Association is the big 'in' for young people who want to get public parks jobs. About seventy percent of the park's workers I've met got their start that way. SCA internships provide a stipend and usually housing as well. There are all sorts of jobs: night-sky study, fire-fighting jobs, kayak instructing, wilderness patrol, and educational camps. Any experience in forestry will help you get hired, but don't distress if you are 'green' to the outdoors. My advice is to call the parks you are interested in and get the name of the hiring official. Politely harass them as much as possible. Make sure they remember your name. Most of the park officials I've met are receptive to anyone who is enthusiastic about working at their park. Furthermore, getting hired by the park or forest service is a confusing process. The hiring officials gave me great advice on how to find jobs and make myself more attractive as a candidate. "

HAVE YOU GOT GAME?

Imagine being paid to play the sport you love. Being a pro athlete seems out of reach to most of us, but if you do a little investigative work, you may find that your dribbling skills or killer kick could earn you a spot on an overseas sports team. Playing or touring in a foreign country could be the opportunity of a lifetime. If you don't have enough faith in your ability to even consider amateur sports, you can always seek employment in a number of sports-related jobs. You could announce for professional sporting events, work publicity or grounds management, caddy for a hot-shot golfer, or assist in a sports camp or clinic.

> "After my senior basketball season ended, I knew I wanted to continue pursuing my passion—basketball—while I was still young. I actively looked at European pro teams and spoke with several agents, coaches, and teams to try to find any opportunity to continue playing. I found a team in England, and I've loved the experience ever since I got here. I have made many life-long friends in England; I have gotten to travel all over the UK; and I have been paid to play a sport that I love, instead of sitting in an office all day."
>
> —Ted Smith, 25

For a unique combination of athletics and global service, check out Right to Play (*www.righttoplay.com*). They place experienced volunteers for one to two year periods in Asia, Africa, and the Middle East to promote sport and play activities. Also consider an internship at the U.S. Olympic Committee that will place you among Olympic athletes in training (*www.olympic-usa.org*). Positions are available in Lake Placid (NY) and Chula Vista (CA) as well as at the headquarters in Colorado Springs. Stipend, housing, and meals are provided. Another perk is access to top-of-the-line athletic facilities.

Sun & Service. Want to combine your passion for the outdoors with community service? Be a counselor at Camp Wakonda, a free summer camp for homeless children in the foothills of Bear Mountain (one hour from New York City). Counselors work at building self-esteem and getting campers excited about nature. Stipend, room and board are provided. Positions include waterfront staff, counselors, unit leaders and activity specialists (*www.backdoorjobs.com/campwakonda.html*).

" Everyone wants to have a backup plan in case their ideal plan doesn't work out. But there is also something to be said for burning your ships. I tried to make the U.S. Rowing National Team the two summers before I graduated, and failed both times. When no jobs panned out during my senior year, I graduated with only one thing to do— make the team.

The following summer I lived in a barren dorm room and rowed twice a day in weather so hot and humid I felt like I was breathing soup. I found that I rowed a little harder and pushed a little farther. Now a member of the national team, I have raced in Spain, Italy, England, Korea, Taiwan and the Dominican Republic, represented the U.S.A. at two world championships, the Pan American Games, won two medals along the way, and will hopefully have the opportunity to represent the U.S. at the Olympics.

Perhaps the smartest thing I did was seek out retired national team rowers. I emailed and called many legendary ex-athletes, told them what I was doing and asked about their experiences and advice. They gave me great advice about what to do and especially what *not* to do so I could avoid their common pitfalls. My advice is that if you have a passion for something, whether it is athletics, the arts, academics, or something totally unique, follow that passion and don't wait. For me there was no possibility of postponing. That urgency may be less apparent in non-athletic endeavors, but I believe that every day you postpone a dream you weaken it a little bit. The longer you wait, the less likely you will ever chase it. "

RESORTS, RANCHES AND LODGES

Tap into tourism to make your ideal outdoor adventure a daily reality. Every getaway, from the enormous beach resort to the quaint family-owned ranch, could use a hand in keeping their guests diverted, happy, and well-fed. This means that there are loads of employment opportunities that could situate you in the most beautiful regions of the country and give you all of the amenities to take advantage of them.

Take your pick from:

• Moose Creek Ranch (*www.mooseranch.com*)

• Verde Ranch (*www.tangueverderanch.com*)

• Prairie Ranch (*www.ranchforlife.com*)

Fly Away to Mackinac Island. Flutter amongst the butterflies at Mackinac Island's Butterfly House (*Mibh@myfine.com*). This remote island in Michigan, which can only be reached by high-speed ferry and is only navigable by horse drawn carriage, offers a whole slew of summer employment options between May and Labor Day. You can work at Mackinac State Park as a naturalist, a historic interpreter, an archeologist or a blacksmith (*www.MackinacParks.com*).

❝ When someone (usually examining my resume and sitting across a desk) asks me what I did last year, I don't think they expect me to say 'Oh, I was a bum.' A ski bum that is. But in fact, I explain my post-college year with pride. Skiing 100 days in one season is something I'll never have the chance to do again. I spent the season of 2002–03 as a ski instructor in Vail, Colorado. The job has some major perks, starting with a free season pass (that's like a $1,000 signing bonus), pro deals on equipment, and endless training opportunities—not to mention good company. The other instructors you work with are a blast. Every job in ski town has its advantages and disadvantages. A ski instructor doesn't get a day off for weeks at a time during the holidays and spring break, but can ski free nearly every day in January. A bartender can ski all day every day, but won't have much of a social life and goes to bed every night at 4AM. And while 'parking lot attendant' doesn't sound particularly interesting, social, or warm, he works only early in the morning and then has the rest of the day to ski and night to party.

Whatever employment you seek in a ski town, the key to getting the right job is to go early—late October or early November. At that time of the year the job openings are endless. There are walk-in interviews and open houses every day, and the classifieds are packed. Check the mountain's website too. Living in a ski town is a fun time (which is why a lot of grizzled ski instructors tell you they never left after their ski-bumming year was over). Oh, and did I mention that I taught Britney Spears how to walk uphill on skis? **❞**

Ski Bum. Don't go back to bartending at that hole-in-the-wall in your hometown. Get a bartending position at a ski chalet, where you can work the bar by night and hit the slopes by day. Many ski resorts offer their employees season passes, and sometimes free or subsidized housing and discounted meals. If you have experience and certification, you can spend night and day in the powdery snow teaching lessons or working ski patrol. If not, there are many standard positions like waitressing, hotel service work and rental counter staff. Get a group of fun-loving friends to work the slopes with you and share housing in ski town. You will learn to fly down black diamonds and earn the regal title "ski bum" for your wise selection of a post-college adventure.

There are plenty of employment options for those who arrive on the slopes without a job in hand, especially if you show up early enough for the fall job fairs. Aspen, for example, has a nearly 0% unemployment rate. So before you run off to the first place that promises you a paycheck, think about where you want to live. Aspen also has a tremendously high cost of living and you may have to get yourself three of those bountiful jobs just to afford residing there. Every resort town attracts a different type, which consequently gives each one a distinct feel (ritzy, quaint, granola-ish, Mormon). Take stock of all of your options, from New Hampshire to Wyoming. Consider the clientele you'll be catering to and what type of community you prefer.

When the summer sun turns your precious powder into slush, you may be able to finagle yourself a ski stint overseas (where winter season is just beginning) through your employer. Some American ski companies sponsor employees in resorts all over the globe. This should facilitate getting a work permit and keep you in your snowy element all year long.

10 THINGS TO KEEP IN MIND WHEN HITTING THE MOUNTAIN

Twenty-two year-old Breckenridge veteran Colleen McCarthy on how to play your cards right in a ski town—black diamonds and all.

1. The ski industry relies on seasonal workers to function. Jobs are plentiful and easy to get. I know people that have moved here and found employment the very next day.

2. Go to the websites of a handful of ski resorts and find their employment information and procedures. You can contact the resort's human resource department for information. They normally tell you to come out and apply for the job in person.

3. Many ski resorts hold job fairs in October that pull in employers from the surrounding region. Many employers interview on the spot. Personality and people skills count for a lot—more than neat appearances. Jeans and sports gear are considered appropriate.

4. Although employers are eager to snatch up energetic young people to keep their slopes running smoothly, you often have to show proof of residence (like a lease or a PO box) before you are guaranteed a job.

5. Take a good look at the benefits each resort offers. You should get a complimentary ski pass, decent health insurance that will cover any skiing accidents and a livable wage ($8–10/hr). Some resorts give their young employees housing or offer subsidized housing. This is a great way to meet other young people quickly. If you do arrange housing yourself, just make sure you're within walking distance of the mountain. Some resorts have organized internships that set up practically everything for you (Crested Butte Mountain Resort , Telluride Ski And Golf Company).

6. You have a whole range of jobs open to you. Investigate and choose your ideal position. You don't have to be that great of a skier to be an instructor for kids. A capacity to deal with children is actually more important. But ski instructors are usually only paid by the lesson and new instructors have last priority in getting groups to teach. You might spend more time waiting around on the slopes than actually earning money. Working the ski lift is probably the most social job on the Mountain. Our lifties are always having a good time! Working in a smaller business in the resort town can be more lucrative than the mountain jobs. Retail is huge in ski towns. I work at a North Face store in Breckenridge and the hours are so good that I can really craft my own schedule and at the same time, always rely on getting solid hours.

7. Every ski town is different: Vail and Aspen are pretty ritzy and draw a wealthier crowd. Other towns like Breckenridge are smaller and more rustic. Park City has the best snow, but is right in the heart of Mormon Country, which is a bit at odds with the ski bum culture.

8. All ski towns are very transitional. About 50% of the population is in their twenties and most of these young people are on the go. Everyone is really well educated and has grand life ambitions, but is also adventurous and fun-loving. We cherish our youth here!

9. Ski season ends in April and most resort towns just shut down. If you don't move out on the same seasonal schedule, you might lose money. Have a plan! I was lucky to find a job at a summer camp for kids that kept me employed and really happy, too. Use the connections you make once you arrive to secure some type of job for the spring and summer. Some resort towns, like Grand Targhee (WY) and Maggie Pond (CO), have summer music festivals. Others have camping and recreational facilities that bring more jobs.

10. If you are female and single, come join me out here! The guy-to-girl ratio is out of control!

Hey, Dude. Situate yourself in a riverside town in the mountains where you lead horseback rides during the day and strum your guitar by the bonfire at night. Most dude ranches not only offer gorgeous locations and a wealth of outdoor activities, but also free employee housing, meals, and a seasonal stipend. Positions range from waitress, housekeeper, receptionist, kitchen worker, riding guide, wrangler, ground maintenance, and kid's counselor. If you don't mind a "western dress code," corny sing-a-longs, and square dancing with old guests, the dude ranch is for you!

Resort to the Beach. Wouldn't it be cool if someone paid you to sit on the beach all day? Lifeguarding is just one of the many coveted positions you can obtain in a resort. Many resorts also employ scuba instructors, sailing teachers, waterskiing instructors, golf caddies, tennis teachers, day care workers, beach bartenders, and waitresses. Take your dream vacation spot and make it your new home base.

Some resorts and hotels aim to hire people who can commit to more than one season, so market your availability. A few resorts, like Amelia Island Plantation, have specific short-term job opportunities for young people. This Florida resort, voted one of the ten most beautiful beaches in the world, offers internships to college seniors as well as regular jobs to qualified young people. Positions range from four-to-twelve months and are available in all areas, like aquatics, marketing, culinary, golf, and nature.

Transport yourself to a foreign location and the perk possibilities multiply. Think white beaches of the Caribbean, coastal villas in southern Italy or isolated getaways in the South Pacific. One of your best chances for a job placement overseas is Club Med (*www.clubmed.com*). Working at this famous all-inclusive resort company will offer you the chance to work with young people from all over the world, not to mention interacting with high-powered international guests. Club Med resorts provide their employees with unlimited use of all amenities, monthly drink tabs, and free housing. They also give you a salary, insurance, and even round-trip transportation (so you don't have to break the bank to arrive overseas). In pursuing employment with Club Med, like any other potential employer in the hospitality industry, just remember that people skills count more than anything else. Present yourself well—as neat, attractive, confident, and bubbling over with enthusiasm as you possibly can. Foreign language skills may also better your chances, so hone up on those as best you can.

THE ORGANIC EXPERIENCE

If you really want to get your hands dirty—in fresh, chemical-free soil—head out to the countryside and join an organic farm community. There you will find a healthy-living philosophy that pervades every facet of your experience, from the meals you share to the daily tasks you are assigned. As an apprentice, you will learn health-based growing techniques and pick up skills you never imagined you would possess, like livestock management, cheese making, or logging. Many organic farms provide free housing (which may mean a barn loft) and of course daily rations of incredibly fresh produce. You can take your pick from a variety of organic farms, from house-powered or experimental farms, to farms with environmental education facilities, bed 'n breakfasts, and yoga clinics.

Job Hunting Tip: In applying for farm apprenticeships, keep in mind that employers are looking for more than someone to do grunt work. Most want apprentices who are interested in the philosophy of sustainable farming and communal effort. They may also be looking for young people who are considering careers in agriculture. Make sure to convey your interest in organic farming and in their farm in particular, as well as your eagerness to learn.

If you want to go global, your best option is World Wide Opportunities on Organic Farms (WWOOF, *www.wwoof.org*). This organization provides a listing of farms across the globe—some commercial and others co-operatives—that are pursuing a simple, sustainable lifestyle and that welcome volunteer assistance in exchange for housing. You join the WWOOF chapter of the country you are interested in and search the database for potential hosts. Arrangements are made between farmers and volunteers; however, WWOOF suggests an exchange of six hours of work six days a week. Chores may range from gardening, harvesting, sowing, milking, cutting wood, and making compost. The minimum stay is two nights, whereas the maximum is up to you and your host.

The National Future Farmers of America offers a World Experience in Agriculture Program (*www.ffa.org*) that is intended for young people who want to work on one specific farm for a long period of time (three to twelve months). The program fee is hefty ($2,000 and up) but covers airfare, transportation, orientation, room and board, and health insurance. Other programs include Mast International Experience Abroad (*www.mast.coafes.umn.edu*) and International Agricultural Exchange Association (*www.agriventure.com/aboutasp*).

WOOF ON BY
BY MARY FINNAN, 21

" When I decided I wanted to go to France for a summer, my bank account didn't look so keen on the idea. A friend suggested that I participate in World Wide Opportunities for Organic Farming (WWOOF), a nonprofit organization that connects willing workers with farmers all around the globe. Perhaps it was a little risky to agree to help a 49-year-old farmer who lived on a remote farm in rural France, but I'm so glad that I took my friend's advice. I spent a month on a biodynamic goat farm in the Pyrenees, where I fed and herded goats, learned the basics of cheese-making, gardened, helped with the hay harvest, canned jam, and made French cherry tarts. In the WWOOF agreement, farmers provide room and board for their workers. In my case, this meant I slept in my own personal caravan on the farm. My only costs were travel and extra expenses, like the occasional pain au chocolat! While the farm was pretty isolated and I could only go into town for two hours a week, solitude was just what I needed after a hectic college semester. The work was physically strenuous but satisfying.

How does one become a WWOOFer? For $25, I purchased a year-long membership to the French chapter of WWOOF and had access to an online list of participating farms throughout the country. The listings include a brief description of the farms, the work to be done, languages spoken (you don't necessarily have to know the language), and the farmers' contact information. There are as many work seekers as there are work sites, but as long as you are truly interested in organic farming, willing to work really hard and want to see something besides major cities, you will definitely have your share of options. You don't need any previous experience and you can do WWOOF alone or with a friend. It can be lonely and a little risky, but since all work is voluntary, you can always leave if you find yourself in an uncomfortable situation. WWOOF is what you make of it. I made a lot of cheese, plumped up some goats, and found myself the best adventure I could hope for in a summer. I highly recommend rolling up your sleeves and joining WWOOF. "

ALASKA FISHING JOBS

Aching to explore a final frontier but not quite ready for outer space? Head north—really north. With vast rugged terrain and glacial wonders, Alaska lends herself generously to the adventure-seeker. For those who are willing to rough it a bit and work until their hands are calloused and blue, fishing jobs are a worthwhile option. Positions are available year-round but particularly in the summer salmon season (when weather is also more favorable). You could work at a remote hatchery cultivating fish eggs, operate machinery on a huge factory trawler, or catch crab on a four-man boat. Work conditions promise to be cold, wet, and harsh but also challenging in a way you might never again experience in your life. Think of it as boot camp, but with astonishing scenery and no angry sergeants screaming in your face (although I have heard tales of hazing on fishing boats). You'll also earn a good chunk of cash, especially if your employer provides housing or if you are in such a remote location that there's no possible way to blow money.

If you happen to live in the Pacific Northwest, one way to commence your job adventure is to track down a ship during off-season in Seattle, which is the point many ships embark from. For three dollars, you can buy five days of access to AlaskaJobFinder.com, which provides listings of employers and helpful insider tips. First check out JobMonkey.com's free section on Alaska fishing jobs to prep yourself on the basics of the industry and peak hiring times.

SEWARD'S FINEST FOLLY
BY GEORGE OVERPECK, 29

" Ever thought about doing one summer's worth of work to pay off all of your loans and debts and then spending eight months in Europe? Well, forget about it. It probably won't happen. Except that it does happen once in while—when someone makes it happen. Go fish!

I spent a summer on a fishing boat in Alaska and made three thousand dollars in just weeks. I met a crewmember who made thirty thousand dollars in a half hour when his boat wrapped the net around a mass of herring the size of a Wal-Mart. Before striking gold, however, he had been working on the shore for at least two weeks, had helped pilot the boat for eight days, and had woken up early for a week.

Fisheries in Alaska go through cycles of boom and bust and boats can have lucky and unlucky days, weeks, or months. The only way to get a fishing job is to be there on the spot when a captain needs someone. Don't write them, call them, or email them. Go

(continued)

to a fishing port in the months or weeks before the season and walk around asking about work and learn as much as you can about the prices and fisheries. Good towns to try are Bellingham, Seattle, Ketchikan, Sitka, Cordova, Valdez, Seward, Homer, Kodiak, Kenai, Naknek, and Dillingham.

Employers seek crew members who have some boat knowledge or at least common sense, have mechanical skills or maybe have worked with heavy equipment before, have safety consciousness (first aid skills are a plus), can work tremendously hard, can cook, and get along with others. Whiners, martyrs, and mutineers are not popular. Some fishermen consider having females on board bad luck. However, others like to have women because they are good communicators and because most girls who make their way north to go fishing are at least as tough as the guys.

If someone offers you a job, take stock of the situation before starting. If the captain and crew don't seem like people who you would get along with, you almost definitely won't enjoy bobbing around in a 40-foot boat for a month with them. A certain amount of abuse is standard for the industry, but most fishermen are pretty good people who just get excited about the stakes. It is a good idea, though, to ask around about the boat's reputation for honesty, safety, and moneymaking ability.

Not every area in Alaska is drop-dead gorgeous, but most of them are, and you will be amazed by the friendly, down-to-earth, tough-as-nails fishermen that you meet when you go to sea in Alaska. The experience, the people, and the amazing history and color of the industry will definitely be more rewarding than any money you make. You can only tour Europe so many times, but you may find yourself fishing forever. "

NATURAL WONDERS

If you view the great outdoors as an intriguing science exhibit as well as a lush playground, find a way to enjoy nature's wonders while learning about them. Teach visitors at an observatory during the day and spend your nights gazing at the stars. Work as a paleontology intern at Florissant Fossil Beds National Monument. Assist in the archaeological excavation of a Native American village in Colorado. Find an opening in a sun-filled botanical garden and tend to your leafy friends. Work as a trainer in an aquarium so you can swim with dolphins and sea otters all day. Observe volcanoes, chase tornadoes, trail humpback whales—whatever grabs your curiosity!

" Majoring in science is hard. Everyone thinks you're a geek and your parents keep hounding you about becoming a doctor. One thing I've learned, though, is that Bachelor of Science degrees are highly employable. And this doesn't mean you have to jump right into the laboratory after graduation. A friend of mine who majored in physics just spent nine months in Antarctica with NASA. I found many summer science internships during my college years. I researched marine invertebrates on a Woods Hole Oceanographic institution ship and also worked as a bird-watcher in rural California and Arizona, observing and catching birds. I had no previous experience in birding, but did have two years college biology and a willingness to live outside.

I have turned that experience into a British Petroleum Conservation Grant, and I am headed to Equatorial Guinea on the West Coast of Africa to gain new knowledge for science about the species of birds that reside there. This trip has no bosses, no infrastructure, and I have to plan it all—from tents to first aid to data collection instruments. My work will influence the conservation strategies for the regions I study.

A science background can bring you many outstanding paid opportunities. The best way to find field jobs is to check the fisheries and wildlife job board on the Texas A&M website (it is widely regarded as the best). For grants, my advice is to befriend the professors of your university. They know about funding opportunities that you might not find on your own. "

Note: *Last news of Britt was that he had just returned to civilization in Equatorial New Guinea after 37 straight days in the wilderness and was babysitting an orphaned baby chimpanzee.*

Considering Veterinarian School, but still unsure if it's the path for you?

Intern at **the Farm Sanctuary** in a picturesque town in upstate New York called Watkins Glen. Here you will care for abused and injured animals. Year-round positions are available for volunteers who can make a substantial time commitment to the Farm Sanctuary. Housing is provided (*www.farmsanctuary.org*). If are willing to jump overseas, consider the **Wild Animal Rescue Foundation of Thailand**. You will work on conservation projects at a wildlife sanctuary, a zoo and an animal rescue center. Volunteers do everything from tracking the nesting patterns of sea turtles to caring for abused gibbons. Veterinary experience is preferred, but some projects accept individuals who demonstrate a love for animals even though they do not have experience. Volunteers must provide their own transportation and pay a program fee. Insurance and meals are provided (*www.warthai.org*).

Now that you are inspired, let's figure out how to get you one of these dream jobs. Hopefully this chapter has already helped you narrow down your choices and you now have an idea of what area you're interested in.

You should begin by obtaining the information you need to contact potential employers. Find a popular resource within your area of interest—a newspaper, journal, or website. Think about the producer side of the industry—what resources would your potential employer use, or print their contact information in? Some examples include Archaeological Fieldwork Opportunities Bulletin, the Alternative Farming Systems Information Center, and the U.S. Forest Service Offices. Also think about the consumer side. What tools would a tourist use if they wished to find an outdoor adventure center? The Internet, of course. Type "white water rafting" into a search engine and browse through the sites to find river sports providers. Copy the names and contact information of the companies or organizations that appeal to you most.

Don't rule out the good old Yellow Pages as a useful resource. There may be a small company with a very local focus that hasn't caught onto the whole web thing yet. Having publicized less, they will have less job seekers contacting them. You might have a better shot at a job at a small operation. Dropping into a local travel agency may help you gather materials for seeking work at a resort in a specific region. Lastly, use any connections you can and give the employment section of the classified ads a look. There's nothing wrong with a job hunt done the old-fashioned way!

Hit the Books: Learning Vacations

There are a number of resource books that are designed to help people find exciting adventure spots and plan quality vacations. Many catalog the diverse array of "learning vacations" or "service-learning travel" that exist, such as horseback riding through the canyons of the American Southwest, photography seminars in Alaska, riverboat voyages down the Amazon River, yoga tours through spiritual India, and hikes through the Japanese Alps. These books contain a gold mine of potential employers. Breeze through them to gather the contact information of the companies and organizations you are interested in.

- *Vacations That Can Change Your Life* by Ellen Lederman (Sourcebooks, 1998).

- *Learning Vacations* by Gerson G. Eisenburg (Acropolis Books, 1978).

- *Fodor's Great American Learning Vacations: Hundreds of Workshops, Camps, and Tours That Will Satisfy Your Curiosity and Enrich Your Life* (Fodor's, 1997).

- *The Back Door Guide to Short Term Job Adventures* by Michael Landes (Ten Speed Press, 2001).

- *Alternative Travel Directory* by David Cline (Transitions Abroad Publications, 2002).

- *Volunteer Vacations* by Bill McMillon (Chicago Review Press, 2003).

- *Healing Centers and Retreats: Healthy Getaways for Every Body and Budget* by Jennifer Miller (Avalon Travel Publishing, 1998).

- *Travel Unlimited: Uncommon Adventures for the Mature Traveler* by Alison Gardner (Avalon Travel Publishing, 2000).

Many of the companies and organizations in these resource books are small (some are even family-owned) and consequently have small staffs. Furthermore, many hire ex-professionals or trained tour guides to lead their trips, making your odds at employment even more difficult. However, like my journalism professor taught me, you'll only find that one pearl if you cast your net a hundred times and pry open every clam. There are enough volunteer vacation companies that hire fresh young people to make your pursuit worthwhile. Go to the websites of the companies and organizations that have piqued your interest, look for an employment section or an inquiry email address, and present yourself as the perfect little apprentice their team has been waiting for.

The next step is to get your application out. Timing is key here. The majority of job openings for outdoor jobs are for the summer season, particularly entry-level positions. Most application deadlines are in the early spring, but a few are earlier. You should aim to have your applications in the mail by early winter to assure that you make deadlines, and also to better your chances. Don't use the same cover letter for many companies (I've learned the hard way, cutting and pasting can get you into trouble!). Many employers will only give a serious look to someone who has taken the time to learn about their company, has shown special interest in being a part of it, and has taken the time to highlight why they are a good match. Lastly, if you are willing to commit a long period of time to your adventure job (i.e. six months, two years), make sure to emphasize this commitment because it will significantly improve your chances of obtaining a job.

In terms of what to emphasize in a phone-interview or email, make sure to provide an example of your leadership. Many outdoor adventure companies want to hire young people with the confidence and capacity to lead groups. If you were a captain of an athletic team (in high school or college), worked as a camp counselor, served as a residential advisor of a dorm, or organized any sort of large activity, make it work in your favor. While the hospitality industry mainly looks for one-on-one charisma and a pleasant demeanor for interacting with guests, the outdoor adventure industry demands a little more. You will have to motivate and guide people of all levels of outdoor experience. As a camp counselor you'll have to command the respect and attention of chatty teen. And, as a white water rafting guide you'll have to speak reassuringly over a boat of nervous first-timers. Your employer has to have confidence in you, so make sure you display confidence in yourself. Another characteristic you should try to stress is reliability. An outdoor adventure job won't be subject to the kind of supervision that your typical job is. So you'll want to show your potential employer that you will perform out on the river, in the heart of the woods, or wherever it is that you will be working.

JOB SEARCH ADVICE FROM THE TOP:

Employers give their two cents about jobs in the outdoor adventure industry:

"We get 25 applications weekly. Of these, about 90 percent appear to know nothing about us, nor do they appear to have looked at our web pages, so we spend very little if any time with them—and focus on the 10 percent who are prepared to discuss what they want within the context of what we may offer."

—Mike Wittig, manager of an adventure company

"Many of our current trip leaders got their start with our company by working in other areas of operations: cooks, housekeeping, driving, office, etc. We love to hire overqualified people for support positions. If they can do a summer of housekeeping with a good attitude, learn about our company, and take the initiative to learn about Alaska, we prefer to hire 'in house' for rafting guides, fishing guides, Kenai guides and trip leaders."

—Catherine McDermott, Alaska Wildland Adventures

"The best thing to do to break into the tour guiding business is to go and live abroad, learn the local language, and get employment learning the treks, walks, or tours of the area. With time, you may start guiding tourists locally. With experience, you then can submit a resume to some of the larger adventure travel companies."

—Julie Wilson, Wilderness Travel

"Since we are dealing with 'nontraditional' jobs, the applicant has to be somewhat 'nontraditional.'"

—Mike Wittig, manager of an adventure company

If you are tempted by one of the jobs in this chapter, then outdoor adventure is more than just a hobby to you—it's a genuine interest. Why should you hesitate to pursue something you care so much about? Just because your pursuit is pleasurable doesn't mean it shouldn't be taken seriously.

And it will be taken seriously by future employers—as long as you make the most of your passion, and present it that way. I spoke with a pre-med college senior who is taking a year off to be a "ski bum." It sounds like a blow off year until you hear that she got certified as an emergency medical technician so that she could work ski patrol at the resort. When she speaks to interviewers in the future, she will present it as a valuable opportunity to be involved in emergency medical treatments. If you have some foresight and think creatively, you can infuse any outdoor adventure with meaning.

But it may not take any stretch or special effort to find meaning in your job. Tour guiding jobs, counseling positions, and national park positions require that you learn about your surroundings and present what you know to visitors and guests. You will most likely be part of a team of employees and have to learn to work effectively with others. Furthermore, the completion of any rigorous physical challenge shows great determination and capacity for hard work. There's not an employer or interviewer out there who won't be impressed when you tell them you ran the Boston marathon or hiked across New Zealand.

And who's to say you will ever switch into a career where your outdoor adventure experience is irrelevant? The adventure industry is booming, especially in the United States, and your options will only expand the longer you are employed in the field. The industry needs entrepreneurs, leaders, and creative minds to meet the growing demand for outdoor contact, both within our borders and overseas. With a bit of commitment and opportunism, any post-college adventure can become a career. In ten years' time you might be printing up business cards with the title "outdoorsman"!

CHAPTER FOUR: OH, SO MANY PLACES TO GO!

F THE HEADHUNTERS AREN'T BANGING DOWN YOUR DOOR just yet, and you find yourself staring longingly at the horizon when mom slips the employment section under your eyes, it's time to succumb to your wanderlust and hit the open road. Travel, like living abroad, offers you the thrill of being in an exotic new place and partaking in its unique flavors, customs, sights, and sounds. There's something intensely powerful about going to a place so foreign that your imagination can't deliver you there. You have to transport yourself across the globe and let distant lands tell you their own story. Travel is truly one of the sweetest things life has to offer.

American culture doesn't put a huge premium on world travel. In fact, as many worldly, slightly snobby Europeans will point out to you, the vast majority of Americans don't even have passports. Not long ago I sat down and paged through a world atlas. Talk about a humbling experience. We're such itty bitty folks and stay in such narrow compartments of the globe. By the time I reached the end of the atlas, I was practically petting the maps (Oh my *lord* is Brazil huge! Oooh! And Sri Lanka! Look at Sri Lanka! I never thought of going to Sri Lanka!) and was overwhelmed by how little of the world I could claim familiarity with. I realized that if I wanted to see even a fraction of this planet in my lifetime, I had to make a commitment to traveling now.

Why now? Let's be realistic. It's never going to get easier to work in a week's trip to New Zealand or a tour of Scotland. Do you want to pass your life without having seen the great Egyptian pyramids or walked the streets of Paris? This is the stuff that great lives are made of. Chances are, soon you're going to have a career, possibly a spouse, and maybe even a little kid. Scary thoughts, I know. Right now you're portable, not only because your obligations and responsibilities are at a lifetime minimum, but also because you can probably fit most of your material belongings in a backpack and be on your way tomorrow.

And as a strapping young person, you've got enough energy and flexibility to journey on overnight trains, leaky gondolas, suspect footbridges, the backs of cargo trucks—you name it! Who wants to see Italy on an overly air-conditioned tour bus with a bunch of fanny-pack wearing retirees? Not when the sun-kissed lanes of Tuscany are inviting your feet for a stroll or the mopeds of Rome roar for company. Getting there is half the fun when you have an adventurous spirit about you. Think of all the cool ways you can experience a place—bungee jumping in an Australian canyon, exploring trails in the Nicaraguan rainforest, and don't forget all of the late night bar chatting you can do with the locals. That is the very best kind of cultural exchange. The best bonus of traveling as a carefree young person is that you will seldom be at a loss for company. There are tons of twentysomethings out there cavorting through any given country. Psyched? You should be. You have the opportunity of a lifetime in front of you.

This chapter not only highlights creative ways to see some of the most spectacular regions of the world, but also suggests ways to finance your globetrotting and work as you travel. Even if you have negative cash right now, don't cut travel from your list of possibilities. There are plenty of resourceful ways to get out and see new places, both within this country and beyond. Let the young adventurers who contributed their travelogues and tips to Chapter Four be your inspiration. They've covered the globe and are probably still going as you read this sentence. Adventurers in motion tend to stay in motion. Give yourself a starting push.

HELPFUL WEBSITES:

Big World: *(www.bigworld.com)* A website with travel links, adventure sports articles, and a hearty dose of inspiration for the young globetrotter.

CSTN: *(www.cstn.org)* Valuable information specifically for those traveling solo.

Transitions Abroad: *(www.transitionsabroad.com)* A comprehensive guide to work abroad, study abroad, international living, and independent travel overseas

Rick Steve's: *(www.ricksteves.com)* Travel tips, suggested itineraries, country information and message boards from the world's most famous "backdoor" traveler.

The Thorne Tree: *(http://thorntree.lonelyplanet.com)* Lonely Planet's comprehensive travelogue filled with reviews, tips, and stories from thousands of of globetrotters..

WHETTING YOUR APPETITE . . .

• Plan a road trip along the breathtaking Pacific coastline.

• Spend a summer backpacking through Europe's hottest cities and charming towns.

• Get to know obscure countries that you can't even spell, let alone place on a map.

• Transport yourself and a bunch of friends across the Australian outback in a VW bus.

• Apply for a travel grant to take an in-depth look at your region of choice and write about it. *(www.mytravelbug.com)*.

• Tour Southeast Asia on a shoestring budget.

- Work as a tour guide for a tour operator or traveling summer program for teens

- Buy an "around-the-world plane ticket" and plan a jaw-dropping itinerary across continents that places you in each country in time for vibrant local festivals

THE PRACTICAL STUFF

Whoa there, cowboy. Before you get all riled up and hop on the next plane to Nairobi, you've got to give some thought to practical matters. Here are a few things you should consider before you and your imagination get lost in the delicious travel options that lie in the pages ahead.

TIME FRAME. Money has the unfortunate tendency to run out, so think timing before you get ahead of yourself choosing destinations. Figure out how many weeks, months, or years you can commit to this journey. Time frame will have a huge bearing on the pace of your trip—whether you wander or plow through a country. If you are determined to see a lengthy list of countries, think about how long a stay your overall allotted time gives you in each destination. Remember that flying to some countries is only worthwhile if you can devote a good chunk of time to visiting. While you might get a $200 Internet special for five days in Paris, rates to India will stay consistently in the thousand-dollar range year round. You'll want at least a few weeks to explore the subcontinent anyway. Also take momentum into account. It's much easier to pack in a string of destinations than it is to plan and execute a number of separate trips. Be realistic about the constraints of the future and consider extending your trip as long as you possibly can.

YOUNG MALE SEEKING (TRAVEL) MATE. Traveling with a group of friends can be a phenomenal experience. Missing a bus sucks, but when you have your best friend there to laugh it off with, your loss is suddenly an adventure. Think carefully before choosing travel mates. Try and find someone who wants the same travel experience as you do, or else you might find yourself prepping for museum tours while your partner lathers on sunscreen for a day at the beach. You should also be on the same wavelength about your travel pace, destination priorities (in case you have to alter your itinerary), and most of all, budget. If you are out of sync in terms of finances, joint expenditures (which means pretty much everything) can become major points of contention.

> "It is far better to travel alone, enjoy complete freedom to do as you like, and go drinking with the ubiquitous Australians you will meet in every hostel."
> —Gideon Maltz, 25

If you think spending every waking minute with one person might be disastrous, you may prefer to have a few travel mates (though not too many or you'll never get anywhere!). Flying solo is another option for those who are ready and able to strike out on their own. Think it through, though, especially if you are a female, because safety may limit you. Thanks to Hollywood, American women have a reputation in many foreign countries, and venturing out alone at night could be asking for a generous dose of harassment. Lastly, choose travel mates of the opposite sex with special care. Pick that fantastic platonic friend of yours and you might find yourself totally smitten by the time you board the plane back home. World travel has been known to have an amorous effect on those who share it together!

> "I went to China by myself, but when I traveled, I was with three other guys I met teaching. Traveling alone can be lonely and two people can wear on each other's patience. The problem with three is that pairs sometimes form, leaving one guy high and dry. Having four is perfect. People pair up periodically, sometimes you go as a group or sometimes everyone does their own thing for the day."
> —Roger Loughney, 24

BY THE BOOK. Most people purchase a guidebook before departing for their trip. They use it for preparation tips, and it quickly becomes their travel bible, guiding their navigation through each foreign country. Some books chart out entire itineraries for you according to your time frame, tell you what towns and cities are worth visiting, and direct you to the hotels and restaurants that have passed their test. Because a guidebook can shape a trip so much, don't be hasty in your purchase. Talk to young people who have traveled with guidebooks, and find out which one is the best for the country in consideration. You can always just plop yourself down in a bookstore and see which style is most pleasing to your tastes. Budget tips, nightlife info, and internet café locations are three sections that may be more important to you than they would be to a forty-year-old traveler. Make sure to find the book that is geared towards your preferences. Also keep in mind that if you buy the most popular travel book out there, you will encounter packs of tourists everywhere you go. If you don't mind lugging extra pages, using two or more guidebooks is a good way to get the best of all travel advice. Lonely Planet has a reputation for having stellar guide books for Asia, while Let's Go reigns over the European backpacking niche. Other good resources for young travelers are the Moon Guides, the Insight Guides, the Rough Guides, and the Shoestring Guides.

> "Don't pack a lot. You never need as much as you bring. Live life simply so you can pick up and move onto your next adventure."
> —Fran Peters, 26

EN ROUTE

Now for the fun part—let's talk possibilities. This section is a compilation of some of the most popular travel routes out there, as well as some that will take you well off the beaten track. These delightful options have been hand-picked to make you hungry for a foreign expedition. You'll also find some random ideas on the zany side that are worth entertaining, if only for a chuckle.

> "If you are working and traveling across the country, call all your friends a few weeks ahead and tell them you're coming out to visit. Make connections in every job you have and take advantage of the cool cities your college friends are from."
> —Jermaine Gaffney, 27

ROAD TRIP! If your cash flow is too low for a plane ticket or you've only got a few weeks to work with, don't fret. Grab the ol' station wagon, a full CD case, and some good company. This country is wide, beautiful, and just aching to be explored. The cross-country road trip is a classic expedition, appealing not only because most of us have only seen a fraction of our own country, but also because it requires little planning, a small budget, and holds endless possibilities. Although you can purchase books on how to tour your way across America, the spirit of the cross-country road trip is usually more spontaneous. Most say the best way is to stop where your whims direct you and make an adventure out of it. Amidst your arbitrary drifting, don't forget to work in the main sights and attractions you have always wanted to see (i.e. the Grand Canyon, Niagara Falls, Yellowstone, the Hollywood sign!). These American treasures will make for a stellar photo collage.

If you are really on a tight budget, buy a tent and a guide to national camping grounds so that you can sleep in the great outdoors every night, rather than staying in regional roach motels. Another idea is to call up all of those wacky relatives you've always heard stories about and pay them a visit for a free place to crash.

> "Camping is one of the keys to staying sane on the road and keeping your trip cheap. It's usually quiet and you meet both cool and weird people. You can cook your own concoctions without having to eat road food. Plus you get to see the wondrous nature along the way instead of bleak strip malls and gas stations."
> —Clay Hastings, 28

If you have always been drawn to water and consider a beach sunset the most breathtaking natural wonder, stick to the coastal highways rather than venturing inland. The West Coast offers quite the scenic route, from southern California up to the Canadian border and beyond. Regardless of which ocean calls you, make sure to bring tons of film, and definitely pack a tent so you can park yourself on any public beaches you pass and fall asleep to the sound of the waves. Another route idea is to follow the trail of great American explorers such as Lewis and Clark through Lower Missouri, the Great Plains, Upper Missouri, the Rockies, and out to the Columbia River. The Appalachian and

Oregon Trails are some other traditional options. And of course, if you're in the mood for a bohemian odyssey, get a copy of Jack Kerouc's *On the Road* and head for the horizon.

Are you toying with the idea of volunteering, but also want to travel and see more of this country? Volunteer for Sprout *(www.gosprout.org)*, a non-profit that leads groups of adults with developmental disabilities on vacations through the U.S. Positions are open year-round, including short-term commitments (three to ten days). Most applicants are between 20 and 30, love travel, and are enthusiastic about caring for people with special needs.

SIX WAYS TO SPICE UP YOUR ROAD TRIP:

1. **Give your trip a theme.** This could be anything from nature photography to the search for the best American cheeseburger. You could compile an American drink list by asking bartenders for the local flavor in every area bar, or set out to see every major league baseball stadium. Use your own curiosities and interests to come up with a creative purpose. It will give you a source of continual entertainment, and of course, a fabulous story to tell for years to come.

2. **Get some funky wheels**. **a)** Rent a convertible. If you and your travel mates can chip in enough money, there is nothing cooler than feeling the breeze as you fly across the country. Brace yourself for troll hair. **b)** Pink Cadillac. You'll be the coolest kid on the interstate. If that's too fruity for you, try for a VW bus. **c)** Oscar Mayer Weinermobile. Believe it or not you *can* get your hands on this puppy and become an official "hotgogger" (driver) if you win their contest. Don't just sit around saying "I wish I was . . . ." Get the details from their website and give it a try! *(www.toomunchfun.com/oscarmayer/index.html)*

3. **Make a mix.** Good tunes make for good times, and your adventure deserves a theme song.

4. For the sake of instant gratification, **invest in a digital camera.** If this is out of your budget range, buy some black and white film for an extra special photo collection.

5. **Name your car.** Think through its look and personality first. The last thing you want to do is mistake the Bessie-like nature of your gentle automobile and name it Zeus. Once named, your wheels are your best friend. Soon you will be whispering encouragements while you rev up the engine, patting its hood as you walk to the gas pump, and including your hunk of metal in every scenic photo you take.

"Stop at all the tourist traps along your road trip. This may seem counterintuitive, but it's time to throw off that college snobbishness towards all things popular and screaming Americana. Haven't you always wanted to see Troll-Land in North Carolina? Or the Screaming Cave in Georgia? And you NEED a picture of yourself next to a 40-foot tall Paul Bunyan in Wisconsin!"

—Christopher Heaney, 22

THE GRINGO TRAIL. Let the rhythms of salsa and the musical Spanish accent draw you into this land of palm-lined shores, indigenous American ruins, thick rainforests, and mountains chains. Because cheap bus transportation will take you everywhere you need to go, you might as well aim for Cape Horn! Arriving at the tip of South America is an impressive feat. If you are departing from California, Central America can easily fill up a full itinerary with diverse sites and scenery. Mexico alone could be a month's worth of traveling. If your thrifty rice and beans diet leaves you with some extra cash, stop in the Caribbean before reentering the U.S. to experience a different Latin rhythm.

TIP: Online travelogues can be great resources when you are in the brainstorming stage of your process. Poke through a website such as Lonely Planet's "The Thorn Tree" to read people's reactions to trips all over the world and benefit from their feedback, advice, and photos collections. You can post questions and get quick replies that will help you get your plans underway before you talk yourself out of anything! *(http://thorntree.lonelyplanet.com)*

" **1. Networking isn't restricted to the professional world.** When planning a trip, mention it to as many people as possible. I talked to my cousin at a party and he had some connections to a language school in Costa Rica. Someone owed him a favor, and I was very fortunately the recipient of free lodging, food, and language instruction.

2. Volunteer. Many programs charge a fee for room and board, though others do not. Searching online, checking out tourism boards, reading guidebooks and talking to fellow travelers are excellent ways to find out about volunteer opportunities.

3. Mix some business with your pleasure. My backpacking partner and I were able to fit in some work on the side. We wrote a magazine article and solicited advertising for a newspaper. Side projects not only offer a break when the sightseeing vision gets blurred, but they're often a great way to make some money and add to that resume.

4. Stay in hostels. They're the cheapest, and this doesn't necessarily mean you have to sleep with the cockroaches (though there's no guarantee!). If you'll be staying in a hostel for an extended amount of time, see if you can work out an even cheaper price. In certain areas of the world, like Latin America, there's no shame in asking for a bargain. Many things are negotiable.

5. Leave on that midnight bus! You're going to pay the fare anyway. This goes for trains too. You might as well save a travel day and the money you would have spent on a hostel.

6. Don't let that budget, well, budge. Don't spend more money than you can. It's a very simple concept, yet many people get halfway through their trip and are shocked to find they have—eek!—no more money. Once you have a pretty good idea of how much you can spend per week, assuming you're having fun and not depriving yourself of food, stick to it. Try not to go overboard with souvenirs and knickknacks. Your family doesn't want that tacky piece of painted tree stump anyway! "

A BACKPACKER'S EUROPE. Take part in this age-old adventure that has been enticing young Americans across the Atlantic Ocean for years. Navigate through remote mountain towns in the Swiss Alps, party in red-light Amsterdam, or wander into cafés on the cobblestone streets of Salzburg. If equipped with an unlimited train pass, a backpacker can allow his whims (rather than a rigid itinerary) to guide him through Europe. Many recent college graduates choose to "do Europe" the summer after graduation or another short transition period because you can definitely see a good portion of the continent (or its main sites) in three or four months of traveling. If you fall under the "I'm taking a personal year" category, then eight months is perfect. That leaves you with four months to work every menial job you can get your hands on, and the rest of the year to enjoy your travels to the fullest, with the security of a good chunk of cash in your money belt.

"Traveling isn't about how many countries you've been to (I call those types 'country counters') but about immersing yourself in your surroundings—which may take longer than one night in the disco. If you have plans to be in a certain place for only a few days or even hours, but become enamored with it, change your schedule and stay for a little while longer. You will be rewarded handsomely."

—Roger Loughney, 24

On Tour. Not all organized tour packages are for retired folks. Luckily, some young entrepreneurs have created tours that appeal to the non-geriatric sensibilities. If you have a decent chunk of money saved and a small window of opportunity to travel, consider Peregrine Tour's Gecko trips. Geared towards the independent young traveler, Gecko offers "grassroots adventures and amazing prices" within small groups. They schedule plenty of free time into their trips so individual participants have time to go off and make their own discoveries. Accommodations are simple and local transport is used, making the trip prices more economical. A company like Peregrine would also be a great place to work (leading groups that don't mortify your cultural sensitivity!) Check them out at *www.peregrine.net.au.*

If you are a liberal arts major who is still lamenting the end of your educational career, traveling through Europe (or anywhere overseas for that matter) offers enough cultural stimulation to keep you learning your little heart out. Architecture majors go out and cathedral hop, artsy folks get lost in the grand museum around every corner, philosophy gurus get your sampling of world religions and photographers just pack plenty of film. Find a way to pursue some interest of yours while voyaging through these rich foreign cultures—whether that means talking politics with your hostel receptionist, biking through a rural area in every country, seeking out quality local musicians, or reading about regional history to pass the time on train rides. Personalize your adventure and it will not only take on an added meaning to you, but maybe also for the interviewer who asks about it down the line.

PACK A SKILL INTO THAT BACKPACK

BY ARIANNA ROMAIRONE, 23

" I had known for a while that I wanted to go to Mexico after I graduated from college. After eight months of working and saving, I'm finally on my way there. One of the first things I did in preparation for my trip was sign up for a one-month yoga teacher training program in Colorado. It was fairly pricey (certification costs almost $2,000), but fortunately between working at a restaurant and using graduation gifts, I was able to pay for it.

After getting certified, I returned home and began giving private yoga classes. Since I was living with my parents, not spending any money on rent, and being extremely careful (perhaps stingy) with extra expenses, I soon accumulated an amount of money that may seem insignificant by U.S. standards, but will go far south of the border. While stockpiling my every cent, I googled yoga and Mexico and got the names of many hotels and retreats. I sent a bunch of emails out on a whim, explaining that I had just graduated from college, was a certified yoga instructor, and was about to start backpacking Mexico on a low budget. I said that I would love to practice yoga but couldn't afford hotels or retreat centers. I asked if they had any work-study opportunities.

One place emailed me back right away and said that in exchange for teaching some yoga, I could be a full participant of their retreat. So although I won't be making any money, I will get a $1,500/week package at no cost. And then I will have plenty of time to backpack around the country on my own! I am of course both excited and terrified—trying my best to keep my expectations in check and just hope that my path will unfold on its own. Somehow, it always does. "

Pilgrim Style. If you are really looking to infuse your trip with significance and learning, organize your trip in the route of an ancient pilgrimage. Some routes, like "El Camino," which starts in France and ends in Santiago de Compostela in northwest Spain, are still journeyed today and lead thousands to a wild celebration at the trail's end. Pilgrims are often offered free (or cheap) housing along the way and even free meals. Every four years the sacred Hindu pilgrimage Kumbha Mela draws millions of Hindus in one day and is the largest pilgrimage gathering in the world. In 1989, 15 million pilgrims gathered in Allabad in northern India, which broke a world record for the largest number of recorded humans gathered for a common purpose. Be part of something big.

10 HOTTEST EUROPEAN CITIES:

Reykjavik (Iceland)

London (England)

Amsterdam (Netherlands)

Berlin (Germany)

Paris (France)

Edinburgh (Scotland)

Barcelona (Spain)

Interlaken (Switzerland)

the island of Ibiza (Spain)

Prague (Czech Republic)

10 QUAINTER EUROPEAN CITIES:

Galway (Ireland)

Innsbruck (Austria)

Seville (Spain)

Florence (Italy)

Cologne (Germany)

Budapest (Hungary)

Aix En Provence (France)

Lucerne (Switzerland)

Salzburg (Austria)

Bruges (Brussels)

10 UNFORGETTABLE & OFF THE BEATEN TRACK EUROPEAN DESTINATIONS:

Cinque Terra (Italy)

Cesky Krumlov (Czech Republic)

Lagos (Portugal)

Naxos (Greece)

Gmunden (Austria)

Breda (Netherlands)

Luxembourg City

San Sebastian (Spain)

Capri (Italy)

Aegean Coast (Turkey)

* Mix the columns together to make yourself a combination of wild hot spots, charming tourist sites, and quiet getaways.

"Instead of doing the typical backpacking tour through Europe, take a couple of thousand of dollars and stay in one place while studying at a language school. You'll pick the language up fast and the skill might help you get a job in a foreign country down the line. Plus, it's a great way to really get a feel for the country, meet the people, and share in local traditions and holidays. For example, in Siena, Italy, the Palio is a huge horse race that brings people from all over the world. It is hard to get a hotel room there or anywhere nearby, let alone transportation into the Tuscan city at this time of year. People I know that were studying at one of the language schools in Siena got prime seats to *both* races as well as the opportunity to celebrate in some of the seventeen neighborhoods' celebrations that are normally closed off to any and all outsiders."

—Ellen Fabiano, 22

Got the travel bug, but no bucks? Every now and then you come across an opportunity that seems too good to be true. The My Travel Bug fellowship is one of them. My Travel Bug offers travel fellowships twice a year to Americans who don't have the financial means to travel. These fellowships provide stipends of up to $1,200 to quality writers. Winning fellows travel overseas for one to three months and write travelogues which are published on the My Travel Bug website. To apply for a travel fellowship, you must submit a basic itinerary and budget, and three 1,000-word essays. For details, check out *www.mytravelbug.org*.

FAR AND EAST. Head to Southeast Asia for a glimpse at elaborate Buddhist temples, rice terraces, and vibrant open markets. You can get by on about ten dollars a day and still have an incredible array of possibilities to choose from: coral reef snorkeling, island jumping, jungle exploring, elephant riding, and mountain trekking cover just the natural attractions. Take a three day tour of Halong Bay in Northern Vietnam, walk through the My Son ruins in the South of the country, plan an extended stay in the incredible town of Hanoi, journey on the Mekong in Laos, and take in the sights and sounds of Thailand's vibrant capital city, Bangkok. If you have extra time and cash flow, end your adventure in Fiji, whose sparkling water, virgin rainforests, and volcanoes will make you ever so grateful you are living your youth to the fullest.

"I recommend traveling with a purpose. When I say purpose, what I mean is that you should find a reason to visit a country beyond just to see someplace exciting. Get a job teaching English, take some classes, be an aupair, pick grapes off the vine—anything that gives you the opportunity to weave your way into the local fabric. You learn more from the guy at the local restaurant than you will from a quick tour of some national history museum. After spending ample time really trying to comprehend your new culture, you can ingest surrounding cultures more easily and can compare and contrast them. I spent six months teaching English in China, and the ensuing two-month tour of South East Asia was all the more rewarding because of my time immersed in China. I was able to recognize certain idiosyncrasies in Vietnam that immediately reminded me of China."

—Roger Loughney, 24

CROWD, COLOR & CRAZINESS: World Festivals

Any one who has ever dropped into a country during a vibrant festival knows how much you can enhance your experience by partaking in local debauchery. Suppose you arrive in a quaint city at the height of its festive celebrations—streets packed with costumed people, decorations draping from balcony to balcony, enough tasty food and drinks to keep you full for days. Intense, eh? If the delectable list below really entices you, organize a world tour around festivals. Since many festivals fall in the months of June through August, this could make the perfect summer adventure.

- *La Tomatina*. **Bunol, Spain**. Last Wednesday of August. Picture six truckloads of ripe tomatoes, 15,000 visitors ready for drunken food fighting and absolute mayhem.

- *Shiva Ratri*. **Kathmandu, Nepal**. Early March. This religious holiday is the only day of the year that marijuana is legal. Locals smoke more than the gigantic bonfires that fill the streets at night.

- *Carnaval.* **Rio de Janeiro, Brazil.** February-March. Though you will encounter a colorful pre-Lenten Carnaval celebration in almost any Latin American country, Brazil's festival is famous for its extravagance, vibrance, and magnitude.

- *Il Palio.* **Siena, Italy**. July 2nd and August 16th. This age-old horse race draws the locals into the city's center, where traditional banners fly high and rivalries rage.

- *Los Sanfermines,* **the Running of the Bulls. Pamplona, Spain.** July 6th-14th. Muster up some macho spirit and take to the streets with a pack of belligerent bulls. Don't turn around to take a picture, just RUN!

- *Oktoberfest.* **Munich, Germany.** Mid-September to early October. Beer, sausages, and more beer.

- Want more? Hit up Las Fallas in Valencia, Spain, Tet Nguyen Dan in Ho Chi Minh City, Vietnam, Carnevale in Venice, and end your festive madness at your home-land's Marti Gras parade. The Testicle Festival in Clinton, Montana is an added American treat for those with time and a stomach for bull privates. Yummy.

THE LAND DOWN UNDER. Head to the Australian outback with a group of friends and buy a discounted used car to turn your tourist visit into the joyride of a lifetime. You can sell back your vehicle at the end of your stay and in the meantime fill your days with road trips through the Tasmanian wilderness and open-ended day trips to the beach. Take pleasure in the magnificent Great Barrier Reef, miles of coastal sand dunes, and more kangaroos than you can count. If you have the chance, get over to neighboring New Zealand, where sheep outnumber humans and hitchhiking is the way to go.

"When I was living in Australia, three of my friends and I chipped in about $375 a piece to purchase a 1976 VW Kombi named Bertha. A 45-minute drive outside the city lands you at a breathtaking empty beach you can camp out on for about four bucks a night. Some of my fondest memories consist of getting a case of beer or a box of wine, camping out right on the beach and surfing near perfect waves. I only wish I had more time to spend in the land of kangaroos and Fosters."

—Seth Burstein, 23

RIDE THE RUSSIAN RAILS. Hop on the "greatest rail journey on the planet," which will not only bring you deep into the former communist superpower, but also across one-fourth the length of the world. The Trans-Siberian Railroad leaves from Moscow and ends in Vladivostock, stopping in enough destinations to show you every bit of the massive country. If that's not enough rail action for you, pick up the Trans-Mongolian and Trans-Manchurian lines that will take all the way through to Beijing.

Advantageous Adolescents: In the interest of traveling as you work, apply to lead trips of high school students to foreign countries. Here are a number of organizations that cater to the younger crowd and use mature twentysomethings to guide gangly kiddies to the far regions of the globe.

Visions Service Adventures (www.visions-adventure.org)
American Institute for Foreign Study (www.aifs.org)
Amigos de Las Americas (www.amigoslink.org)
Global Routes (www.globalroutes.org)
Global Works (www.globalworksinc.com)
International Christian Youth Exchange (www.icye.org)
Breakthroughs Abroad (www.breakthroughsabroad.org)

"Avoid tours to see remote villages and indigenous people. They are either scams or take advantage of the people trying to live their modest lives."

—Roger Loughney, 24

AFRICAN ODYSSEY While almost everyone has a story of their trip to Europe, most Americans know zilch about the diverse nations that comprise the continent of Africa. Dedicate yourself to getting to know a section of the world unfamiliar and distant from your country and lifestyle. Your trip could carry you through gorgeous landscapes, diverse wildlife, and hundreds of different languages and cultures. Shoot four rolls of film of black rhinos in Etosha National Park in Namibia, go white water rafting on the Zambezi at Victoria Falls, explore the rock-hewn churches at Lalibela in northern Ethiopia, and take the unforgettable 52-hour train from Kapiri Mposhi in Zambia to Dar es Salaam in Tanzania.

> "Visit countries that your friends have never heard of. Everyone visits France. No one is really interested in hearing about your special experience at the Louvre or seeing your photos of the Eiffel Tower. However, if you visit Togo or Kyrgyzstan or Bhutan, you can hold your friends rapt."
> —Gideon Maltz, 25

THE COUNTRY LESS TRAVELED: For those who cringe at the sight of tube socks and visors and actively seek out authenticity in places that others won't touch, don't hesitate to boldly go where few tourists have gone before. And that hardly narrows down your options! If anything, you've got more possibilities if you want to do the unconventional. There are probably at least twenty countries in the world that you have never even heard of. Get a map and test yourself: Did you know that Georgia is not only the Peach State, but a country in Eastern Europe? Any recollection of Eritrea, Chad, Tajikistan, Myanmar, Oman, Belarus, or Gabon?

In researching for this book, I couldn't help but notice how the volunteer and work abroad programs all concentrated in certain regions of the world—mainly Asia, Western Europe, and Latin America—while almost none offered placements in the countries of the former Soviet Union and the Middle East. It isn't hard to pinpoint where our country has few ties and little cultural exchange. Personal travel gives you a small window of opportunity to counteract these trends and make an ambassador of yourself.

Safety will be a consideration when heading into countries that have little in the way of organized tourism. Your best approach may be to find a contact within that country (perhaps through one of the alternative accommodation organizations listed in this chapter) and navigate the country with their help and advice. I traveled to Port-au-Prince for a week with a Haitian friend and realized as soon as the trip began that it would have been impossible without her companionship (we fought our way onto a jam-packed bus of people yelling in Creole and she actually had to push a man off of the bus to maintain breathing room). There are some regions of the world that are just not amenable to independent traveling and you'll have to make extra preparations and connections to ensure that you don't end up completely overwhelmed, lost, or taken advantage of. All that said, my week in Haiti was the most profound travel experience I have ever had and has transformed the way I view the world.

On top of the countries whose names you can't even pronounce, there are plenty of lands we've all heard mention of, but our knowledge ends right there with the country's name. To name a few: Bulgaria, Laos, Wales, Uruguay, Tibet, Madagascar, Papua New Guinea, and Jordan. Seek out the unique and you'll find it in spades. Oh, and save the caves of Afghanistan for a later point in life. That's one experience in this book that's safe to delay.

ROUND THE WORLD. Now that you have had a sampling of specific destinations, it's time for the craziest proposal: go everywhere! Circling the globe is every world traveler's dream and definitely one of the most awesome things you can do with your young years. Imagine being able to trace your finger around a globe and say, I did *aaaaall* of that. Pretty cool, eh?

If you think about it, traveling around the world in one fell swoop actually makes a lot of sense (bear with me on this!). If you go through all of the preparatory efforts to visit another country and get yourself on a plane, you might as well keep that backpack packed and let your momentum propel you on to a dozen other destinations and take the "scenic route" back home. Buying one "around-the-world plane ticket" saves you taxes and extra fees while offering you a great package of flights. This magic ticket might also deliver you to countries that are not cheap to reach in a single flight, like Vietnam or Nigeria. While leaving your country and visiting another takes such a concerted effort, once you're on the road and in global curiosity mode, it's easy to keep on moving and rack up a jaw-dropping itinerary. It's a wide world—wide enough that you can chart a course no one else has ever followed.

IT'S A SMALL WORLD AFTER ALL

BY TIM GREENE, 24

"I ate a fried beetle the size of my thumb in a Thai street market—for the equivalent of half a penny! How can you beat that? Sampling kangaroo, porcupine, guinea pig, chicken feet, emu, and other unusual foods was just one aspect of my wild four-month around-the-world adventure. When I finished college the prospect of crossing continents—and meeting a variety of people while learning about their history and culture—was too good to pass up. Yet many graduates choose to immediately commit to jobs and graduate programs, sometimes without fully considering their options. My friends in this predicament often wonder aloud to me why they didn't first do some exploring before getting 'stuck' in the real world. Although the employed are in better financial shape than me and the graduate students have finished a year of their schooling, I wouldn't trade either of those situations for my experiences in Thailand, Cambodia, Vietnam, Malaysia, Australia, New Zealand, Tahiti, Easter Island, Chile, Argentina, Bolivia, and Peru.

To answer the question I get most often ('How did you do it?'): I moved home for six months to work, save money, and find a friend to see the world with. My parents fed me and let me sleep under their roof, and I put every available dollar from my paychecks into the bank. My travel companion and I planned with Airbrokers.com, an agency specializing in around-the-world travel. We picked general areas we wanted to visit and the agent pieced together deals for us (an example being that Lan Chile flights from Auckland to Santiago stopped on Tahiti and Easter Island to refuel, allowing passengers to get off and catch the next leg a few days later—for free). The fare was $2200—a hefty sum, but a great value considering the number of flights and destinations we spread across three continents.

On the trip we stretched every dollar by sticking to street vendors (Southeast Asia and South America) and the supermarket (Australia and New Zealand) for food and by staying in the cheapest budget hotels and hostels. From kayaking Milford Sound in New Zealand to hiking the Inca Trail in Peru, my eight thousand-dollar investment was well worth it. The trip was an unforgettable adventure in absorbing and comparing cultures, seeing some of the world's natural wonders, and enjoying a perfect bridge from college to the next step. My only advice is to just make it happen. The real world can wait until you get back. And eat a bug. They are quite tasty."

Traveling around the world requires a long time commitment (four months to one year) as well as a good chunk of money. Costs vary greatly from trip to trip, depending on where you choose to go, how you get there, and how long you stay in each area. Here are some ideas of ways to cut down the costs:

- Shop around and get the best deal on an around-the-world plane ticket. This will cost you about $1,500 to $3,500, which is a pretty sweet deal considering what it gives you. You are allowed a certain number of plane rides, usually about five. For example, one ticket deal gets you from California to Thailand, India to Russia, Egypt to Nairobi, South Africa to Argentina. You connect the dots with land travel.

- Organize the length of your stays according to the costs of living in each area. You could float around Southeast Asia for a month and spend less than you would in Switzerland for a week. If you are really looking to cut corners, leave out some expensive areas completely. Maybe do Eastern Europe rather than Western Europe, Vietnam instead of Australia, and China, not Japan. You will be able to stretch out the duration of your trip immensely by staying in the cheapest areas.

- When you chart your course, investigate land transportation prices. Find out how much trains, busses and planes cost in each area to compare with parallel courses. For example, one long train ride through Russia may be cheaper than many shorter bus rides through India, Pakistan and Turkey.

- Stick to the mainland. Islands are enticing, but most ferry and plane rides to get to them will suck your money away.

- Equip yourself with good information so you can always compare an array of options. *First-Time Around the World* (Rough Guides) by Doug Lansky is a good buy, while *The World's Cheapest Destinations: 21 Countries Where Your Dollars Are Worth A Fortune* by Tim Leffel and *The Traveler's Atlas: A Global Guide to the Places You Must See in a Lifetime* by John Man, Chris Schuler, and Geoffrey Roy are also worth poking through.

WORK YOUR WAY AROUND THE WORLD

Here it is—the dream tour—for any adventurous, but financially strapped college grad who wants to see the world. Keep in mind that these are job *ideas* that will not be open to everyone. Obtaining these positions or other international jobs takes a lot of planning, persistence, and luck. This itinerary simply gives you an idea of what you could line up if you planned a work or volunteer stint in each of the destination cities on your around-the-world plane ticket.

June: Depart for Cape Town, **South Africa**. Start with a volunteer gig for the South Africa Sports Coaching Program (*www.score.org.za/programs/pro_pc.htm*). Serve as a sports coach to young kids for this Dutch-run summer program. For income, look for a tourism service job in Seapoint.

August: Arrive in Cairo, **Egypt**. Look for work as a film extra. Egypt is the capital of the Arab world's film industry and there is usually a demand for western extras. You will most likely play the drunken degenerate.

September: Raise tents, cook sausages, and keep beer steins full at Oktoberfest in Munich, **Germany**. 12,000 people employed every year, 5.7 million liters of beer consumed.

October: Bounce around rural **Europe**, and look for some agricultural jobs through WWOOF memberships. Take your pick from the orange groves of Greece, the tulip farms of the Netherlands, and intoxicating Italian vineyards (*www.wwoof.org*).

November: Ride the rails through **Russia**. Start in St. Petersburg and head east. During stops and trips to Russian towns, arrange to stay with Russian families in exchange for housework or English lessons to their children (*www.russia-hostelling.ru/index_e.php, www.globalfreeloaders.com*).

December: Stay in a center for yoga or a utopian community in **India** where you can participate in daily rituals and food production in exchange for cheap or free housing (*http://india.yoganet.org*). Also spend two weeks working with Mother

Teresa's Sisters of Charity in Calcutta, where unskilled volunteers are accepted on a short-term basis. 78 A.J.C. Bose Road, Calcutta 16, India.

January: Teach ESL in **Thailand** for the spring semester. With the money you earn, travel through Southeast Asia during weekends and holidays (*www.eslcafe.com*).

May: Work on a sheep farm in rural **New Zealand**. When traveling throughout the small island, hitchhike and sleep on beaches. Both are easy to do and acceptable here (*www.wwoof.co.nz*).

June: Make your last plane stop in Central America and earn your keep at **Casa Guatemala**, an orphanage that relies on travelers to do maintenance chores and teach English (*www.casa-guatemala.org*). Depart to the U.S. from Costa Rica so you can make your final journey through the coastal rainforest.

That's one year you'll never forget!

CRUISING TOGETHER: If a certain region strikes your fancy (Caribbean, Mediterranean, Alaskan coast) but you don't have the funds you need to travel throughout it, apply for a cruise ship job. The advantage of this unique option is that you are financing all of your travel expenditures as you work. You won't need to save up a penny for this journey. The three biggies in the industry are Princess, Carnival, and Royal Caribbean. Other major employers include Crystal Cruises, Disney Cruise Lines, Holland America Line, and Seabourn.

The most sought-after jobs in the cruise industry are the activity and entertainment jobs, which include hosting, DJing, performing, lifeguarding, and planning on-shore excursions. You can also work as a deck hand, manage the restaurants, bars, gift shops, and passenger cabins, or work as a beautician, hair stylist, massage therapist, personal trainer, fitness instructor, or medical assistant. Keep in mind that cruise ship jobs are not a walk in the park; the hours are long, private space tight (cabin dimensions may even make your old dorm room look palatial!) and on-shore free time may be limited. Nevertheless, young people working on the seven seas hail their jobs as the best positions anyone could dream up.

How can you get yourself a coveted position on board? First of all, you can improve your odds in the hiring process by committing a long period of time to the job (six months is typically the minimum, so offer longer if you can). Also, knowing a foreign language or having a special skill will help you get your foot in the door. Having a CPR or lifesaving certification betters your chances as well. Figure out how you can tinker with your resume and present yourself as someone who has experience in the hospitality industry (ie. anything working with people). Aim to send in your application in time for a peak hiring periods (winter holidays, summer, spring break).

SAIL AWAY, SAIL AWAY, AND GET PAY

BY KATE ANDERSON, 26

"At graduation parties, people would talk about what they were doing after school and most would mention so-and-so corporation or graduate school. I will never forget the look on this one guy's face when I said I was going to work on a cruise ship. He just looked at me and his eyes were practically glistening. He said, 'I never thought of that.'

I thought to do it because I figured this was the prime of my life. I should do whatever I want. I had experience working with children, so I was able to get a job on the youth staff of a cruise line, which basically means that I hosted activities for kids. The salary is decent because while you are working you don't have to pay rent or buy food. Of course you'll want to eat real Naples pizza when you dock in Italy, but other than a few rare splurges you will save your earnings.

The crew lifestyle is a great way to make the transition from college to the real world. You are surrounded by people who like to have fun and travel. In the meantime, you are traveling around the world. I got to see almost all of the Caribbean, the Mediterranean, including France and Italy, and then northern Europe, including Norway, Sweden, and Russia. It was a fabulous experience. I am in graduate school now and so happy that I took two years to do exactly what I wanted to do. "

While requesting any position on the ship might strike you as a good approach, remember that this suggests to hiring officials that you just want to travel and are less interested in a specific job. Instead, take time to figure out what position you are best qualified for. You can always call the personnel office and just ask them what is available. You have to present yourself as an ideal match for both the position and the cruise line if you want a real shot at employment.

" Step 1: Getting started. A journey of a thousand miles begins with a single Google search. The best way to start is to get acquainted with the cruise lines themselves—see where they go, what positions they offer, how much they pay, etc. The Internet is full of good and bad information. Don't be deceived by companies or services requesting payment for applications. Due to some misinformation, I purchased an application packet from a company which guided me through the process and guaranteed employment. Although, the information was helpful because I was a first-time applicant, I could have easily avoided this mistake. I recommend going straight to a U.S. Hiring Partner like Shipboard Staffing, the company I eventually applied through (www.shipboard-staffing.com). .

Step 2: The application. My application process consisted of completing a standard application, designing a resume, and cover letter tailored to my desired position, enclosing a photo, and sending it to the ships that appealed to me. I learned that, at least with Royal Caribbean, there are seasonal/temporary positions (around three months) and long-term positions (usually six-plus months). I applied for a seasonal, youth staff position. Had I wanted a more permanent position, I could have applied for other jobs like shore excursion staff. It's important to show those reviewing your application that you a) are qualified b) are confident and c) have the personality to work on a cruise ship. In addition, it helps to apply for positions with which you have experience. Remember that some jobs are more popular than others and if you're not absolutely set on something, it might be wise to apply for the less sought-after position. You may want to call the hotline and ask what positions are more difficult to get and what sort of qualifications they require before applying.

Step 3. Waiting. From the time I sent my application in May, I waited approximately three months before I received a call. Apply early, allowing several months before you expect to begin employment. Even if you aren't positive you'll be ready to take the job, it's best to apply. I was able to postpone my interview with Royal Caribbean until after my three-month backpacking adventure in Central America.

Step 4. Phone interviews. Because I applied as youth staff, the interviewer asked me questions about my experience with kids, previous jobs, leadership skills, whether I had the required CPR/first aid certification, and when I would be able to start. Jot down

(continued)

FIVE STEPS UP THE GANGPLANK TO CRUISE LINE EMPLOYMENT · BY MEGAN MCDONNELL, 22 some answers to questions you think they may ask. Have past experiences fresh in your mind and think about how they relate to the position you're applying for. They'll probably give you situational questions and ask how you would ensure that guests enjoy themselves. Also, come up with a few questions for them. For example, asking about advancing within the company shows serious interest and dedication. I had to use a web cam for my second interview with Royal Caribbean's Human Resources Department. I think the questions, which were mostly the same as those from the first interview, were there for the purpose of distracting me as he scanned for excessive amounts of facial hair or other unsightly features that might offend guests.

Step 5. Rejection. Nope, I didn't get the job, but best of luck to you! Ok, just kidding. I got a call a few days after my second interview and was offered a youth staff position that started less than three weeks later. Preparing for departure did cost me (buying wacky costumes and getting a thorough physical) but from here on out, I expect it'll be nothing short of smooth sailing! "

To better your chances of scoring a job, also send out applications to regional cruise lines based in the U.S. that are more likely to hire Americans. Many big chains pull from foreign employee pools. Some small ships and "adventure cruises" can give you experience that will aid you in getting a job on a larger cruise line in the future.

There are a few other floating employers out there that you might have luck with. Semester At Sea takes college students on educational trips around the world on the "SS Universe Explorer"(*www.semesteratsea.com*). Apply for a job in student life that will draw on your college expertise. Take a peek at all of the places your new drifting home will dock: Vancouver, Japan, China, Hong Kong, Vietnam, Malaysia, India, Suez Canal, Turkey, Croatia, Spain, Cuba, Brazil, South Africa, and Kenya. Hot damn.

If you want to get even closer to the water and more involved in the navigation, take a sailing certification course and try to obtain a job on a private yacht. Look in the classified ads of yachting and boating magazines and send out letters, proclaiming yourself a world-class cook and cleaner, in addition to shipman. With a little grunt work, you may earn yourself a free passage from the West Indies to the Canaries, up the Californian coast to Alaska, or through the Grenadines. Bon voyage!

" I had always talked about 'time off' after college, but had never really considered what I might actually do. When a friend told me about Peace Boat (*www.peaceboat.org*), I investigated and found out it was a Japanese NGO that takes Japanese passengers on around-the-world cruises to learn about global problems firsthand. It sounded so wacky that I decided to apply as an English-Japanese translator on board the 43rd cruise. Before I knew it, I was waving to my friends from the top deck of a ship as it pulled out of Tokyo harbor.

For the next three months as we slowly made our way around the world, I learned more about the world than I had ever learned in any college class. All kinds of speakers—journalists, academics, NGO representatives—were invited on board to hold lectures on anything from media coverage of the war in Iraq to the AIDS problem in Eritrea. Until I joined the Peace Boat, I never imagined I would have the chance to share a joke with someone born and raised on a refugee camp in the Gaza Strip, or to help preserve sea turtles by releasing new born babies into the warm El Salvadorian ocean.

Anyone interested in the Peace Boat should definitely look into it. Even if you don't speak Japanese, volunteer English language teachers are recruited for every cruise. I've also found that NGO's are excellent networking vehicles. Check out websites of groups that might interest you and see where their links take you. With a little patience and some creativity, there is always a way to travel without driving yourself into debt.

As I learned following my first voyage, volunteer work can be a gateway to securing paid work. I maintained my ties with Peace Boat and now have a job with them helping to coordinate an onboard program called Global University. I research topics for students to study, and help design exposure tours for them to participate in at ports of call. I'm learning a ton, and I get paid for it, too! "

FLYING THE FRIENDLY SKIES

Would you hop on a plane to a new country every week if you could? Well, if you happen to be "height-weight proportionate," you have the chance to become a flight attendant. Yes, you have to be nauseatingly polite all of the time, perform safety demonstrations that no one ever pays attention to, and be chronically jet-lagged, but at least you get free lifts overseas! Honestly, if you have the personality for it and would reap the benefits of the global transport, flight attending isn't a bad deal. Training periods are long (four to six weeks) and most likely unpaid, but the salary and benefits are pretty decent once you get started. Perks include layovers in destinations worldwide (mini all-expense paid vacations!), some flexibility in work schedule (you could have between 10 and 21 days off a month), major discounts on flights and vacation packages, and all the salty peanuts you could ever want!

KEEPING IT CHEAP

Now that you've got a travel plan, let's talk budget. If you are like the average twentysomething, you want to do it all, but need a way to keep costs down.

1. **Aim to get free plane vouchers.** Every time you fly, from now until the day you strike it rich, volunteer to be bumped from your flight when you check in at the counter. If you do this ahead of time before any overbooking is announced, you will be the first one offered the chance to give up your seat in exchange for ticket vouchers. You can rack up hundreds of dollars by playing this smartly and passing a little extra time in the airport (bring a good book!). Most ticket vouchers are only good for a year, which may be just the push you need to make your travel plans happen.

2. **Serve as an air courier to get discounted plane tickets.** As an air courier, your job is to assure that important packages arrive overseas to their designated destinations. You are only allowed one piece of carry-on luggage and must travel on specified dates, but plane fare for couriers is a fraction of the regular price. Join the International Association of Air Travel Couriers for a small fee to find out when bargain air courier flights are offered. Going through the whole process is really only worth it if you are very flexible and planning to fly to a number of separate places. Check out the following websites for details: www.aircourier.org, www.courier.org, www.courierlist.com.

3. **Push for the best value.** Spend some time on the phone when booking your plane ticket and fiddle around until you find a low fare. Ask about flying out of a number of different cities, flying on weekdays, departing from a different city you arrive in (the "open jaw flight"), taking indirect routes, staying for various lengths of time, and qualifying for a youth discount. Inquiring is the only way to assure that your booker tries for the lowest price possible. Stress your flexibility. Lastly, remember that one-way tickets are almost always a bad deal.

Check out these websites that offer discounted plane tickets. Before you go punching in your credit card number, make sure you read the fine print. The terms of your purchase may contain special restrictions regarding exchanges and refunds.

www.cheaptickets.com
www.travelnow.com
www.travel.com
www.priceline.com
www.orbitz.com
www.airtreks.com
www.airtech.com
www.flights.com

3. **Before your trip, talk to everyone you know to get names of native people** living in the region you are headed to. Being connected everywhere you travel may earn you a few free stays. But more importantly, the advice from locals in terms of where to stay, eat, go out, and visit is incredibly valuable. Tourism is set up to milk money out of foreigners (i.e. people who don't know the area). If you can get hooked up with an insider, their scoop will lead you to the most economical places and help you avoid getting ripped off. Lastly, remember that almost everyone knows someone who knows someone who knows a travel agent. Take advantage of any connection that gets you inside expertise on the travel market and might alert you to one-time deals.

5. Follow this cheesy motto: **Always put an 's' in your hotel.** Hostels are usually much cheaper than other tourist accommodations. Some even have kitchens so you can cook your own meals. If you encounter high prices, don't hesitate to

investigate alternatives, like YMCAs, religious establishments (such as convents and churches), and family homes. Volunteer organizations may have a place for you to crash if you lend a hand. Other good options include private rooms available through local tourist agencies and out-of-the-way pensions. If you are really on a tight budget, offer to do some housework or to work the hostel reception desk for a few hours in exchange for your night's stay. Some hostels have organized work stints for their guests.

Think about investing in a membership to Hostelling International—American Youth Hostels ($25 per year). Like an AAA for young backpackers, this membership offers you a whole slew of convenient services that will make your travel go more smoothly. Members receive the best rates in over 4,500 hostels in 60 countries. If you are going to be bouncing to a number of different places, the membership will pay for itself in discounts (*www.hiayh.org*).

7. Flee tourism. In most areas, particularly Third World countries, the farther away from mainstream destinations, hokey tourist sites, and large hotels you go, the lower prices drop. People have the tendency to get excited by prices that seem a little less expensive than what they are used to. But often, seemingly "cheap" prices are still extremely overpriced. Be sure to adjust to the local currency.

8. Think up ways to make your travels lucrative. In this day and age, you can sell anything and everything on the Internet. While roaming through distant lands, think about what local goods, artwork, and unique souvenirs might sell for a good price back at home. If you come across large inconsistencies in your travel guide, email the author and offer your services in obtaining the updated information.

ALTERNATIVE ACCOMMODATIONS

About one third of a budget traveler's costs are spent on accommodations. Cut out expenditures for a nightly roof and a bed and you'll be able to afford a lot more during your daytime escapades.

• **Global Freeloaders** was started by a twenty-four-year-old, "travel bug"-afflicted Australian with a vision of a worldwide network of willing hosts, enriching one another's travel experiences and making them more affordable. He defines a free-loader as "a person who takes advantage of the charity, generosity, or hospitality of others." You can only be a guest through Global Freeloaders if you also sign up to be a host (*www.globalfreeloaders.com*).

• **The Hospitality Exchange** is a database of kind souls who are travel veterans and want to open up their homes to travelers passing through their region. This exchange, like Global Freeloaders, is reciprocal. You host travelers in return for the hospitality (www.hospex.net).

• If you want a longer-term stay done the budget way, get yourself a subscrip-tion to the *Caretaker Gazette*. This magazine is a listing of international properties, from ranches in Baja California to estates in Brussels that are in need of "caretakers." Housing is usually free for caretakers and some duties like pet-care and plant water-ing may be included. As a young person you might have to sell yourself a little harder to convince homeowners that you are a reliable house sitter. These house-sitting stints are really fantastic opportunities, especially for someone with an independent art, writing, or academic project that they can do from any location (*www.caretaker.org*).

• **Homestays for Peace** is an international network aimed at promoting peace through visits between diverse people. During homestays, travelers partake in daily duties of hosts. There are more than 14,000 homes in 130 countries (*www.usservas.org*).

• **Women Welcome Women World Wide (5W)** is an organization fostering inter-national solidarity among women visiting one another's countries. Membership is open to all females, though the organization warns that its purpose is not facilitating cheap holidays (*www.womenwelcomewomen.org.uk*).

"My friend Nick and I were traveling around southern Spain when we heard from the 'traveler's grapevine' that Africa's largest music festival was kicking off in a few days in a Moroccan town called Essouira. On a whim we hightailed it down there and made it just in time to catch the start of the festival—and also to discover that every hostel bed, hotel room, and bus shelter had been claimed months in advance of the event.

As we were discussing our prospects of sleeping on the beach, a young guy around our age wandered over to our table. In a surprisingly understandable pidgin of Spanish, French, Arabic, and English, he introduced himself, told us that he had overheard our plight and invited us to stay with his family just around the corner. We were a little dubious at first but went on to enjoy an unforgettable week of Moroccan hospitality. Receiving this first-hand insight into Mohammed and his family's day to day existence was absolutely amazing. A week passed and they would not take payment other than our laughter and conversation, so we had to move on. With sadness in our hearts we boarded the bus back to Marrakesh.

On the ride it occurred to me that I'd spent almost two years traveling intermittently around Europe, and while my diary was filled with hundreds of email addresses of friends from Australia, New Zealand, and South Africa I'd met along the way, I could count on two hands my European friends. Surely that's not what travel is supposed to be about? Inspired by the previous week's events, I realized that just about any of my friends would happily accommodate a 'friend of a friend' at my referral. Why not extend that circle a little and create an online travel community that would accommodate other members, free of charge?

I flew back to Australia and enlisted the help of a few friends to set my ideas in motion and several months later, GlobalFreeloaders.com was launched. Three years running, the site now boasts thousands of members in more than 130 countries. As the site is still completely free, I'm certainly not rich because of it, but that was never my intention. I still get a thrill every week when I read through all the new references on the site describing friendships that have been forged because of one hospitable Moroccan family. "

Worried that your future employer won't find your travel escapades so impressive? Anxious about having a hole in your resume? Don't be. First of all, you shouldn't rule out the possibility of making travel into a career, or at least a really fantastic job for a few years. Over 600 tour companies in the U.S. and Canada hire tour guides. Get to know the areas they traverse and you've made yourself a prime candidate. People nowadays expect more in-depth and quality travel experiences than the traditional tourism packages offer. In future years, travelers will only become more selective and create greater demand for alternative vacations, educational travel packages, and small, specialized tour companies. It's an exciting and promising niche that you could insert yourself into and let your entrepreneurial and leadership skills flourish.

A broader, global perspective is highly valued anywhere in the current interconnected, globalized world. Have you ever heard the word "worldly" used with anything but the most positive connotations? Don't fret about getting "real world experience" from a job when you have the chance to go out and *experience* the real world for yourself. You can very easily market your adventure to an interviewer as "a learning experience," a "study of other cultures," or even "intensive foreign language development." It's all how you present it. The stories you will bring back with you—of the time you chased down a purse snatcher in Portugal, or the night you spent at a traditional Malaysian wedding ceremony—will make you the star of future job interviews and cocktail parties.

But as you travel, there *are* ways to build your experience for advantageous use in the future. Keeping in mind your personal interests and your future plans, find a way to infuse your travels with meaning at every chance. For example, if you were a pre-med in college, visit a clinic or volunteer in a nursing home in every city you travel to. Not only would this be an interesting cultural practice and helpful community service, but also something you can draw on to advance your future. Imagine how you could blow away your med school interviewers by talking about the advantages of the Dominican model of long-term care in comparison to the U.S. model, or the availability of AIDS drugs in Botswana. If you are interested in the effects of globalization, take a tour of a clothing factory while in Thailand and talk to workers about their job alternatives. The word "Fulbright" usually blows people away. All it really means is pursuing your interest or area of expertise in a foreign country. Who's to say that you can't do the same without an award? It is easy to draw any serious interest into your travel escapades.

There is a recent graduate from my college named Gideon who has earned himself fame in the young alumnae community. He left a high-paying financial job to go globetrotting in un-touristy regions. Throughout his travels he sent vivid emails of his latest adventures to a large group of people. Mind you, I have never even met Gideon but heard about him constantly from the people who received his travelogues. One girl even printed out all of his tales and put them in a binder. Suspecting he might be the poster child for this book, I tracked him down. What had become of Mr. Gideon? Well, he'd gotten so much positive feedback on his famed emails that he was planning on making them into a book.

Go to any local bookstore and park yourself in the travel section. Before you get lost in the photo-filled guidebooks of countries around the world, take a peek at the travel-writing shelf. These books are endlessly impressive because they show how personally valuable an odyssey can be and the potential of what you can produce with thoughtful world travel.

CHAPTER FIVE: WHY NOT CHANGE THE WORLD?

WHAT BETTER WAY TO START OFF YOUR YOUNG LIFE than by working for a cause you believe in? If you are reading this book, you probably haven't been enticed by the work world yet, and are still holding out for something more inspiring, more novel, more you. Public and community service programs like City Year, the Peace Corps, and Teach for America have become the answer for our generation's idealists, and for good reason. We are in the perfect position to volunteer our time and talents—with a college education in the bag, no current commitments holding us back, and a desire to make a positive step in the right direction. And we young people also have the passion to drive forward social movements.

With thousands of well-run nonprofits of both the domestic and international variety, you will find many organizations that champion the causes you are interested in. Whether you feel called to lend a hand in your city or work for hunger alleviation on the other side of the world, there is an organization eager to harness your energy and utilize your talents. And don't be deceived by the word "volunteer." While your remuneration will certainly not make your friends envious, most organized volunteer programs (at least the long-term ones) provide you enough benefits so you can manage financially. Many of the programs listed in this chapter provide food, housing, health insurance, and a modest stipend.

But the benefits of joining a service program go far beyond these perks. In devoting yourself to full-time service, you will make an impact on the people you work with and will also walk away with a heightened social awareness, valuable problem-solving skills, and intense appreciation for your exposure and growth. So go ahead, put your heart and soul into your work for a year or two. You may never consider doing otherwise again.

WHETTING YOUR APPETITE . . .

- Build houses for low-income families in Kentucky's Appalachia.

- Join the Peace Corps and immerse yourself in your assigned country while pioneering agricultural projects (*www.peacecorps.gov*).

- Live with a Honduran family outside of San Pedro Sula and volunteer teach at a small high school.

- Volunteer aboard a global charity ship and bring health care and spirituality to poor communities around the globe (*www.mercyships.org*).

- Volunteer teach at an environmental education program for middle school students in the Rocky Mountains.

- Intern at an AIDS education project in San Francisco (*www.ucsf-ahp.org*).

- Lend a hand in a therapeutic community in a beautiful rural region of Vermont and serve as a counselor to adults recovering from mental illness (*www.spring-lake-ranch.org*).

HELPFUL WEBSITES:

Idealist: (*www.idealist.org*) The most comprehensive source for information about domestic and international nonprofits. Users can sign up for daily emails with job openings according to their specifications (location and issue).

One World: (*www.Oneworld.net*) A website with news, jobs, and volunteer positions in the international, relief, human rights, and development arenas.

Quaker Information Center: (*www.quakerinfo.org/oportnty.htm*) A website that highlights overseas opportunities (volunteer, internship, and study programs) related to social justice, relief, and development.

The Points of Light Foundation and Volunteer Center National Network: (*www.pointsoflight.org*) A website whose mission is to mobilize millions of volunteers to solve serious social problems.

Response: (*www.cnvs.org/vo-rdir.htm*) A website that lists overseas opportunities through Catholic and Christian organizations.

Volunteer International: (*www.volunteerinternational.org*) A website that allows you to search overseas volunteer opportunities by location, type of work, and project duration.

EENY MEENY MINY MO: HOW TO CHOOSE THE PROGRAM FOR YOU

If you are a socially-minded person, researching the multitude of service programs is overwhelming for one reason: you'll want to do it all! There are so many organizations that have impressive mission statements and need help to accomplish their aims. Everything can look appealing at first glance, but once you give each program a thorough look, you see how much they vary in terms of the length of service, affiliation, benefits, and a variety of other factors. While some of the programs in this chapter are strictly volunteer—you donate your time and they (hopefully!) help you make the donation feasible (by providing room and board, for example)—others are public service-related jobs (like teaching through a salaried inner-city teaching program) that will provide you an income and job benefits.

So to start, take some time to figure out what specific elements you're looking for in a program. Below are some questions that will get you thinking about the conditions and circumstances under which you want to volunteer yourself.

"I went into the Peace Corps and one thing I was worried about was missing out on all the cool stuff family and friends would be doing while I was away. But even after two years, I didn't miss a beat. To sum up what happened, I was away having an amazing experience while my friends who entered the "real world" were hating their jobs and wishing they had done something more exciting. I also got a lot more comfortable with life decisions when I realized that I didn't have to have the whole thing planned out. You just have to figure out your next step at this point—not your whole life."

—Rob Marek, 28

WHAT IS YOUR MOTIVATION FOR DOING COMMUNITY SERVICE?

Devote some time to pinpointing your motivations, and then keep them in mind as you read through the more specific questions below. Your motivations will play a large part in determining exactly what type of program you want. Is it a particular cause that motivates you? A new experience or unfamiliar place? Religious devotion? Practical experience for your future career? Some time to figure out life? If you are honest with yourself, you will think through your choices more clearly and make a better decision according to your genuine aims.

WHAT KIND OF VOLUNTEER WORK DO YOU WANT TO DO?

Look at your own volunteer history. What issues have excited you? What service projects have you loved doing? Think about your talents, interests, and the things you could seriously devote a whole year or two to. You can find volunteer positions that require nearly every area of expertise, from economic development to sex education. Go to some service websites and poke around for positions that match your interests and skills. This question should narrow down your options quite a bit.

HOW LONG CAN YOU COMMIT TO VOLUNTEERING?

The question of how long you want to volunteer is a big one, and one that will very quickly cut your enormous pool of options down to size. If you can only commit a few months or a summer, then you can limit your search to work camps, service vacations, charity camps, nonprofit internships, and any other short-term options you can find. Six-month programs are rare, but they do exist.

> "If you are interested in social welfare issues, the experience of living in a developing country is a must. I never trust people who talk a lot about poverty reduction or equitable trade unless they have some real practical experience outside of their own borders. By living in a developing nation, you gain firsthand field experience that you can draw upon to better understand how the world functions and how you might make it a better and more equitable place. It won't be easy or luxurious, but it will most likely be the best 'education' you can hope to obtain."
> —Emily Hurstak, 22, from Bombay, India

If you are considering a longer commitment, then some other issues come into play. Beyond the obvious considerations of money and time away from home, you should take into account where and what you would be doing during your volunteer time. Two years may make more sense if you are volunteering internationally, since it can take a long time to adjust to cultural differences and become proficient in a language. Two years also gives you more time to really get into a community and connect with the people. Volunteers in teaching programs usually serve for two years because developing lesson plans and learning how to teach effectively is a lengthy process. Furthermore, a number of the teaching programs offer participants the chance to do free course work for a master's degree in education—an opportunity which is worth taking advantage of and committing time to. However, a one-year program may be more sensible if you are doing service for the overall experience and not because it is not relevant to your future career plans. For example, if you are interested in advocacy law, you may be ready to move onto law school after one year of working in a soup kitchen.

DO YOU WANT TO GO OVERSEAS?

Whether you choose to do a domestic or international service program will largely determine the character of your experience. To start, let's be honest about the reality here at home. Our country is fairly stratified and segregated. As a result, most of us are unfamiliar with pockets of our own towns, cities, and states. Before you send yourself off to Burkina Faso, think about whether you could immerse and devote yourself to your own community first. Next, language is a huge factor. When considering whether or not you want to live in a foreign country, keep in mind that some programs offer language classes to help you pick up the language fast once immersed in a remote community. Distance from home is another factor here, particularly if you are doing a two-year program. If you are placed in Pakistan, you may not see your family for the full period. One Peace Corps volunteer I met in the Dominican Republic said that proximity to home was the one thing that got him through his two-year term. He was able to fly home four times.

While dealing with poverty anywhere is a challenge, the poverty of the Third World presents its own array of problems. Oftentimes, fundamental issues like garbage removal, clean water, and passable roads are the major concerns. Conditions may fall below your level of comfort. The only way to be sure that you are up for the challenge is to know exactly what the challenge is. So give it some thought, and if you do have a specific program or country in mind, research and find out what your lifestyle and daily tasks would be like if you were to volunteer there. And don't assume that your living situation will be any more dangerous in a Third World country. Often, U.S. cities are no safer than locations in developing countries. Just do your homework. If the statistics and stories you hear do sound a bit risky, then you have one more thing to think about. Are you willing to go somewhere where you are more vulnerable to disease, theft, or violence? Talking to past volunteers in your prospective location will help you sort through this personal question.

> "The Peace Corps isn't easy and the two-year commitment turns many people away. But it is the most rewarding thing I've ever done and something I'll carry with me for the rest of my life. Of course you have some tough days, but seeing the smile on someone's face when you accept an invitation to his home or sharing a cup of tea while making friends in the village bazaar are profound experiences. You learn how the majority of the world lives."
>
> —Jim O'Neil, 22, from Bangladesh

SHOULD YOU WORK FOR UNCLE SAM?

The U.S. government sponsors a few major volunteer programs, the most well-known being the Peace Corps. Because the program is well-funded by the government, there are a number of Peace Corps perks that might play a role in your decision. The government will pay for plane fare, health insurance, and language training. You will also receive a $6,000 allowance once you complete the two-year term, and can defer payment of your government loans. Nice, eh? Another thing to consider is that you will be an employee of the U.S. government and will receive job placement assistance upon your return. It *also* means that you will be a representative of the government and will be placed in strategic areas. You might find yourself trying to improve conditions in a country where U.S. interests and policy have a clearly detrimental effect on development. Get in touch with former Peace Corps volunteers in your areas of interest to address any doubts you may have.

HOW MUCH COMPENSATION DO YOU NEED?

It should be no surprise to you that public service work won't bring in the big bucks. But if you are really low on savings and high on loans, you should give a thought to the financial conditions of your time of service. Some organizations, like World Teach, actually charge their volunteers or require them to fundraise. But many long-term volunteer programs are free and include housing and a stipend as well. This is key if you are located in a city that has a high cost of living. Other programs, which are public service related jobs, like Green

Corps, provide salaries and benefits. Also, find out whether you can defer loan payments by becoming a volunteer in your prospective program.

GET WITH THE PROGRAM

Now that you've given some thought to the program details, take a look at how awesome the real thing can be. Read on to get an idea of what the diverse array of programs are like—from the most popular to the least known options—and to get your imagination running wild with altruistic possibilities. Don't limit your search to the listings here. Instead, treat this chapter as a small sampling of the rich variety of public service programs.

LARGE DOMESTIC PROGRAMS

If you plan on sticking to your home turf here in the States, but want to make an impact in a big way, check out these programs that will immerse you in a local rural or urban community and give you the tools you need to make positive change.

Americorps: (*www.americorps.org*) For those who want to see change happen within their own borders, this "domestic Peace Corps" offers forty thousand volunteers the chance to work on a whole gamut of issues in the U.S. You might renovate low-income housing, lead outdoor cleanups or assistant teach in a school for the mentally challenged. Health insurance and living expenses are both covered and you can receive a $4,725 education award after completing the year of service.

City Year: (*www.cityyear.org*) This ten-month program will give you a chance to combine theory with hands-on practice in the community. With the goal of advancing new policy ideas, volunteers serve in the heart of the city mentoring children, building urban gardens, and organizing community events, among other things. City Year places a special emphasis on eradicating social barriers and racism. Volunteers are between the ages of seventeen and twenty-four, and receive similar benefits as AmeriCorps volunteers (the $4,725 education award, health insurance, modest monthly stipend, and loan deferment).

Green Corps: (*www.greencorps.org*) This one-year Environmental Leadership Training Program will equip you with concrete skills for leadership in the environmental movement. Thirty-five young people are selected each year for Green Corps' unique, three-part training program that includes intensive classroom orientation, hands-on experience running environmental and public health campaigns, and placement in leading environmental groups for full-time social change work. Benefits include a salary of $19,000, health insurance, and a student loan payment program.

The Population Institute's Future Leaders of the World Program: (*www.populationinstitute.org*) For young people interested in reducing excessive population growth, the Institute offers The Future Leaders of the World Program. A one-year commitment, the program includes a media coordinator position, a field coordinator position and one to three public policy assistant positions. Includes an intensive training session on global population growth and other issues.

Habitat for Humanity AmeriCorps: (*www.habitat.org*) If you want to help low-income families achieve their dream of owning a home, consider this eleven-month term of constructing houses. It includes a living allowance, insurance and an AmeriCorps education grant of $4,725.

Boys Hope, Girls Hope: (*www.boyshopegirlshope.org*) If you've got a strong maternal/paternal instinct and a desire to help at-risk children gain stability at home, serve as a surrogate parent for this special program. Year-long "residential volunteer" positions are available through this nonprofit multidenominational organization that provides at-risk children with positive parenting, high-quality education, and mentoring. Volunteers live and work in a home of six to eight children (ages 9–18) in 38 homes across 17 U.S. cities. Volunteers receive room, board, health insurance and a monthly stipend of $200.

"What attracted me most to the Americorps' VISTA program (Volunteers In Service to America) was the unique opportunity to serve a community for a year, but with a stipend that was at least enough to ensure I'd be able to eat and have a roof (of some kind) over my head. We each get a stipend, set at 105 percent of whatever the poverty level in the region we're working in is, but it's not enough to qualify as any kind of salary. We are essentially full-time volunteers and full-time volunteers are what your average nonprofits need most. There are six of us "Vistas" at my non profit and we really are a vital part of the work done here. My co-workers are the most idealistic, good-hearted young people. I've gotten an invaluable look at what poverty really looks like, and how it affects families and kids."

—Laura Bufford, 22

Want to give a little, but don't have much time to give? These two reputable volunteer programs offer short-term projects all over the world for reasonable prices.

Volunteers for Peace (VFP): Take your pick of two- to-three week work camps in over seventy countries. VFP has a long tradition of providing affordable and meaningful overseas experiences and promoting "citizen diplomacy." Most program fees are $195, which includes room and board, and the majority of participants are twenty to twenty-five. You must become a member of VFP ($20) to register for a volunteer program. If you submit any feedback on your work camp experience—even a postcard—VFP will renew your membership for the coming year. They often use former volunteers as trip co-leaders (*www.vfp.org*).

SCI—International Voluntary Service USA: Join a two-to-four week summer volunteer project in one of fifty countries all over the world. The application fee for international programs is $125 and the participation fee is an additional $35–80, depending on the work camp. The program covers room, board, health insurance, and a year's membership to SCI. To find out about projects you must purchase the Directory of International Workcamps ($5) (*www.sci-ivs.org*).

NATIONAL TEACHING PROGRAMS

Always thought you have what it takes to be a teacher? Dedicate your passion and youthful energy to a classroom for a year or two and you will learn more about the art of instruction and our country's school system than you ever thought possible. As any young teacher will tell you, teaching is as tough as anything, but more gratifying than nearly everything. Take a peek at this list and pay special attention to the degree programs offered by some of these organizations. You could walk away with a Master's degree as well as valuable public service under your belt.

New York City Teaching Fellows: (*www.nycteachingfellows.org*) Think you're up for the challenge of teaching in the Big Apple? This program places 5,000 individuals (without teaching experience) in New York City public schools with the greatest need for teachers. The application process is selective and those accepted go through an intensive six-week training program. Fellows receive the normal teacher's salary and work on a subsidized masters degree program.

Teach for America: (*www.teachforamerica.org*) This well-known two-year national teaching program places young college graduates in low-income public schools throughout rural and urban America. All teachers go through intensive training the summer before the first school year begins. Government teaching salary is provided.

Alliance for Catholic Education (ACE): (*http://ace.nd.edu/ace*) If you are interested in teaching for two years in a needy school and would like to volunteer your services to a Catholic school, check out ACE. Based out of the University of Notre Dame, this program places college graduates (without teaching experience) in under-resourced Catholic schools across the southern United States. Housing, insurance, living stipend, loan deferment, and the Americorps education award are included. ACE volunteers receive a cost-free master's degree in education by the end of the two-year program.

Red Cloud School: (*http://redcloudschool.org/volunteers.htm*) Why not combine your teaching stint with a geographic jump and an interesting cultural experience? Every year this Jesuit-run elementary and high school for Native American children invites 18–20 volunteers to live and work at the Red Cloud School in South Dakota. Volunteers from all faiths live in houses with other volunteers, and commit to the core values of "simplicity and spirituality," while performing all types of teaching jobs.

Sorting Through the Mixed Reactions. Organized service programs can be hit or miss. While one volunteer might have a positive, life-changing experiences, another volunteer in the same program might walk away with more than his share of disillusion. In planning your experience, you not only have to look thoroughly at the program—its philosophy, its leadership—but also at the smaller details of your daily experience, like what kind of support you will be given and what your work assignments or sites might be. When committing a year or two of your life, you can never ask too many questions. Of course, there is a limit to how much you can anticipate and be sure about your experience before diving in, but exercise caution nonetheless. These quotes from Teach for America volunteers below illustrate how service program experiences are neither consistently good, nor consistently bad, but rather as diverse as the classrooms, communities, and projects that young people are assigned to serve.

"You have to be totally devoted to make a Teach for America experience successful. You not only have to overcome a lack of resources in the school system, but you often must overcome skepticism from others, inexperience, lack of formal training, and students' previously formed negative opinions of education, among other things. Just because this laundry list of obstacles begins to sound as if accomplishing anything is impossible does not mean that's actually the case. Perseverance, strategic thinking, support from administrators and experienced teachers, camaraderie and advice from critical teacher friends, enthusiasm for learning, and a strong relationship with students' families will begin to dwarf these problems in order to make actual and substantial positive change."

—Josh Griggs, 22

"Teaching in an inner-city public school is one of those incredible challenges that makes you want to keep doing it day in and day out. You work yourself hard because you have kids looking up to you every day. You have to use creativity and compassion in ways that aren't required on most college campuses."

—Jordan Pearce-Bristol, 22

"Some days I love my job and am exhilarated by it and some days I hate it and am exhausted by it. I am thankful to Teach for America for the opportunity to teach and learn, but I am also disappointed in their disorganization. Too much of the program is overseen by young, hardworking idealists without enough experience to make it great. I did not have a school or grade level assignment until two days before school started in September. Teaching is an unquestionably tough job and it is not a job that you can prepare for in 6 weeks (the length of Teach for America's 'Institute'). Yes, we're smart and well-educated, but teaching is an art and teaching in a struggling school is a massive challenge and this program is not going to do much to help you overcome either of those hurdles. However, willpower, resourcefulness, and dedication to children and their education will. I think I will continue to teach and work with children and I am glad that I have had this opportunity to learn more about education. But I love my students and I worry that my education comes at the expense of theirs."

—Teach for America volunteer who wishes to remain anonymous

NATIONAL RELIGIOUS VOLUNTEER PROGRAMS

If you feel a strong link between your desire to serve and your religious beliefs and would like to bridge them together even more intimately, take a look at these religious programs.

ADOVAH (Jewish Service Corps): (*www.avodah.net*) This year-long program combines anti-poverty work, Jewish study, and community building in the New York City or D.C. areas. Corps members live together and the program offers a stipend to cover rent, food, and personal expenses. Exit stipend and education grants are also provided upon completion of program. Loan deferment is possible.

Jesuit Volunteer Corps : (*www.jesuitvolunteers.org*) A one-year program sponsored by the Catholic Church, JVC sends young volunteers to the region of their choice (i.e. Northwest, Southeast) to live together in community and work on a variety of service assignments, from distributing clothes in women's shelters to organizing Latino PTAs. Room and board is included and a very small monthly stipend is provided. Program also includes the $4,725 AmeriCorps stipend and loan deferment.

Christian Appalachia Project (CAP): (*www.christianity.com/cap*) Are you eager to develop your Christian spirituality and also drawn to work in the Appalachian region? This nondenominational Christian nonprofit which mainly serves the Kentucky area assigns volunteers to different areas such as elderly services, spouse abuse, housing, employment, summer camps, and counseling. Short-term, medium-term (nine-week camp counselors), and year-long commitments are all available. Volunteers live, eat, and pray together. CAP offers loan deferment and health insurance.

REGIONAL VOLUNTEER PROGRAMS Whether you've got your heart set on a special corner of the country or feel called to get your hands dirty in a distant state, breeze over these local service programs and see if one of the unique options catches your interest. Also, start asking around and poking through the service opportunities in your ideal location.

Rocky Mountain Youth Corps: (*www.rockymountainyouthcorps.org/byc.html*) To help equip young teens with job skills and self-awareness in the Rocky Mountain region, join the ranks of the teachers and volunteers at this program in northwest Colorado. Volunteers help sixteen to nineteen year-olds develop outdoor skills, job ethics, financial management skills, and independent living skills. Also check out Northwest Youth Corps (*www.nwyouthcorps.org*).

Milwaukee Community Service Corp: (*http://my.execpc.com/~mcsc/*) By dedicating three months to a full year to this Milwaukee program, you will have the chance to renovate homes, intern at youth organizations, do outreach activities, plant gardens, distribute food at pantries, and so on. Corps members have the chance to earn the Americorps education award.

University of California at San Francisco Aids Health Project: (*www.ucsf-ahp.org*) This unique one-year program is geared towards college graduates with an interest in health professions, social services, or nonprofit management. Interns work about thirty-two hours a week on HIV and AIDS projects, like counseling and testing programs. A $800 housing stipend is provided each month and most interns find part-time work for supplemental income.

"Right now I work trying to help children of migrant farm workers meet educational standards in an after-school program funded by the No Child Left Behind Act. I'm pursuing what I'm passionate about and that—for me—was an important decision to come to. Not settling into a well-paying job for its financial security, but being contented and happy with *what* I'm doing. Right out of college, I spent a year working for an NGO in Honduras, which was an even bigger leap of faith. But again, it came down to pursuing my passions. That has been my mantra, I think, and it's made me very happy (if not driving a nicer car or wearing nicer clothes)."

—Ben Lewis, 25

INTERNATIONAL PROGRAMS

Are you set on heading overseas to do a service project? Your generosity is inclined in a worthy direction. You will find the need and level of poverty in developing countries much greater and graver than what our domestic reality can prepare us for. Get ready to make a profound impact and to be profoundly affected yourself. Such intense service work often makes volunteers want to give away the clothes off their backs. You just might come with an empty suitcase and an altered perspective for the rest of your life.

STEEP HILLS AND DEEP POTHOLES
BY KRISS BARKER, 40

" I began my strange journey as a result of a 'double dog dare.' Although I was dead-set on going to medical school, and had actually been accepted to my top choice, a friend challenged me to join the Peace Corps. Although this friend never did sign up for 'the Corps,' I soon found myself on a plane bound for Swaziland. I'd never heard of Swaziland, so when I got the call from the Peace Corps office in Washington to tell me about the assignment, I thought it was a joke. 'Check an atlas, and I'll call back in 10 minutes,' the recruiter patiently offered.

Peace Corps was a great experience. I taught science and math at an all girls' school, and while I was there, King Mswati III was crowned. He took three wives during my Peace Corps tenure, and all three of them became my students! Working in Africa changed the course of my career. Not only did I not return to study for an MD (I have a Masters' Degree in public health and work in health communication), but I learned that

(continued)

sometimes the best choices in life are the most illogical; that sometimes the road less traveled is the very one where your footsteps fit best.

I've been shot at; emergency evacuated twice due to civil unrest in the country where I was living; and I've seen more poverty and disease than I care to remember. But, I've also been a part of some really wonderful things. Some of my most poignant memories include working with voodoo priests on HIV/AIDS education in Haiti; teaching traditional midwives to provide better care; working on a national immunization campaign (and delivering vaccines in a U.S. Blackhawk helicopter); and working on communication campaigns for everything from breast feeding to prevention of child slavery. It's been quite a ride—and it's far from over! Although the road less traveled is often plagued with steep hills and deep potholes, the journey is guaranteed never to be dull. 〞

Note: *Kriss is humble and left out some exciting accomplishments. She also sailed around the world while working on a yacht, worked on an archeological dig in Latin America, and is just recently back from India for a work assignment. Who said adventure is limited to the twenties?*

"I've done two short-term volunteer projects through Volunteers for Peace (*www.vfp.org*) in Croatia and am hoping to do one in Belarus this summer. They are easy to get involved with and also a great, inexpensive way to fill down time between adventures and really live in a place of the world you'd never get to just by traveling."

—Andrea Gregovich, 28

Volunteers in Asia: (*www.viaprograms.org*) A program started by Stanford students in the sixties, Volunteers in Asia sends between 30–40 English teachers to Indonesia, Laos, Vietnam, and China every year. Participants volunteer their English language skills in a variety of different ways, like teaching school children in China, translating on the Vietnam border, or editing for an Indonesian newspaper. Commitment can range from a summer to one or two years. Benefits include language training, pre-departure training, country orientation, round-trip airfare, medical insurance, room and board, and a living stipend. Program fee is $1,975 for one year and $975 for two years. Those who make a two-year volunteer commitment will receive a stipend to cover living costs. Scholarships are available.

Peace Corps: (*www.peacecorps.gov*) Introduced by President Kennedy in 1961, the Peace Corps is one of the largest work-abroad programs for U.S. citizens. Corps members are placed in countries all over the world on assignments ranging from agricultural development to environmental education. Intensive language and cultural and technical training are provided (two to three months). All expenses are paid (housing, food, clothing, spending money, medical and dental care, transportation and twenty-four vacation days per year) and a "resettlement allowance" of $6,075 is granted after completing the two-year assignment. Job hunting assistance is also provided.

"Volunteering in a different corner of the world or country than the one you are used to is invaluable. We all tend to be products of our environment. Going outside of your comfort zones pushes you to challenge and reaffirm how you live your life. In the end, you will come out a stronger and more genuine person. This comes at a price; you will also experience intense culture shock. But it's all part of the learning experience." —Beth Conradson, 24

Pondering a service project as a short-term relief from your day job?
Take a vacation you'll never forget. These organizations will value your professional expertise enough to finance your trip costs and make good use of the skills you have to offer. Volunteers for **Financial Services Volunteer Corps** devote one to two weeks to projects utilizing their financial experience in Croatia, Kazakhstan, Macedonia, Moldova, Poland, Romania, Russia, and Ukraine. Room, board, and transportation costs are covered. Another organization that sends American professionals overseas is **Winrock International.** Volunteers commit two to six weeks promoting agricultural and business development, and Winrock covers all costs including travel expenses.

Concern America: (*www.concernamerica.org*) If you have some valuable professional skills and want to use them to promote social betterment overseas, join the ranks of non-salaried volunteers that drive Concern America. Professionals work for two or more years sharing their skills and knowledge with community leaders in developing countries. Applicants must be at least twenty-one and have a degree or work experience in a certain area (education, agriculture, public health, etc.). Room, board, round trip transportation, health insurance, a monthly stipend, support services, an annual trip home and a repatriation allowance are provided.

IndiCorps: (*www.indicorps.org*) This nonprofit organization was created to encourage people of Indian origin to reconnect with their roots through an intensive service experience. The IndiCorps program includes a one-year competitive public service fellowship, emphasizing both personal growth and international development. Selected fellows are given individual responsibility to execute and complete projects that are created and defined by local developmental experts. A one-month orientation is held in Bombay, India and fellows come together every six weeks for retreats. Housing, food, and a monthly stipend are provided.

Feeling web-fatigued? Stop clicking around and get your hands on some real pages. These handy guidebooks will help you sort through international service prospects.

Alternatives to the Peace Corps: A Directory of Third World and U.S. Volunteer Opportunities (Food First Books) by Jennifer Willson and Meagan Rule.

How to Live Your Dream of Volunteering Overseas (Penguin) by Joseph Collins, Stefano DeZerega and Zahara Heckscher.

INTERNATIONAL RELIGIOUS PROGRAMS

If you are interested in combining overseas work with your religious beliefs, breeze over these options to find a program that will implant you in your ideal work and faith community.

Kibbutz Program Center: (*www.kibbutz.org.il*) If you have two to six months to work with and are interested in living in Israel, consider the Kibbutz experience. Volunteers generally contribute eight hours a day, six days a week in return for accommodations, meals, and a small stipend. An extra $25 per month charge covers health insurance.

Mercy Ships: (*www.mercyships.org*) Torn between adventuring on the seven seas and dedicating yourself to global charity? Do them both as a volunteer short-term crewmember aboard this fleet of hospital ships that bring Christian ministry and health care to the poor in over 75 port cities. Both skilled and unskilled positions are available for two-week to two-year stints. Various positions available (cook, translator, deck hand, etc.).

Maryknoll: (*www.maryknoll.org*) If you are seriously committed to lay missionary work in the developing world and have three and a half years to offer, take a look at this Catholic program that serves fifteen nations in the areas of health, education, community organizing, and grassroots economic development. Maryknoll has a spiritual element and volunteers must be at least 25 years old to join. The program commences with an intensive four-month training, including language-training if necessary.

" Ever since my first trip to Israel at age 12, I've wanted to live there for a year. I've also had this crazy childhood dream of working with sea turtles. After college, I was able to do both with Project Otzma, a ten-month volunteer program offering a variety of experiences through living and working in Israel (*www.projectotzma.org*). Though I was tempted to go straight to law school, I knew I wouldn't have a chance like this again: a period of time with no responsibilities other than to my dreams. How could I pass that up?

During the ten months I spent in Israel with Project Otzma I worked three months in an absorption center for new immigrants primarily from Ethiopia, three months in a religious development town, one month in Jerusalem, and three months on the Mediterranean with the Marine Turtle Rescue and Rehabilitation Center. I decided to do this program after college because its sheer breadth of experience appealed to me and the structure of the program appeased my parent's fears about security. The cost of

(continued)

the program is $1,850, which is substantial, but considering that the program already subsidises each participant $6,000, it is not unreasonable.

There are plenty of other ways to live in Israel. For instance many kibbutzim take on volunteers for a few months at a time and provide food and housing in exchange for work. Unfortunately, because of the general economic shift away from socialism, working on a kibbutz is not what it used to be and you may likely end up doing kitchen work. Nevertheless, it can be a great experience.

Safety is probably everyone's main concern when considering travel in the Middle East. There's no such thing as being one-hundred percent secure anywhere. Every person has to take the precautions they feel comfortable with. In my case, that means not riding buses. Luckily, Israel has another form of transportation, *moniot sherut*, or service taxis—which run along most bus lines and are as cheap as the buses. It was important to me to be wary and put limits on my activities for safety's sake. But it was equally important not to let fear keep me from pursuing my dreams. **,,**

Project Otzma: (*www.projectotzama.org*). Want to develop your Jewish faith through a stimulating variety of community work and study in Israel? This ten-month leadership development program for young adults (ages 20–25) assigns interns to live and work in immigrant absorption centers, to study Hebrew, and to carry out community service projects. Program fee is $1,850 and covers most expenses, though airfare is not included (read Lara's personal account above for a fuller picture of Project Otzma).

Lastly, why not **CREATE YOUR OWN SERVICE PROJECT?** You may be interested or involved in a small nonprofit that has a very specific mission, and want to devote a year or two of your time to it. Contact them and propose your idea. Or maybe you envision something bigger than what has already been established. Strike off on your own and do something that only you can do, and that won't get done if you don't take the risk and initiative to do it. Teach for America began because a student named Wendy Kopp decided to put her senior thesis into action after graduation. There are countless other examples of recent college graduates who saw a gap in social services and envisioned a way to fill it, through charter schools, community clean-ups, or groundbreaking organizations. Bring your ingenuity and personal flair to a unique project and you really will make your mark on the world.

> "Starting your own project or organization is not as daunting a task as you may think. If you have an idea, go for it! It's definitely hard, but there are people out there who will help you. And it's the best way to learn—by doing."
> —Abigail Levine, 23, founder of Jews for Equal Rights for Immigrant Communities

PREP SCHOOL PIONEER
BY EMILY ROEBUCK, 24

" 'We're opening up a new school down the street...by any chance, do you have any fifth graders?' I found myself saying these words to random strangers on the street shortly after leaving the comfort zone of my college campus. Having signed up to be a volunteer in the Nativity Prep Program, I joined ten volunteers to open a school offering a tuition-free, college prep education to at-risk kids in San Diego. No building? No principal? No curriculum? No experience? No problem. Through a lot of ambition and hard work, we somehow made the dream happen and now seventy underprivileged kids are one step closer to getting to college. As a pioneer in a grass-roots organization, I've had the most bizarre, rewarding, and empowering experience of my life.

The best advice I can offer is to trust your instincts when making a decision, but also do your homework before you commit a year or two of your life to something. Understand the program's vision and make sure you agree with every part of it. For example, if you were challenged in living situations with college roommates, don't sign up to live with a community of ten people. Oh, and don't make plans for after your scheduled 'time' is up. You might just find your niche and postpone the real world forever. "

AND THE FUNDS?

Samuel Huntington Public Service Fellowship: A year-long public service fellowship anywhere in the world. Applicants submit a proposal of a volunteer project to the committee, which selects one to two winners every spring. Open to graduating college seniors only (*www.nationalgridus.com/masselectric/about_us/award.asp*).

American Association of University Women (AAUW) Community Action Grant: An award for women who propose nonpartisan projects that have direct public impact. Twenty to thirty grants of $2,000–$7,000 are awarded every year. Up to five grants are available for two-year projects (*www.aauw.org/fga/fellowships_grants/ index.cfm*).

Ella Lyman Cabot Trust Grants: Grants for graduating seniors and recent college graduates to support projects that are personally meaningful and benefit others. Awards range from $7,000–$12,000. Contact: Ella Lyman Cabot Trust, Inc c/o Palmer & Dodge, LLP 1 Beach St. Boston, MA 02108.

Echoing Green Public Service Fellowships: Two-year awards for innovative public service projects anywhere in the world. Includes $60,000 stipend ($30,000 each year), health insurance, training, technical assistance, and access to Echoing Green's network of social entrepreneurs (*www.echoinggreen.org*).

KEEPING IT REAL

It doesn't take a stretch of the imagination to come up with ways that volunteering is a valuable experience. In fact, you probably wouldn't be able to fit all of the job skills you'll gain onto a one-page resume. You will walk away with great problem-solving skills after a year or two of assessing social problems and remedying them. Furthermore, as a volunteer, you will have learned tremendous self-discipline. You will know how to motivate yourself to get a job done, either independently or as part of a team. Because of the community nature of your work, you will also have developed a capacity to work with people of other cultures and gained a more in-depth understanding of social problems, in a general sense, and also in regard to the specific needs of your community. Leadership is another skill that any sort of community service project or program will teach you, simply by nature of the fact that you must motivate others, organize efforts, and serve as an example. Lastly, you will walk away with great practical, real world experience under your belt. In other words, you'll be an employer's dream.

CORE VALUE

They call it "the toughest job you'll ever love." See what these two former Peace Corps volunteers say about the personal and professional value of the two years they dedicated to public service overseas.

"When you join the Peace Corps you are more or less saying, 'I'm willing to do what you need me to do—wherever or whatever it is.' This ability is really attractive to employers. And when you actually enter the working world you will excel, because for two years you made things happen with so much less at your disposal than most workplaces in the U.S. have. After finishing up the Peace Corps in Namibia, I moved to Puerto Rico to be with my girlfriend and was able to find a good job quickly. I went to the University of Puerto Rico in San Juan and started talking to biology professors who told me about the fieldwork that was going on outside of San Juan and put me in touch with the right people. My employers later told me that I was hired because of my Peace Corps experience. The fieldwork I was hired to do was often grueling because of the constant rain, mud, and heat. My employers thought I could handle it."
—Rob Marek, 28

"Peace Corps has a huge effect on your personal and professional life. Doing what you love is not going off track from your career, but could actually boost it. The Peace Corps is a tremendous network of professionals. They offer career fairs, returned volunteer clubs, and resource directories that help you network with RPCVs (Returned PC Volunteers) in every profession. Some of these volunteers were in the first wave of volunteers of the sixties, others have just returned. Most are eager to help newly returned volunteers with jobs because they recognize the value of the experience. The experience stands out on resumes to any future employer. Take the time to frame it well, and bring up the obstacles you overcame in interviews. The challenges, from making do with scarce resources to learning a new language to working with the rules of another culture, require extreme innovation. In the Peace Corps you are the manager of each community project from the get-go. You learn how to deal with all people. You learn that, no matter what part of the globe you are in, people are people, and they come first. Common courtesy, patience, consideration, and genuine concern are valued in rural communities and most countries (a little more than in our own, perhaps). All of these lessons go a long way!"

—Colleen Quinlan, 25

If you wisely choose a program that matches your interests and talents (i.e. teaching, the environment), then you will have a whole new set of skills to market to any prospective employer. And after an extended period of service, you may even want to remain working in the area you devoted your energies to. You will not only have experience in that area, but you will know which organizations hire people full-time. Opportunities may even open up within the nonprofit in which you volunteered. Keep your ears open and connections strong throughout your term of service.

Volunteering after college gives you far more than job skills. It will not only serve as a springboard into the future, but also shoot you there with perspective, awareness, and dedication to your community. When the real world comes a knockin', you will not only be prepared to greet it, but will have established a strong, lifelong commitment to service.

CHAPTER SIX: ALL THE WORLD'S A STAGE

ONE OF THE MOST COMMON COMPLAINTS of young people fresh in the working world is that their full capacities aren't being utilized. Without some room for creativity, you start to feel like a cog in the system. Monotony takes its toll. Weeks pass and you can't remember the last time you created something you could proudly attach your name to. Even weekends cease to be exciting. HEY! Snap out of it! You thrive on expression and creation, not dollars and narrow work tasks! Why are you sitting in a cubicle manufactured for Joe Schmoe when you should be out there crafting your own work space—one splattered with paint, covered in words, draped in costumes, or filled with music!

It is crucial to recognize your creative gifts and find a way to feed them at this early juncture in life. Make a personal commitment to expression, dynamism, and diversion and be okay with a humbler salary and fewer comforts so that you can keep your personal priorities untouchably high. Otherwise, there will always be a million voices—in TV commercials, phone conversations back home, or happy hour chats—telling you that you need numbers to subsist. Your salary should be above X marker by now, it's time you bought a car, you *need* your own apartment, and if you were *really* successful, you'd be throwing around money like Mike.

First of all, you don't want to be like Mike or you wouldn't have bought this book of non-conventions. Second of all, be honest with yourself about what exactly you *need*. Have you ever gone hungry? Slept in the rain? Had to beg from strangers? Didn't think so. Before you go reading the expression "starving artist" like a death sentence, give yourself a reality check. There *is* a way to make a living off of what you love to do, in some capacity or another. The average forty-year-old won't quit his job to become an artist or entertainer because he has established a lifestyle he needs to maintain or racked up three mortgages and a load of kids. You, however, have only yourself (or perhaps a loan or two, at worst) to answer to. Act in your best interest now and you may just save yourself a pricey mid-life crisis! Aren't the twenties about scraping by to do what you love, anyway? Sure your raw creativity might not generate a salary to write home about, or even bring the glory you had secretly hoped for. But in creating and inventing, you'll discover something so rare and precious that you should be willing to live on peanut butter and jelly alone to maintain: work that ceases to be work, because it's exactly what you want to do with your time, your day, your life.

In this chapter, you will find dozens of ideas for how to pursue your passion in a variety of artistic and creative fields, from classical theater to historical expositions, musical production to fiction writing. Though some positions require specific talent and training, other jobs are attainable for anyone who has the slightest interest or appreciation in the art. And while some artistic pursuits are geared at recognition and advancement, others are simply about enjoying a community of like-passioned people. They can be full-time commitments, side ventures to complement an adventure like world travel, or weekend activities to work in with your studies or day job. For the truly gutsy folks out there, the "Leap of Faith" sections offer suggestions for how you can take your artistic gifts all the way. Regardless of your level of skill or seriousness, every artistic involvement has the potential to inspire and satisfy.

For those in search of a highly entertaining creative venture, the second half of this chapter is a list of fun-filled and challenging jobs in the entertainment industry. Many ideas will demand artistic talent, while others will require a spirit of adventure, passion, and perhaps a sense of humor. Flirt with the whole bunch of them. Remember, if you think that a certain job is out of your reach, chances are that most people will think the same and won't bother to apply. Someone has to get the job, and if you can muster the enthusiasm and confidence to present yourself with a bit of pizzazz, the odds turn in your favor.

So let the Mikes of the world keep tossing around their wages like monopoly money. You've got a higher calling. *You,* my friend, are an *artiste.*

> "All the great advances in the history of the arts were made by the people who threw convention out the window!"
> —Graham Norris, 22

WHETTING YOUR APPETITE . . .

- Earn your keep at an artist community in New Hampshire *(www.macdowellcolony.org).*

- Lead poetry, acting, dance or drawing workshops at a grade or high school.

- Work in a Vegas casino or join the ranks of the circus *(www.soyouwanna.com).*

- Write overseas for a small magazine, newspaper, or travel publication.

- Work as a dancer, musician, or photographer at a resort in the South Pacific.

- Intern at "the Kitchen" a nonprofit that promotes emerging artists and their work in the Chelsea area of New York City *(www.thekitchen.org).*

- Design exhibits in a natural history museum *(www.museumjobs.com).*

- Choreograph, critique, or jam at a summer dance festival *(www.americandance-festival.org).*

BECAUSE YOU LOVE IT

Think of what makes you tick—the hobby that you lived for as a little kid, the class you used to get psyched for, the thing you would do 24/7 if you could. If any kind of artistic field comes to mind, read this section to see how you can use your passion to kick off a career.

HELPFUL WEBSITES:

Global Art Jobs: (*www.globalartjobs.com*) Listings of art jobs worldwide.

Entertainment Jobs: (*www.entertainmentjobs.com*) A membership website that lists jobs and internships for TV shows and films. Includes a company directory.

Productionhub.com: An online resource and industry directory for film, television, video, and digital media production

U.S. Directory of Entertainment Employers: (*www.EntertainmentEmployers.com*) An entertainment industry job search and reference guide providing current information on over 3,000 top companies, career resources and key organizations in the entertainment industry.

Maslow Media: (*www.maslowmedia.com*) A staffing company for the broadcast industry that includes information on jobs in television, camera crews, production management, and so on.

"When you're in the midst of a job search at the end of college, you tend to put way too much emphasis on getting absolutely the right job, based on the idea that the direction you take after graduation will play a huge role in determining what you'll be doing when you're forty. As far as I'm concerned, the predictive value of your first job is pretty much nil. Finding out what you want to do for a career involves being willing to muddle through and learn from the process. Today, I'm not doing what I thought I would do when I started college, and it wouldn't surprise me if in ten years I'm doing something else entirely."

—Nathan Littlefield, 22

VISUAL ARTS

Always been an art buff? Why not find a job that surrounds you with artistic creations or demands the visual creativity you are bursting with? Here is a broad palette of possibilities to give you a sense for just how much is out there:

•**Tour guide in an art museum.** Imagine having a job that pays you to learn about great works of art and show them off to visitors. Tour guiding is just one of many positions you can secure at a museum. Others include exhibit designer, historian, curatorial assistant, special events coordinator, fundraising officer, brochure designer and librarian. If you are looking to relocate, take the initiative and look for museum job opportunities in a cool city. To browse through listings of full-time jobs, part-time jobs, paid internships, fellowships, and volunteer opportunities in museums, libraries, archives, and galleries, give these online resources a look: *www.globalmuseum.org, www.museumjobs.com, www.museum-employment.com, www.aam-us.org,* and *www.museumstuff.com.* You can also just go to individual museum websites and find out if they have fellowships or internships. Many museums and galleries, including the Metropolitan Museum of Art (*www.metmuseum.org*) and the Smithsonian Institution (*www.si.edu/cms*) offer short-term stipends, internships or fellowships for assistants.

> "For someone who really wants to break into museums and doesn't have any training or experience, I would recommend applying for preparatory work. Preparators are the people who do the framing, set up, and installation of the exhibitions."
> —Emily Wright, 22

•**Counsel at an art camp**. Remember when the highlight of your summer was making lanyard bracelets and macaroni art? Take a job at an art camp and inspire a whole new generation! You might find a camp that focuses largely on crafts, which will give you an excuse to break out the finger paints on a daily basis. If teaching older kids interests you, apply for an art teacher position at a private school. Check out resources like *www.campresource.com* and *www.joltcamps.com* for listings of art camp jobs. Also take a peek at *www.the-clearing.org* for a unique adult art school.

• Revive the art of the past— **join a restoration project**. Use your skills to revamp a crumbling church, paint a street mural or restore an ancient façade. This could take you anywhere, from the center of your own city to the international destination you've been daydreaming of. For leads, get in touch with art history preservation societies. Ask around to find a crew that could use an extra hand.

• **Live and work in an art community.** Join a group of artists to contribute and develop your skill. Whether you have a knack for sculpture, pottery, painting, beadwork, photography, or furniture, your company will inspire you on to create great works. Most art centers offer classes, practice areas, and some sort of instructional guidance. Aim to waive fees with work-study.

Check out The MacDowell Colony, founded in Peterborough, New Hampshire in 1907. About 200 artists a year receive room, board, and a studio. All that is required is an application and there is no financial obligation. Some grants and fellowships are awarded (*www.macdowellcolony.org*).

For overseas ambiance and tropical muses, check out The Julia and David White Artists' Colony in Costa Rica, an artist colony founded by an American man in memory of his children. You pay $550 a month for half your board and a fund pays the other half (*www.forjuliaanddavid.org*).

Ladies, you have the opportunity to join an all-female art community in the Hudson Valley called the Women's Studio Workshop. Internships are available (*http://www.wsworkshop.org/internships.html*).

• **Be a caricature artist**. If you pick up and move to the location of your dreams and need a moneymaker that will keep your creative juices flowing, consider sketching people into cartoons at an amusement park or another highly touristy area. This could be great practice at facial study and plant you in a colorful work environment.

• **Work or volunteer for an art coalition or NGO.** You might try beginning with practical tasks like grant writing and fundraising, and then work your way up the arts promotion ladder. Idealist.org is a fantastic resource for art NGO's.

• Surround yourself with classic and funky contemporary pieces of art by **working behind the scenes of an auction house**. Everyone's heard of Sotheby's and Christie's, but there are thousands of other auction houses around the world for every item possible, from ancient record albums to seized property. Spend time mooning over your favorite pieces before they're sold.

•**Paint scenery and props for a theater.** Turn a wooden stage into a colorful wonderland, and enjoy the free shows. There are thousands of theaters of all sizes that could use your artistic talent, from small community playhouses to well-known opera houses. Networking is the best way to get involved with show prep. Go to performances and readings and talk to people in the community afterwards. Theaters, companies, and producers are also always looking for people to work sound, lights, and props on the cheap. Give *www.backstagejobs.com* a peek.

•**Draw political cartoons, greeting cards, or illustrations for children's books.** The trick here may be to start small and build up a solid portfolio that you can shop around to local or free art newspapers and publishers.

•Having trouble selling your article, magazine, or comic? **Self-publish a ZINE.** All you need are paper, ink, staples, and of course, that brilliant idea. Spend some time getting six pages of art, comics or original writing together, publish them for 50 cents a copy, then hawk them to friends, family, and strangers at shows, coffee shops, and on the internet for a $1–2 a pop. They won't pay the rent, but will let you print up a second issue, which will be twice as cool. Check out *www.zinebook.com* for examples and inspiration.

•**Sell folk art at craft shows**. Whether you're an expert at beadwork or holiday ornaments, you can tour the nation marketing your darling designs. Check out: *www.artandcraftshows.net* and *www.horizons-art.org*.

•**Use your sculpting skills in a stop-motion animation studio**. Even with today's computer animated characters, there's still something awesome about a clay gorilla pounding toy planes into sawdust. Check out *www.stopmotionanimation.com*.

•Why not do a service to your fellow artists by serving as a bare-all muse? **Nude modeling** will bring in a few extra bucks and hey, a classroom of eyes never killed anyone. Check out city art schools and local universities and make some very subtle inquiries in the art department around the beginning of the semester. Just be careful when the gig is with an "independent" photographer or for an unclear purpose. And if something feels sketchy, grab your undergarments and go!

• Most people don't think as creatively as you do . . . **PROPOSE SOME-THING!** Paint murals on the cabins of a dude ranch in exchange for free room and board, offer to touch up the crumbling sculptures of a neighborhood church, apply for a grant to study Renaissance art in Florence, or propose an after school drawing class at an inner-city school.

Combine your artistic endeavor with a geographic switch. Browsing through *100 Best Small Art Towns in America* (Avalon Travel Publishing) by John Villari should give you a wealth of ideas of where you might plop yourself down. If you would like to surround yourself by artists and artists only, check out *Artists Communities*.

"I began my summer stint at the Albright Knox Art Gallery by simply calling and offering to volunteer. Luckily, my offer coincided with the visiting Phillips collection from D.C. and the museum needed extra help in nearly every department. I greeted guests, aided with tours, and helped in guest relations. With the traveling Phillips collection came all the greats, from Renoir to Monet to Matisse. If I'd seen the collection in D.C. I would have been there for an afternoon, but instead I was able to view "The Boating Party" again and again, finding new details each time. For an art lover like me, it was fabulous! I moved on to a full-time job in the fall, but one of my fellow volunteers, who also had a BA in history, was offered a permanent position at the gallery by mid-summer."
—Ellen Fabiano, 22

Art Corps: Check out this organization that places artists in Central American NGO's with the goal of employing their creative talent to convey the NGO's message. A $1,000 stipend is provided for travel costs. Art supplies, room and board are also covered. You will need to be fluent in Spanish to score this fantastic opportunity. Visit the Art Corps website at *www.nebf.org/artcorps_brochure_web.html*. While you're at your web post, check out the Latin American Art Resource Project (*www.hood.edu/academic/art/laarp/volint*) and Art Workshops in Guatemala (*www.artguat.org*).

" I'm from Israel and have lived in the States for most of my life. I never really got over leaving the Mediterranean, and Barcelona was like a lilting star in my head, constantly distracting me and telling me to come. So I did.

I lived in NYC for a year, working the graveyard shift in a photography print-house from 7 PM to 4 AM (the city really never sleeps). Eventually I got a more normal job, assisting a photographer in his studio, which paid well and allowed me to save money. By the time I left NYC, I had almost $5,000 saved up. I bought a book on working in Spain, took Spanish classes, and got ready to be a photographer living on the other side of the Atlantic. I had a couple friends in Barcelona who let me crash with them for a few days and threw a huge party my first night in the city. I told every single partygoer that I was looking for a place to live, and within a week I was sharing an apartment with two German girls in a colorful part of town. It was a large room with tons of light, a balcony, and a roof deck—for only $250 a month!

For ten months I fruitlessly hunted down work as a photographer. The Catalans were not so eager to give a young American/Israeli any work, so I did my own projects. First I did a long project on bullfighting in the south of Spain which brought me to Granada, Sevilla, and Rhonda for two weeks. I also did lots of street photography, and a bit on the changing architecture of the city. I had to be a self-starter and the work was all financed by me, edited by me, and had no real prospect of getting published anywhere.

But when a photo editor at the _Washington Times_ really liked one of my bullfighting shots, my project directly helped score me my current job. Furthermore, some of my Barcelona street photography is soon to be published in a new lifestyle/travel magazine based out of Miami. Not only did my Spain experience pay off professionally, but it was probably the best year of my life. Barcelona is an amazing town, beautifully situated on some prime beaches and filled with art, culture, dance, hiking, architecture, and the notoriously fabulous Spanish nightlife. It's cheap, so some dollars can get you a long way, but don't go expecting to find work. Go expecting to have the time of your life. "

FROM THE GRAVEYARD SHIFT TO BARCELONA DRIFT
BY ROEY YOHAI, 27

PHOTOGRAPHY

Want to capture the world through your lens? Do a little searching to turn your hobby into a purposeful source of income or even a career.

- **Submit those killer photos from your last overseas adventure to a photo stock house.** If you think people (other than your mom) might want to see—and maybe even purchase—your photos, contact a stock photo agency. These places rent photos to clients, usually advertisers. If they bite, they'll showcase your photos in their magazines to clients, and then you take a cut of whatever is purchased. You could also contact them to find out what kind of photography they are in need of, and customize an upcoming adventure according to their demand.

- **Try photojournalism.** Contact news wire agencies and find out where they're lacking photographers. If you want to start small, get in touch with the photo editor of a local arts newspaper or free publication and find out how you can be of aid.

- **Work as an assistant at a photography kiosk at an amusement park or historic site**, developing photos of open-mouthed roller coaster riders and taking pictures of sunburned tourists stuffed into period costumes.

- **Work at a photo lab or a professional dark room**. Develop those embarrassing or scandalous photos for free, and in the meantime mingle with photographers (and potential bosses!) in your city.

- **Appeal to your heroes.** Track down your favorite photographer in your area and ask if he or she could use an assistant. You'll learn from a master and get your feet wet.

- **Have a soft spot for true love?** Work as an assistant to a wedding photographer and you will have a taste of marital bliss every weekend. By the time your lucky day comes around, you'll have had enough to elope and save yourself a few grand!

- **Work your way into commercial photography**, shooting anything from tennis tournaments to interior design.

" I spent six months in Chile working for a Chilean newspaper in the gorgeous port town of Valparaiso. I didn't go down there with anything. I spoke rudimentary Spanish and my experience with a camera was limited, but I was determined to get a job as a photographer. Through the help of a language program I was enrolled in, I ended up getting a job with the biggest daily paper in the city within a few weeks. Although they only paid me in limitless free meals and film, the six months in a foreign work environment were priceless. That experience sealed it. I wanted to work abroad after graduation.

I was lucky enough to receive a fellowship from my university to fund a one-year photo project documenting the Three Gorges Dam in China. Halfway through the year, I am building up a huge archive of photos, improving my Chinese dramatically, and gaining what I hope will be a deep and profound understanding of China and the Chinese. Although I was lucky enough to get a fellowship to fund the whole thing, there are many national fellowship opportunities for similar projects (for example, the Fulbright, the Hays-Brandeis, and The Alexia Foundation Fund). If you don't have luck with any of those, you can always go abroad to places like China and teach English. I know a lot of very interesting and motivated western artists and musicians that work ten hours a week as English teachers, leaving them the time to practice their craft.

Photography has allowed me a fascinating insight into the world. Instead of glazing over everything I see, my eye wants to scrutinize ever closer. It makes literally every moment a situation to be compartmentalized in the neat package that makes up every single photograph. Most of those photos turn out to be lacking in the fundamental 'IT' that makes the great photograph. But when that moment appears and you know it and it all comes together the way you envision it, that is the moment and a feeling that can rarely be duplicated. But its euphoria lasts until the next one. "

- **Set up shop at a flea market:** If you think your photos are worthy, try to sell them at a flea market, fair, or an open-air market. Ask friends and family to do some free advertising for you to ensure you pull in some customers.

- **Think outside the box.** Every media source needs photos—everything from boats, to coffee, to dogs, to hairpieces. Browse through magazines, check out their style and submit your best work to the photo editor.

- **Find your subject** Find something that draws you—whether it be a street performer, a chess player in the park, or your favorite cashier at the supermarket. Follow them around (with their permission of course), find out what they're doing when they're not on the clock or in public and capture the story on film.

Tip: It Takes Two to Tango. Why go at it alone? Be it theater, writing, music, or art, two heads can be better than one. Even if you're a solitary writer, you need a community to give you criticisms, support, and understanding. Go to your local coffee shop and look at the bulletin board. Pick up your local art newspaper and find out about writing groups. Go to open mikes, find other musicians, start an art-jam band, or writer's group of your own. Truck your art around to coffee shops and restaurants for display, or even sale. In addition to making yourself a community, you're also getting yourself some recognition, which is really the best you can hope for in the early years of artistry.

MUSIC

Stick with your natural rhythms by choosing a job in the music industry. Whether you sing opera or simply can't live without your headphones, there are plenty of inviting opportunities out there for you.

"Being a rock star does not come along with all the glamor the title implies. As in any kind of artistic pursuit, the most important thing is to believe in and love what you're doing. Different forms of rejection will always be there—whether it is from club bookers, audience members who came to see a different band, or your grandfather who doesn't understand your music or message. But during the moments on stage when the music clicks just right, and you can feel every person in the audience breathing with you, the countless trips of moving heavy equipment, massive hours logged in your van, numerous dirty floors slept on, and underpaid shows are worth every second. No education can prepare you for life on the road, but if you enjoy what you're doing you won't mind the learning process."

—Evan Cobb, sax player and booker for Chicago jam band Buddha's Belly, 22

- Get a starting position as a late night **radio DJ** and rock the early morning hours away. You might be able to break in most easily at a local community or college radio station. Make a demo tape of a sample radio show that you can hand out as an audio resume of your on-air voice, style, and taste in music.

- If you have the talent, take it to the local hot spots and **sing or play at a bar or coffee shop**. How fantastic would it be to come home from a night on the town with full pockets instead of empty ones? If you have an international itch, be bold and try performing overseas, where American tunes are often in high demand. I remember hearing Tracy Chapman songs belted out in a small café in Rome and thinking, 'I could do that.' Fact is, I can't. But you certainly can!

- **Work as a counselor at a classical music camp** where you can take advantage of practice spaces and talented company.

- If you have a good voice and don't mind being a big cheese ball, **sing advertising jingles** for extra cash. Mom will be so proud when your chipper voice comes on the radio advertising denture cream!

- Whether you have to lug equipment or take photographs, do whatever it takes to **work for a favorite band or musical group**. Choose a lesser-known group and your chances for getting on board their tour perk up. Community bulletin boards and coffee shops are good places for these.

- **Work at a summer music festival** and fill your sunny days with jazz beats, country rhythms, or classical tunes. Get into the event-planning side of things and you may get to meet some well-known musicians.

- **Volunteer.** You have the power to project your creative gift and raise spirits. Bring your gift to a children's hospital or nursing home between gigs, jobs, and classes. A small generous effort goes a long way and may come back to serve you. You never know who is in your audience.

WRITING

If you were born with a pen in your hand, you have plenty of ways to keep on writing without selling out or starving. Some of today's most famous writers never held "real" jobs. Here are a handful of options.

- Thinking in verse? **Sell your poetry** as song lyrics or to greeting card companies.

- Keep your perspective young by **writing for a children's magazine.**

- **Write travel articles** for a hometown newspaper, a travel book or local English language publications abroad that will invest in your insightful reviews of foreign destinations. Even if this generates zero cash, it will equip you with valuable clips for future endeavors.

- **Organize poetry readings** in a funky coffee shop. Whip up double lattes as you listen to the lyrical shows.

- Got a healthy appetite as well as a thing for writing? Offer your services as a **restaurant critic** for a local newspaper, city magazine, or Internet site. Many publications will take volunteer submissions. Once you prove your tongue to be king connoisseur, your may be able to work out some kind of payment for your contributions (or at least free dinners!).

- Join forces with some techies to make their new Internet company a grammatically correct hit. **Freelance write or edit for a website** and you may land yourself a portable job that you can do from anywhere.

- Want to share your passion with blossoming young writers? Be a **counselor at a creative writing camp or poetry workshop for kids.**

Leap of Faith: Got a good story in your head? Give fiction writing a shot. There are all kinds of awards you can get for a good short story, as well as grants for first time novelists. Plant yourself in a stimulating environment, slow down the pace of your life, and write, write, write. You may just have the great American novel in you, and turning it out in your twenties will make you an even bigger hit. If nonfiction is your thing, plant yourself in a rich environment or quirky job that you can use as material. Also consider starting your own publication with a group of people that share your vision. This is a tough venture for a youngin' but the Internet may facilitate getting your words out there.

A MAN THAT LIVES ON WORDS ALONE

BY JIM SWEENEY, 25

" Trying to make it as a writer just after college is a daunting and usually dispiriting path to follow. Master of Fine Arts programs are one way to go, especially if you can get yourself accepted to one with generous funding. But the last thing you probably need now is more debt, and with too many graduate programs in creative writing, you end up either working forty hours a week teaching freshman composition, or incurring huge debts.

Fortunately, you can hone your storytelling skills and develop your voice without living impoverished in a garret. Find a friend, a fellow aspiring writer, whose work you admire and whose advice you trust, and exchange your work every couple of weeks. Then, find a job, even one you're not thrilled with (you're not going to be doing it forever, right?), just to pay the bills. Write at night or in the morning before work, and when you feel they're ready, submit your stories, poems, or essays to literary journals. (Search for the O. Henry Awards online: they maintain a helpful list of journals and contact information.) Submit again and again—just about every writer has a drawer full of rejection slips, so you might as well start collecting them.

At the same time, search out contests with no entry fees (*Poets & Writers* magazine offers a helpful listing, both online and in their print magazine). And, if you want to see what it would feel like to dedicate yourself to your craft full-time, apply to an artists' colony—you can find a list at *www.artistcommunities.org*. Most of these offer financial support and some offer full fellowships to cover your expenses while you're there.

Most of all, be patient: I've been doing all of this for more than two years since graduation, and I still don't have an agent, let alone a book deal. But my novel's almost finished, and I'm starting to place my stories in magazines. I have a sense that it will all start to come together soon. "

Another valuable resource is **Grants and Awards Available to American Writers** *edited by John Morrone and the Pen American Center.*

THEATER

Drama kings and queens: hear your curtain call! The stage awaits and it would be a crime not to put those theatrical skills to use.

- **Act for a dinner theater company or a local first-run show.** If you don't end up with a part, work backstage for the production to get a peek into the making of a show. Look for a theater with extra ambiance, like a Victorian opera house or a converted barn playhouse. Connections are key so start talking to the dude next to you in the coffee line. Put yourself out there and someone will eventually scoop your creative energy right up.

- **Counsel at a theater camp**, offer to teach an acting class at a local school, or start up an acting workshop.

- Snap your fingers in the aisles as you **usher for plays and musicals**. By the end of the season, you will know all of your favorite show tunes by heart and might have an in to a more technical job backstage.

- **Start up a local theater group** by drawing on dramatic friend circles and students at nearby colleges. A close-knit theater scene will be invaluable in keeping you motivated and connected.

- **Act in a children's theater company** to bring the magic of drama to the kiddies.

Leap of faith: Audition for a part in a play or musical you love. Even if you don't come out with the lead, a spot as an extra could get you on tour with the whole company. If nothing else, a gutsy try out will bolster your courage for the next long shot or soothe your nerves for smaller pursuits.

" Figure out how to go on a cross-country adventure with your friends and get the government to help pay. In 2001 my friends and I received a government grant to tour a piece of performance art across the country. On most road trips people go on boring, schlocky tours or peruse local tourist-dump stops with postcards and other assorted gimmickry. Going as part of a performance group gives you more purpose (which means you don't have to feel like you owe it to your life to get back to your allotted cubicle). Remember, you're a working artist.

We developed a performance that used inflatable costumes and performed it in galleries, outside at some festivals, and in parks. We rented a van and camped to save money. In every city we had arranged for the art gallery to represent us while we were there. Many artists love to network and meet other artists, so we just put down our foamies and crashed at their places. Often they'd show us around and go out on the town with us. We partied in Halifax, Toronto, Montreal, Chicago, New York, and even in little towns like Sackville, New Brunswick.

While you peruse the classifieds and eat mac & cheese, you'll never regret taking this kind of opportunity. Just take stock of the situation: you've travelled with friends for free on your own terms, you've met tons of interesting people from around the country all the while adding to your resume, and you've made many contacts and connections (which will make applying for the next grant easier). If you're lucky, you might make a whole life out of this kind of behavior. Who wouldn't? "

AS FESTIVE AS YOU LIKE IT: Shakespeare Festivals

Thousands of communities around the globe celebrate the great William Shakespeare every year with a line-up of productions. If you love the literary master and never tire of a good soliloquy, then join the troupe! Most Shakespeare festivals take place during the summer months, and many are located in beautiful areas. Central Park's Delacourte Theater is an outdoor theater that was designed specifically for Shakespeare productions, "Bard on the Beach" is Vancouver's waterfront Shakespeare festival, and Shakespeare Sedona sets up stage in Arizona's red rock country. You could take a scenic trip across the country or around the world by way of Shakespeare festivals!

You don't need to be an actor to play a role in the production. Many Shakespeare festivals employ or gather volunteers to usher, work on scenic production, assist in hair and makeup, manage wardrobe, photograph performances, fundraise, advertise, organize membership and do prop construction. So whether you're eager to propel yourself into the spotlight or just looking to extend your literary experience beyond college, join the festive company and enjoy every mid-summer night production.

FILM

The lights and camera are waiting, take action! If you are fascinated by the artistry behind the silver screen, give some thought to pursuing a job in film.

- **Volunteer on film projects**. Join a listserve (such as "women in film and video") and scope opportunities to be a production assistant or a volunteer. If you are willing to work for little (or no) money, you can find yourself killer film projects to dive into. Show up early, work hard, and the chances are good that you'll get called for the next film project (and this time even get paid for doing what you love!).
- **Get that screenplay that has been floating around in your head down on paper**. If you need moral support or guidance, take a screenwriting class or join a screenwriter community (online or in your town). Get additional feedback and help from friends so it's in tip-top shape to mail off.
- **Raise money to make a short film**. You can't move up in the industry without having produced something solid. Hit up friends and relatives, throw a fundraising party, and promise to mention your contributors in your first Oscar speech.
- If you are a movie buff and have a thing for butter-saturated popcorn, try **working in a small movie theater** that shows independent films.
- **Volunteer at a film festival**, whether it be a tiny, fledgling project in your hometown or a bigger name competition that helps you make valuable connections.
- **Join a team in your city's 48-hour film project** and write, shoot, and edit a short film in just 48 hours. Think about it—in just two days you could be a total hit! (*www.48hourfilm.com*).

• **Work at your local independent video store**. The perks are obvious: free movies, endless entertainment, and the company of fellow film buffs!

DREAM JOB AT DREAM WORKS

BY KELLY COONEY, 24

" People say it's all about who you know in Hollywood. But what they forgot to mention is that it's also about who your friends know, who your family knows, or even who your best friend's brother's girlfriend knows.

To make a long story short, I got my job as a storywriter at Dreamworks Animation because I knew someone who knew someone who knew someone. Through this network of people, my resume landed in the company's human resources department. They offered me a job working as a production assistant, which basically meant I was an extra set of hands. I pinned and hauled storyboards, set up meetings, and killed a few forests making copies of scripts, artwork, and reference material. Eventually I was asked to help with *Shrek 2* and was given more challenging roles. My job now consists of tracking script changes, managing deadlines for storyboard artists and writers, coordinating recording sessions with actors, and maintaining communication across the story and editorial departments.

People make the mistake of thinking they need to choose their 'career' immediately after graduating, but the most important thing is to pursue what you are interested in, whether it's business, travel, service, sports, or entertainment. I would have taken any job they offered if it meant working in the film industry. Now I'm doing a job I love and have even found a way to make it my 'career.' My most successful friends are the ones who are doing work they enjoy. "

ARTS UNLIMITED

Don't stop there! Keep your imagination running to find a venue that matches your interests and demands ingenuity. Sharpen your culinary skills as an assistant chef, be a fashion show runner while you perfect that catwalk strut, do stand-up comedy shows on the weekends, intern under a graphic designer, or teach ballet to adorable mini-ballerinas. Whether you are just looking to do some volunteer work on the side or searching for a career, finding your creative niche provides crucial, daily food for the soul.

" I went into college with a very specific goal: to eventually work as a classical dancer. I cannot tell you how many times I was told I would never make it. I ignored people's warnings and forged ahead. About halfway through my degree I realized that although I loved taking classes in ballet, I absolutely loathed performing it. I was the one on stage during Swan Lake cracking jokes to the girl next to her. I then began to consider that I could still be a dancer without being a ballerina. The last place I imagined myself was on a cruise ship in the Caribbean doing Las Vegas style shows. But like I learned, you have to take advantage of every opportunity that comes your way, no matter how scary or crazy.

I don't regret accepting my cruise ship job for a second. I hardly work, get paid to do what I love and get to see some amazing places. What a life! The best jobs fall under the category 'staff positions.' You have a lot more privileges and more time off the ship in ports. Staff positions include entertainment, shop, casino, photography, pursers (information desk), information techs, spa, and security.

Cruise ship employment is especially great for those in their twenties and early thirties. We have two 'crew only' bars where most of our evening time is spent. We live in a dorm-like setting and make friends from all over the world. I am currently living with an Australian, and there are dancers from Romania, Russia, England, Canada, and Mexico on our crew as well. I know if my ship ever docks in these countries, I'll have a home in each one. "

JUST FOR KICKS: JOBS IN THE ENTERTAINMENT INDUSTRY

Ready for a job experience that's totally off the wall? Keep yourself entertained by getting a job in the entertainment industry. Here are some of the most out-there options, guaranteed to make every day a blast and a give you stories that'll have your friends roaring with laughter.

WORK AS A SINGING TELEGRAM. If you like to be the center of attention, could prance around in a French maid costume and a fluorescent leotard in the same night, and know how to embarrass the hell out of people, the singing telegram industry could use your fine skills. Just imagine all of the parties you will attend—even if you do only get to stay for fifteen minutes. You will have the chance to impersonate celebrities, dress scantily on occasion, and most importantly, make around six hundred dollars a week if you really devote yourself to the job. So go ahead, be silly and give it a shot. You'll never have a boring day.

BY TIM ERNST, 22

I'VE GOT A GOLDEN TICKET!

" At a young age I decided that I wanted to change the world through video games. Sound silly and impossible? Thank goodness I didn't think so and kept the dream alive. When I visited my first gaming company towards the end of college, the work world suddenly transformed into Willy Wonka's Chocolate Factory. I was certain that I had found my 'thing.' The game industry is small and hard to get into, as the entertainment industries are, but I had the luck of getting a job and starting less than a week after graduation.

Unfortunately, I am now an oompa loompa. Just kidding. There are a lot of real world duties that accompany this job. Sure I play video games at work, but my responsibilities go far beyond that. I'm learning so much about business, the workplace and an industry that I care about. My advice is to follow your professional dreams right out of college, no matter how crazy they sound.

Call and email people in the industry to make contacts. Networking is arguably the most important skill in finding a job. Look at all the websites and check out what jobs there are. If you are an aspiring gamer, look at publisher and developer sites. Read through the credits of your favorite video game and try to find the email address of someone you admire. Don't be afraid to practice what you want to do before you get a job in it. If your interest is developing, make mods or maps for your favorite PC game. Get involved in whatever community you wish to join, whether it be through the Internet or through a group like the International Game Developers Association. Finally, when you get that job, wake up every morning and enjoy the fact that you are doing what you love. "

JOIN THE CIRCUS! Although you might not have the natural gifts necessary to be a nimble trapeze artist or the darling bearded lady, many circus positions are within your reach. You can work as a clown, ringmaster, animal caretaker, or roustabout (putting up tents, driving buses, and feeding animals) without much experience. Imagine what an experience it would be to see the country with a colorful cast of characters from the greatest show on earth. Take a look at *www.soyouwanna.com* for more ideas. Want to combine your knack for working with children with your passion for the Big Top? Check out Circus of the Kids at *www.circusofthekids.com*.

HEAD TO VEGAS. Work casino security or the poker table, and witness the madness of the glitzy gambling world. If you are female, at least 5'5, and don't mind scandalous attire, try out to be a Vegas showgirl. You can make up to a thousand dollars in one night. Just stay away from the topless shows so your parents can speak proudly of your new venue!

Coming of Age in Sin City

Las Vegas offers a whole slew of service jobs that are surprisingly lucrative. As a valet, you could pull in $50,000 a year (of course, that's assuming you aren't gambling-inclined and don't slap down all of your tips on the nearest black jack table! Those with addictive personalities, beware!). Vegas is a popular choice of conventions and trade shows, which means hotels and conventions centers hire thousands of workers to manage meetings, activities, and the extra influx of tourists. You shouldn't have a hard time finding a job. Call a hotel's Human Resource Department and ask what positions they are currently looking to fill. You will probably have to pass a drug test to get a job in a casino.

Housing in Vegas is also easier to come by than in other resort towns, not to mention cheaper. Browse through online classifieds to get an idea for what job positions are open and what your living options are. You might get lucky and find a notice for an apartment that offers the first month rent-free as an enticement (believe it or not, this sometimes happens in Vegas). This would give you some time to get on your feet, find a job and adjust to the flashing neon lights. Just remember, high roller's room = bad, slot machines = not good either (they don't call them "one armed bandits" for nothing!).

DO STAND-UP COMEDY for a club's amateur night and see if you can make people roar for a living.

" On any given day, I will find myself monitoring cardiac sounds in a pediatric patient and pondering whether a sketch idea about Yasser Arafat on Maury Povich is remotely funny. You see, my life is what one might describe as moderately absurd. I'm willing to bet I'm the only medical student in my class doubling as a sketch comedian. Riding the train into New York City wearing my scrubs from the anatomy lab just reminds me that yes, I am that oddball.

Getting into medical school was far easier than putting on a sketch comedy show in Manhattan (plus, the whole medical school thing isn't as funny. So many different ways to vomit on me). There are six strapping young men in my comedy group, recently given the name 'Trophydad.' We hail from all over the country but met in college where we all did improvisational or sketch comedy. Coordinating schedules to get together to write out the sketches for the next show is always a challenge. One of the initial obstacles was finding a location where we could perform. Luckily, the Drama Bookshop on the West Side was willing to take a chance with our unique brand of ribaldry. Unfortunately, we had to pay them a relatively substantial fee out of our own pockets.

The week before our first show was a bit of a mess. I was attending classes in Connecticut in the morning and commuting into the city for rehearsals at night. Our first show ran for three nights during which there were moments of hilarity and some of awkward silence. But overall the reception was splendid. We also earned back all of the money we put down, and then some. Medicine is an insular little world. Comedy is what keeps me sane. "

WORK AT A LIVING HISTORY MUSEUM and get paid to be a smiling artifact. You might even get to fire cannons or better yet—churn butter! Many museums and centers also have archive research opportunities as well as architecture and archaeology positions. Give these sites a look:

•**Conner Prairie:** An open-air living history museum showcasing 1800's America on a 1,400 acre property in Northeast Indianapolis (*www.connerprairie.org*).

•**Colonial Williamsburg:** A 1700's colonial era museum in Virginia (*www.history.org*).

- **Astors' Beechwood Mansion:** A Victorian mansion in Newport, Rhode Island complete with balls, teas, and murder mysteries. Company members must have singing and improvisational skills (*www.astorsbeechwood.com*).

- **Historic Deerfield**: A New England history museum that offers a unique summer fellowship for a historical study and behind-the-scenes view of a museum. The $7,500 fellowship sponsors room and board, studies and travel for nine weeks (*www.deerfield-fellowship.org*).

- **Chautauqua Institute:** A 750-acre educational center beside Lake Chautuaqua in southwestern New York that hosts a nine-week season featuring art, music, dance, theater, opera, writing, and a world-class speaker series (*www.chautauqua-inst.org*).

THINK OF THE LOCATION OF YOUR DREAMS, and apply to be an entertainer at a resort there. With any musical talent and the ability to schmooze with guests, you could earn yourself melodious and margarita-filled nights on the beach.

WORK AS A STUFFED CHARACTER and morph into the lovable persona you adored when you were little. Hop into a ridiculous costume and head to the baseball stadium or theme park. Wave your arms to the little kiddies, sweat like it is your job, and watch the people fall in love with your furry alter ego. If you're the extra cheery type, aim for employment in "the happiest place on earth"—Disneyland that is. The magical kingdom offers many jobs to students and young people.

DELAY THE REAL WORLD BY STARRING IN THE TV SHOW. If you are a public person who enjoys drama, test your luck and apply to a bunch of **reality television shows**. You might not make money but you may find instant fame (or notoriety) that jump-starts your career down the road. Get started by making a video of yourself—the wilder the better. The popular show *Survivor* claims that they select contestants on the basis of the following traits: "strong-willed, outgoing, adventurous, physically and mentally adept, adaptable and interesting" (they seem to have forgotten to mention hot). You just can't be running for public office at the time of the show (shucks!). Even if you don't make the final cut, you might at least earn a free trip to Hollywood. Some shows fly their finalists out for interviews. If exposing your life on television is not your cup of tea, think about seeking a job behind the scenes of reality television. How entertaining would it be the guy who sifts through people's entry videos all day?

GIVE DJing A WHIRL. Invent a funky new name for yourself like "DJ Exquisite" and bring your turntables to the nearest club. For some extra cash do some club promoting.

> "I started DJing when I was 17, and now as a 25-year-old, I have DJed all over the world, from France to South Africa. I have found that dedicating yourself to the arts is much more rewarding than any day job. I may not make as much money, but I have the opportunity to pursue my love of music. In order to do overseas gigs, I branched out to subsidize trips and networked a lot to utilize connections of friends. Business took off from there. I also do freelance web design and development which has supplemented my income."
> -Aaron Hedges, 25, owner, artist & repertoire agent for label District of Corruption

Apply for a variety of game shows and see who calls you back**.** Who *doesn't* want to be a millionaire? Even if you don't strike it rich, you might return home with a new refrigerator or at least a picture with Vanna White!

A PRICE THAT'S RIGHT

Imagine being paid thousands of dollars to play a game for a few hours. Yes, we're talking game shows, folks. Whether you want to rally all your relatives for a round of *Family Feud* or secretively make an appearance on *Supermarket Sweep*, it's all worth a stab. Even if you don't earn a cent, you'll have a fabulous story to tell for the rest of your life. Remember, this book is all about making you that awesome person everyone wants to date, invite to dinner parties, sit next to on the subway *and* employ—NOT about pulling in the big money. But hey, every so often you get the best of all worlds. Check out the tales of these two young contestants to see what your thirty seconds of fame could be like. A small little fortune might just come along with it.

Fabulous Cash and Prizes

By Conor Knighton, 22

Without a car or anything resembling a paying job, I spent my first couple of weeks after graduation as a struggling actor in Los Angeles stuck in my apartment with the TV on. One afternoon, while cycling through our seven measly channels, it dawned on me that just a few miles from my apartment, happy housewives were walking away with "fabulous cash and prizes" every day. Why couldn't that be me?

I proceeded to spend the rest of the afternoon chuckling while calling various L.A. game shows (listed online) to see if they were looking for contestants. A few auditions later, I was appearing on a nationally syndicated show called *Pyramid*. While it took the check over four months to finally arrive, I won $11,000 and a $2500 ski trip. Years from now, should I become a famous actor, I have already given Leno the perfect clip to drag out during an interview. In the meantime, it plays on loop on the TV in my parent's living room.

do-Do-do . . .

By Tom Ogorzalek, 24

I got my chance to appear on *Jeopardy* like all contestants do: a mixture of luck and skill. Trivia has always been a hobby of mine. From time to time, the *Jeopardy* production team travels the country to hold tryouts. When Washington, D.C. was next on the list, I emailed them to see if I could have a shot. My name was drawn from a hat (lucky break number one) for the chance to try out.

At the tryout, about seventy people sit in a room with a big projection screen and do a free response test, answering the *Jeopardy*-style prompts that appear on the screen. Most of the people in the room are revealed to be incompetent at this point— they're fans of *Jeopardy*, not Trivia nuts. Something like the top ten people pass that test and then you have to turn on the charm. They take you to the front of the room, and you play a mock game of three or four questions.

Being dynamic and charismatic—and really loud—is key here. If you're lucky enough to be picked, it's off to Culver City, CA for the show (you pay your own way). They film several shows in a day, and everything is done randomly, from question selection to contestant matchups. There's no way to really predict what the questions will be, so the best way to prepare is to pay attention to life as it goes by.

Note: Tom did not win his game of Jeopardy *but says it was an honor just being nominated.*

HEADING OFF TO HOLLYWOOD

Show biz is calling you. Well, maybe not by name, but L.A. invites all who want to try for a piece of the classic American dream! Save up some cash, get your glossy photos done, and head west. You will probably have to get a job on the side to keep you generating money between auditions. Try leading tours of a major studio for the hordes of tourists that pass through Hollywood. You can always pick up work as an extra, though you won't make a fortune. If you're a hot young thing, aim for soap opera gigs. They can always use some attractive figures to fill the backdrop of wedding and bar scenes.

Extra! Extra! Check out www.*beinamovie.com* for opportunities to serve as an extra. You won't pay the bills this way, but you will get some cool freebies and might just lollygag for hours beside someone that knows of an opportunity or try-out that can help you get on your way.

ALMOST FAMOUS... And Getting Closer Everyday

To get you extra jazzed up about heading to Hollywood, here are two accounts of ambitious young folks—a rising star and starlet—who have invented their own approach to success in L.A. Keep an eye out for their names in movie credits and play-bills of the future. These two are unstoppable.

Learning the A, B, and Double D's of Hollywood

By Elizabeth Shapiro, 22

Buy any actor's manual and the first thing they will warn you against is naivete. I'm pretty sure all of those books have in mind that their reader is fresh in from Kansas equipped with only a calling for stardom and a piggy-bank for the boob job that will get her there. And so the author makes sure to remind you of the difficulty of the industry, the unlikelihood of success, the sketchiness of trying to get there, and most importantly, the rules.

I should have prefaced this by saying, "You shouldn't listen to me. I am fresh-off-the-boat myself, and my size A cup gives you an idea of the size of my piggy bank." But with that said, I have one great advantage—and so do you—we don't know the rules. And since we don't know them, we cannot be paralyzed by them. One of the great rules that you will quickly learn from any actor's manual, or jaded vet, is that blind mailings to agents are useless, and blind mailings to important agents are criminal. But forget the rules, and let me tell you a different story.

My junior year in college, I decided to go to L.A. and meet with some agents. I was completely in the dark as to how to go about it. I had done extensive research into who was good, but having no connections to make an introduction, I was left with a less discreet method: the telephone. A week after my mailings went out I made follow-up phone calls to a handful of the biggest agents in Hollywood. Using my most important voice—one part nonchalance, two-part condescension, with a dash of impatience—I was able to fool their secretaries (the dreaded gatekeepers) into thinking that I was a Hollywood player rather than a girl sitting in her dorm room. Once I got the big guys on the phone, they were usually so impressed that I got through to them that they agreed to give me a meeting. But with all of this said, there is one rule that you should know. Ignorance can only work when rooted in the knowledge of two things: your talent, and your drive.

The Muffin Man Hits Los Angeles

By Graham Norris, 22

In L.A., no one takes you seriously as an actor until you have an agent. So I dutifully studied up on all the hundreds of agencies out here, put together some nice mailings, and sat back and waited for the movie deal. Shockingly, I had no luck. Didn't anyone care that my Mom thinks I'm the best Hamlet she's ever seen? When I called to follow-up, I heard the same refrain again and again: You can't get an agent until you've had some roles. "But," I'd say piteously, "you can't get roles until you've got an agent." "Welcome to Los Angeles," they'd say.

You want to be an actor? Great. So does everyone watching the Oscars, not to mention the thousands of people moving to this city every year to get the job that you want. Standing politely in line isn't going to cut it. First off, agencies usually ask you not to drop by in person. I started dropping by in person. I started telling agents that I had several interviews lined up with other agencies, often fictional. I flirted with receptionists, regardless of gender. I once brought in a box of muffins from a deluxe bakery and pretended that I'd won them from my acting class for being "Actor of the Month." When one agency called to say thanks but no thanks, I showed up at the time when they were having callbacks for the people they liked and faked confusion about the phone message.

We have been taught all our lives not to do things like that—it'll be so embarrassing if you get caught! The shame! You'll be disowned! Well, it *is* profoundly embarrassing if you get caught, but if everything works just right, then you can stand out for the unique, charming, sparkling genius that you are. And, remember, it only has to work once to get you an agent. I got hired at the place where I pulled the muffin trick.

KEEPING IT REAL

Pick any of the options mentioned in the arts section of this chapter and you'll walk away with a valuable, motivating experience underneath your belt. If you are committed to pursuing your creative passions, now is absolutely the time to make a go of it. Not only will you find out what it takes to make it in the industry, but you will also figure out whether you *want* to devote your energies to making it. You may decide you need to go to graduate school or find some secondary source of income. Regardless, you will walk away with a mature understanding of your artistic discipline and a realistic sense of your future path. One nice bonus of working in your field, on any level, is that you will meet people with the similar interests who are moving in the same direction you are or have already established themselves. Both groups of people can provide you with inspirational company and also connections for the future.

As someone with artistic ability, you can use any out of the ordinary or especially challenging experience as inspiration or fresh material for your work. What famous filmmaker or writer doesn't have a story or work of art that took root in their "poverty" period, before any one had recognized them and they were slaving away at that first big work? Whether you have your eye on greatness or would just like to release and share some of your creative energy with people in your local community, the hunt for artistic opportunity and the adversity that accompanies it will be formative, totally unique, and a source of nostalgia for the rest of your life.

The same goes for the wild array of employment options in the entertainment industry. Though your job might be a bit bizarre and a constant source of amusement among friends, it will carry with it a host of experiences. As the entertainment industry is about pleasing people, a job in the industry will hone valuable job skills. You will be working as a team with your co-workers to make your customers very happy people. If you take that spin on your job, you will be able to market the experience to almost any employer. Portray the lessons you learned with a dose of humor, tell a few anecdotes, and you will get your foot in the door.

Like all of the other possible areas covered in this book, you never know where a short-term job in the industry could lead you. When I emailed Kerry Prep, the owner of a singing telegram company called Prepgrams, asking for information for young job seekers, he responded, "How ironic that what started out for me 23 years ago as something designed to do exactly what your book intends to cover (delay the real world) ended up being a full-time business because I was so damned successful!" Making inventive use of your talents can open unexpected doors. You might spend the rest of your life a clown—but a happy clown with stellar profit margins! Combine your wacky job experience with your fine creative skill and you've got an award winning documentary or best-selling book about the modern day circus. Do something out of the ordinary and you'll always have an audience of interested listeners, readers, or viewers.

CHAPTER SEVEN: A BLAST IN YOUR OWN BACKYARD

I F YOU'VE READ THROUGH ALL OF THE OTHER CHAPTERS, your head is now filled to the brim with ideas for how to make your young years the best time of your life. You feel tugged in a thousand different directions—Southeast Asia, Route 66, New York City, Mount Everest, Las Vegas, Uzbekistan!—and at the same time, reality is gluing your feet to the floor. As much as you may *want* to delay the real world and entertain every thrilling option you come across, life is holding you right where you are. Maybe your parents are pressuring you to come home, or maybe a family situation or illness demands you stay close by your loved ones for a while. Perhaps your numerous loans are starting to whisper, "Pay me, pay me!" or you need to get a start on that lengthy graduate program right away or you'll have gray hair by the time you finally lose the title "student." You've thought it all through, considered all risky alternatives, but you know that at this point in your life, you just can't make it happen.

First of all, personal satisfaction is not an all-or-nothing pursuit. You can always find a way to work in what you love on the side or make it a priority for the near future. If you can't afford a full-time commitment to volunteer work, travel, outdoor adventure, or your artistic passion, keep in mind that there are thousands of ways to incorporate these things into your life on a smaller scale. Don't make the common mistake of abandoning all efforts just because your big plans don't pan out. Sometimes you can't control what you do, but you can control what you make of it and what you devote your free time to. It's just a matter of attitude and resolve.

And who says you have to go flitting around the world to find adventure? Okay, I did—but it's not the only way to give your life a shot of excitement! Sure, it's much easier to spice things up when you parachute your life into exotic lands, but a change of country, or location for that matter, is not essential. In almost any community, you can find all of the elements you need to construct your ideal lifestyle. Downsizing your grand plans just takes a little digging, creativity, and commitment. This chapter is filled with ideas for recent college graduates who don't have the resources or time to pursue their ideal adventure, but are still committed to giving themselves a positive, challenging, and fulfilling experience. Whether you are returning to your less-than-thrilling hometown, or working a monotonous job, there's a way to keep dissatisfaction at bay and make the years ahead ones you'll cherish.

" After a year of volunteering overseas in Puerto Rico, the time came to return to the States, and I didn't have a clue what I was going to do or where I was going to live. I thought that one of those funky jobs in San Francisco that lets you take your dog to work sounded like fun, but when I went home to St. Louis to ponder the decision ahead of me, my priorities changed dramatically. My mother was diagnosed with cancer.

There was no doubt in my mind that while she was undergoing treatment, I would stay in St. Louis. My fear was that if I stayed, I would be missing out on an urban adventure somewhere in the big city. As a self-proclaimed adventure-junkie, that was a big concern. But I came to the realization that life is the adventure you make it out to be, and there is one to be had even in my hometown. The longer I stayed at home helping out at the family business, the more this midwestern city felt like the very place I should be.

St. Louis, like most medium-sized cities, has most things large cities have, just not in the same quantity. I sought out interesting organizations, quickly became involved in volunteering, learned to whitewater kayak, and joined an organization for young professionals that want to contribute positively to the community. Moving back to where I grew up and building connections required just as much energy as moving to a completely new place would have.

Three years later, I still work at the family business (reporting to my healthy mother), and I love my job. I have wonderful friends (none of whom I went to high school with) and I entertain myself with great culture and cuisine. If I need a break, I make sure I allow myself the opportunity to head to the big city or a remote mountain for a little while, but in the end, I'm always anxious to return home. "

After four years of living in the heart of a lively college campus with total freedom, we can't help but cringe at the thought of moving back to our native neighborhoods to live with our parents. But when credit card bills are piling up and you suddenly have to pay for things like medical insurance (the horror!), it's hard to resist the allure of free rent. Many young people move back home after graduation to rack up some savings, to be closer to their families, or to have some transition time before heading out on their own. It's a good temporary solution to the shaky post-college transition. And moving back home doesn't have to be a recipe for stagnation. If you have a positive attitude and a spirit of adventure, your experience can be as worthwhile and stimulating as any other adventure in this book. Here are some ideas about how to do all of the cool things mentioned in previous chapters right in your own backyard.

PROM NIGHT REVISITED
BY MATT VOGEL, 23

" I never thought I would have the opportunity to go to prom again. Yet there I was, a year after college, chaperoning the big event. While just about all of my friends headed to professional school or business jobs right after graduation, I knew that those paths were not for me. Instead, I headed home to teach for a year through an alumni program at the all-boys Jesuit institution where I myself had gone to high school.

The pay (or 'stipend,' as places like to call pathetically low wages for idealistic people) was meager, but the experience was extraordinary. The year allowed me to teach a subject I love, to live with high school classmates who were also teaching for the year, and to have an impact on the lives of still-impressionable youths. I applied for the position in November of my senior year, interviewed over Christmas, and had the job by March. The school wanted responsible college graduates who majored in the subject they wished to teach. In my case, that meant U.S. history. In addition to the stipend, the school provided housing, health insurance, and most importantly, a lot of support and mentoring.

The flexibility of the program also allowed me the free time to pursue activities that I would have had neither the time nor the energy for had I been working the 9-to-5 grind. At what other point in my life will I be able to find the time to coach a sport, tutor multiple students, volunteer several times a week, and train for and run marathons and ultramarathons? And of course, don't forget those high school dances. Wild nights indeed! "

CHAPTER ONE REVISITED: FINDING THE HIGH LIFE IN YOUR HOMETOWN

Approach your hometown as if it were a new place. You are bound to have a different outlook and spin on things as a curious twentysomething than you did as a self-centered teen. Explore all of the things you took for granted and discover all of the area's hidden treasures. A town or city guidebook can help you uncover everything you overlooked growing up. If you were raised in the suburbs, the nearby downtown area might be totally foreign to you, or at least an area you don't know well. You might find a new strip of chic cafés, a sports club or center, free concerts in the park, ample community service options, or a vibrant nightlife in the downtown center. Find out about area bands and musical groups that might give your music collection a shot of novelty. There may also be a young scene of college students and twenty-somethings that will keep your social circle wide and your nights rowdy.

Cool jobs that will help you rediscover your hometown:

- Lead tours at a local historical or tourist spot. You will learn a wealth of information about your local treasure, as well as the history of the region.

- Bartend or waitress in the area's newest night hotspot.

- Work at the local chamber of commerce or tourist office.

- Work at a restaurant or store in an unfamiliar part of town. Hostess at a restaurant in a traditional Italian neighborhood or work at a karaoke bar in a Dominican neighborhood. The new faces, flavors, and rhythms will be a nice change of pace.

CHEAP, RANDOM, AND FUN
Ways to make your homestay worthwhile:

- Go on a pub-crawl and hit up every fine drinking establishment that ever shot you down as a minor. You might even discover that your city has unexpected classy joints, like a martini bar!

- Explore a rural part of town or go fruit picking at the nearest orchard.

- Gut your closet and have a yard sale with all your old stuff. Make some neighborhood kids elated by selling your old He-Man and She-Ra dolls.

- Hang out with your old childhood friends in grown-up ways. Have them over for a tasty barbecue and have a laugh at your awkward days. Go to a wine tasting, rent a box at a concert or playoff game, or take a trip to the nearest big city.

- Trace your family lineage and start planning an exciting trip to visit distant cousins in distant lands. You might arrange that family reunion that your relatives are forever talking about but have never made happen. Push an exotic vacation spot and you could end up scoring a complimentary trip!

- Have a Tuesday night movie club with some friends and watch all of the classics you missed.

- Plan a reunion of quirky old grade school friends and see where life has led the class bully, glue-eater, and smarty-pants.

" I thought my biggest challenge upon graduation was to decide where to go. Bali for the summer? Teaching in Thailand in the fall? The possibilities had my mind whirring. So imagine my disappointment when, a week after graduating from college, I found myself back in my far-from-exotic hometown. It turns out my biggest challenge was not picking an adventure, but financing one. Like so many of my classmates, I left college with a diploma, amazing memories, and zero cash. Soaring idealism comes face-to-face with a crushing reality.

I vowed, however, to make that summer as adventurous, exciting, and cheap as possible, while keeping in mind that the whole experience would eventually get me to that aforementioned dream world. I got a job leading tours of nearby Niagara Falls and met people from all walks of life and all corners of the world. This stint as a tour guide will go down as my absolute favorite job not only because it allowed me to tell ridiculously corny jokes, but because it helped transform my surroundings from 'Ugh, the place I grew up' to a surprisingly fascinating region. And it also showed me that spending a summer at home does not necessarily have to mean boring temp jobs.

With the generous tips I earned with my corny jokes, I was able to finance the kind of adventure I had always envisioned. Just a few short months and many paychecks later, I set out to live in Portland, Oregon for a year to work for a nonprofit. "

CHAPTER TWO REVISITED: GO INTERNATIONAL IN YOUR HOME TOWN.

Although it is virtually impossible to have the abroad experience in your comfortable domestic atmosphere, there are plenty of ways to give yourself a taste of what life could be like transplanted in another country and gear you up for making your dream happen soon. Get some travel writing books that place you in exotic corners of the world and let you feel the nuances and cultural idiosyncrasies of a foreign country, keep your television parked on the travel channel, and rent international films to watch with someone who has a similar case of wanderlust. Seek out an international crowd in your town or city and share with immigrants from all over the world right in your backyard.

Let the incentive to move abroad be like a fire under you; take advantage of every spare minute to advance your goal. Many of the expatriates in this book worked for a number of months at home before taking off for Mexico

City, Milan or Bombay. Think of this time as a crucial stepping stone and funnel your energy into launching yourself "across the pond." As corny as this may sound, make a fundraising sign for yourself. I know someone who had a $5,000 thermostat poster on her wall and filled it in with red marker while waiting tables until she had raised every penny she needed to make her move. This not only motivated her to work a million odd jobs, but also deterred her from blowing any of the money she was making. Thanks to minimum wage laws, a dollar goal is attainable to almost anyone who commits all of his energy to earning and saving.

Cool Jobs That Will Help Get You Overseas:

• Nanny for a wealthy family for a summer. As a young adult with a driver's license, you will be the prime candidate to lead a troupe of kiddies around on their summer adventures. I have friends who scored big time overseas opportunities by nannying. One got an all-expense paid trip to Italy in exchange for her around-the-clock childcare.

• Work at an independent movie theater or rental store. Take advantage of international pickings that will multiply your desire to live on foreign soil.

• Get involved in your local Rotary Chapter, make connections and start the long application process for a Rotary scholarship to study or live overseas.

• Join one of the alternative accommodation organizations listed in Chapter Four and host world travelers in your home. This is a generous way to get your international appetite raging, and also to earn you valuable connections worldwide that will aid you in your future travels.

CHAPTER THREE REVISITED: TAKE IT OUTSIDE IN YOUR OWN BACKYARD. Every region is host to its own unique natural wonders. A gorgeous desert landscape, lakeside-hiking trail, or steep mountain peak might be right under your nose. Find a book about nearby national and state parks or trails, or just start asking around. You will soon have more outdoor adventure ideas than you can possibly carry out. Plus, a physical challenge is a great way to get in shape and ward off the stir-craziness that you might feel at home. It is also a healthy, productive way to funnel your energy and future jitters into an attainable goal. Join a local running club, pound the pavement in good company, and aim to enter some festive local road races. Dig that ancient curly handlebar bike out of the garage and use it to branch out into your surrounding regions while sweating up a storm. Check out *www.backpacker.com* to find outdoor adventures in your neighborhood.

Cool jobs that will give you outdoor adventures in your area:

• Counsel at an area summer camp. You'll get all of the perks of working outdoors, but be close enough to sleep at home instead of with mischievous raccoons.

• Be a guide at a local outdoor adventure company.

• Coach a local school's sports team. You may even be able to assistant coach on your old high school team.

• Lend a hand at a nearby farm or orchard to fill your 9-to-5 with fresh air and sweet nectar. You'll earn your share of fresh goodies to bring home.

• Join a local environmental campaign or cleanup effort.

CHAPTER FOUR REVISITED: EVEN MORE PLACES TO GO. If the travel chapter piqued your interest, don't give up and suppress that wanderlust just because you have to be stationed in one place. Seize the opportunity to explore your area now and then, using your hometown as a home base. Take road trips with old friends. The long ride will give you a chance to catch up on each others' lives (and music tastes), and you will surely discover sites, views, and towns that you had never come across before. Even the smallest states have hundreds of towns, landmarks, parks, and other worthy attractions.

" At age 22, having found myself scooping chocolate-covered almonds into plastic bags for a living, I decided to leave the big city of Vancouver and head for the village where I was born—New Denver, British Columbia.

The choice was practical: if I needed a few months to figure out what it's all about, I might as well do it somewhere beautiful and cheap. New Denver is both, tucked in a spectacular mountain range, and coming up on a hundred straight years of very nearly emerging from its recession. Besides, the move seemed historically fitting. New Denver has long been a place where folks just kind of end up, from steely-eyed prospectors at the turn of the century to bleary-eyed draft-dodgers in the sixties. So off I went.

What I discovered was this: New Denver is really bloody small—under 600 people, not including me. In a place like this, you've got to make your own fun, which for me meant hanging out with friends and family, hiking, reading, writing, and working odd jobs precisely as little as I could manage. And from this experience, gradually, as if by magic, I figured out what I wanted to do with my life (filmmaking, as it happens). I returned to Vancouver with renewed resolve and I've been pursuing my goal ever since.

The point of this, I suppose, is that you can't predict where your sense of purpose or direction will come from. So stay flexible, don't settle, and most of all, don't rush. Put yourself in situations that are comfortable but stimulating, and where you're not so busy struggling to make ends meet that you can't let inspiration in. If no such place comes to mind, I recommend heading for New Denver. You wouldn't be the first. "

DRIFTING WHERE THE HEART STRINGS TUG

BY CHRIS HEANEY, 22

" At my five-year college reunion, after my friends compare the pursuit of Taoism in China's emerald forests to the call of artistic purity in a Mexican art commune, I will slap this less exotic—but no less brave—accomplishment down on the table: I followed love!

Yes, LOVE! That magnificent and terrifying emotion turned this thrill-seeking college senior into a lovesick graduate, happily attached to a wonderful girlfriend and a future that seemed twice as bright as before.

I faced the lonely June after my graduation with only my heart and a beautiful girl to guide me. Throwing caution and our generation's overblown sense of independence to the wind, I got a job in the city she had made her home and drove my overloaded station wagon into the rest of her year. She couldn't get rid of me! But seriously, by following my heart, I let our senior-year fling become a far more lasting and meaningful relationship. The biggest surprise is that we make quite the creative team: she writes, I edit; I make mini-comics, she gives me inspiration. We push each other on and on in love and creativity.

After almost a year and a half of finding fuel for my dreams in those of my girlfriend, I can proudly say I have but one complaint: it's damn hard to fit a job description for 'Romantic' on my resume! "

CHAPTER FIVE REVISITED: CHANGE YOUR COMMUNITY FIRST, TACKLE THE WORLD LATER. Every community has its share of social problems, as well as an entourage of nonprofits struggling to remedy them. Pitch in for a cause that you believe in and give back to your neighbors. You shouldn't have any problem finding volunteer opportunities in your hometown. And sometimes you can accomplish more when you have the stable resources of home such as a car, proximity, and family help. Sign up for Habitat for Humanity and borrow dad's work gloves and hammer. Work at an after school program at a community center and bring your old board games. Be a baby-cuddler in the hospital and draw on mom's expertise. Or use the spacious mini-van to help out a local Meals-on-Wheels chapter. All of these part-time opportunities will put you into contact with fellow community members from all different age groups and backgrounds. If you have a special vision for change in your community and extra time on your hands, create your own niche in community service. Maybe start up an organization in your town like the one you worked at in college, or create a completely unique project in your community.

Cool jobs that will get you involved in your local community:

• Organize an overseas volunteer project for your religious group and you might earn a subsidized trip for your efforts.

• Work at the local United Way chapter.

• Organize holiday community projects in needy areas for your church or a local nonprofit.

• Work as a teacher, volunteer, or tutor in an area school. Drop into your old grade school and high school to see if there are any openings. If you went to a private school, you may not need a teaching degree. As a twentysomething who is actively fighting off the real world, you'll be the coolest kid in school.

• Work or volunteer for a local political campaign or get involved with an upcoming election.

CHAPTER SIX REVISITED: LOCAL CREATIVE JUICES. Tap into the area's arts and entertainment scene to find an activity or job that stimulates your creativity. You may encounter a flourishing community of artists that you never knew existed. More importantly, you will find dozens of opportunities to exercise your passion.

Cool jobs in local arts and entertainment industry

• Get trained to lead tours at a local art or history museum.

• Get a temporary job helping at a local music or theater festival. You might get to run the beer tent and treat all of your friends.

- Host your own cable show to liven up the public access network.

- Join a local culture club to make yourself an avid opera, ballet, and symphony-goer.

- Work behind the scenes of a local TV show. You will have a much easier time breaking into the local television industry than in Hollywood.

- Join in painting a mural for a neighborhood revitalization project.

- Write for an alternative newspaper or magazine.

WHAT TO DO WITH THAT OFF-THE-WALL SCHEME

As a young twentysomething living in Brooklyn, Brandon Chase started taking notes on the edgy coffee shops and salons that splattered the city's artsy district. Then, at age 27, he returned to his hometown of Buffalo, determined to bring something that upstate New York had never seen. Meshing art, dining, drinking, and shopping into a funky hot spot, "Off the Wall Lounge and Eatery" is truly a one-of-a-kind establishment. Seven-months after launching "Off the Wall," Brandon shares some of the secrets to his success as a creative young entrepreneur.

1. "Use your passion. Passion drives you farther than anything. You have to have an eye for funkiness and give people something they're not expecting, but at the same time you want to make the atmosphere welcoming so that everyone has a smile on their face as soon as they walk in the door.

2. "Restaurants are the hardest business to succeed in. Banks are skeptical of loaning money to a young person who wants to open a coffee shop. You have to propose something that is a little bit different than what is already out there."

3. "If possible, look for private funding. Give your idea a lot of thought and put together a detailed mock business plan that you can present to potential backers. If family and friends help you out, you might have lower interest rates than the bank would charge you."

4. "Look for breaks—either grants from your city or state. I've gotten matching grants (for $5,000) and tax breaks because I am located in a 'renaissance' area that the government wants people to redevelop."

5. "Free information is the best information. Look for mentors who can give you advice. I was blessed to have a great businessman behind me—my father-in law."

6. "Interacting with people is not only a perk of this job, but it's the most important part of the business. I meet and work with artists all the time. I have developed a great rapport with my workers, who are about my age. And lastly, but most importantly, you have to be present for your customers. When we opened I was around this place 110 hours a week. People are always taken aback by how young I am and I just say, "I didn't know there was an age requirement on owning a business!"

"You bum off my parents, I bum off yours."

Still cringing at the thought of going home even though you need to save money in a bad way? Propose a casual "exchange program" within your family or circle of friends. Maybe one of your Louisiana cousins would be interested in working in your quiet Pennsylvania town for a summer and you are itching to head south. Work it out between the two families and you've got yourself a new location, with all of the comforts and financial perks of home (no utility bills!). If this doesn't pan out, throw the idea by some friends—or find out if any more distant relations could take you in.

KEEPING IT REAL

If you are coming home for the sole reason of making money as quickly as you can, you can take another approach to your homestay. A popular "get-relatively-rich-relatively-quick" plan is to take on enough jobs to fill up every second of every day, and in the meantime, not spend a cent. This game plan is the best way to earn your freedom quickly. After a summer of working around the clock and focusing only on your goal, you should have enough money to take off and embark on the adventure of your dreams, be it world travel or a job in an expensive city. So as you are frying onion rings or chasing around toddlers, keep dreaming about all the amazing things you will do with that stash of cash that is piling up by the hour. Every time you feel down about your life of menial labor, give this book a read through and start daydreaming up an awesome new adventure.

A Temporary Fix: Temping will help you pack every spare hour with work and wages. While local temp agencies may be your best shot, also give web services a look. Try Kelly Services (*http://jobsearch.kellycareernetwork.com*), Net-Temps (*www.net-temps.com*), and MonsterTrak (*www.monstertrak.com*).

You should however, consider taking the time to enhance your daily life while living and working at home. Doing this will not only prevent burnout and abject misery, but may also help launch you into the future. A solid bank account isn't the only thing that will facilitate a dream job or overseas stint. Your opportunities multiply with every skill you develop. There must be *something* you have always thought it would be cool to be able to do. Why not enroll in some fun classes or free community activities to equip you with handy skills? Here are some ideas:

- **Massage classes:** Knowing how to give a good massage is not only a killer skill for any aspiring heartbreaker, but it could also give you a one-up if you are trying to get a job in a resort. Official certification is a big investment that only makes sense if you are really serious about massage. Otherwise, take a low-key class and make your friends the happiest people on earth as you practice on them.

- **Cooking classes:** Learn how to cook up scrumptious feasts and you will better your chances of getting onboard a private yacht or into the kitchen of any restaurant. Your mother or father may be the best and nearest teacher in this subject area, so hang around during dinner and uncover their culinary secrets.

- **Guitar lessons.** If you are aiming to get an outdoor job, knowing how to strum a guitar will be a major plus. It could help you get your foot in the door of a dude ranch, summer camp, or any type of alternative community. Job or no job, this is just a fantastic talent to have.

- **Lifeguarding:** It is always handy to have lifeguarding certification up your sleeve. Use this skill to rack up money during your time at home, and then to secure a job in a tropical destination.

- **Foreign Language:** Spend time working or volunteering in an ethnic neighborhood to turn your classroom language knowledge into a practical skill. Use your language proficiency to break into the lucrative and perk-filled tourism industry.

- **Bartending:** Use your local connections to get a job as a beginning bartender and pick up the tricks of the trade. It can be hard to get work in nice urban bars without any experience, so informal training will definitely come in handy ("official" certification is not necessary and often a money-making scam). Bar skills will ensure you can pull in money wherever you place yourself. You'll also be a more adept host and party-thrower for the rest of your life.

- **That Class 101:** Keep learning. Invest in your education. It's not just a degree, but an ongoing process. If you have the chance to take a seminar or lecture on a topic that interests you, go for it. You might just appreciate it more than you did in the college daze.

"After graduation, I forked over $250 to Georgetown University's continuing adult education program for eight classes on "Comics as Literature." I got to apply literary theories like deconstruction, queer theory, and post-colonialism to comics' unlikely canon of 'Batman: The Dark Knight Returns,' 'Maus,' and 'From Hell.' I would heartily recommend taking courses after graduation, if only to teach you that education is something to which you can always return.
—Chris Heaney, 22

- **Standardized Tests.** If you are pretty sure you'll apply to graduate school in a few years but can't bear to think about returning to academia just yet, at least consider taking whatever test you'll need. Sometimes it's nice to cram and get these out of the way so you can go off and have your adventure worry-free. I took the GRE two days before leaving the U.S. for a year and although it was a headache (SAT revisited, but this time feeling considerably dumber and paying the criminal test fee myself), it would have been a much bigger pain had I tried memorizing obscure vocabulary words while also learning a foreign language. I was very relieved to have the test behind me when it came time to apply to graduate schools.

"My job as assistant director of admissions at Canisius College has given me the chance to tour all through Central America, meeting with high school students in Guatemala, Nicaragua, Honduras, Costa Rica, and Belize.
—Katie Kinder, 26

ON A COLLEGE KICK

You may have more of an attachment to your university than your hometown. If you don't mind being the big kid on campus, take a look at some of the ways you can extend your college years and take advantage of all your school has to offer:

- Work as an admissions counselor. One of the best perks of this job is that you will probably have the chance to travel. If you are in charge of international students, this could mean a free ticket overseas.

- Get a job in student affairs, coordinating events, or organizing meetings.

- Work for your favorite professor on a research project, experiment, or book. If you are lucky, this could earn you some prestigious recognition and maybe the chance to travel as well.

- Be a residential counselor. This will keep you in touch with college students and also provide you with free housing right in the heart of campus.

- Work as a student director of a study-abroad program and accompany the whole gang of gringos overseas. A good way to better your chances for obtaining such a job is to start off in student affairs and build experience in university services.

- Part-time moneymakers:
  - Be a test bunny for psychology department experiments. Get paid ridiculous amounts of money by the hour to do wacky things, like petting tarantulas.
  - Promote a campus bar or work as a drink promoter for your favorite alcoholic treat.

SAYING NO TO SELLING OUT
BY BRIAN WALLACH, 22

" My shock in leaving college was softened by the fact that I had a nice job as an investment banker lined up as soon as I graduated. However, within two months of working sixteen-hour days and almost every day of the weekend and sitting in my little cubicle in a suit and tie designing an Excel model for a potential pitch, I realized that this was not the life that I saw for myself when I had entered college four years ago. The fear of not having a job was not enough to prevent me from leaving the investment bank.

Amazingly, I ended up working at the admissions office for my alma mater. I honestly love my life now. It's a little weird living in the same town where I went to college and not being a student anymore, but I realized very quickly that the real world of suits, long days, and repetitive work will always be there for me when I want it. Many people have asked me if I regret leaving my high-paying banking job and I can honestly say no. When I look back on life, I want to be able to say that I experienced a lot, lived a lot, and had fun while doing it. "

Remember to use your time at home to launch yourself into the next exciting stage of your life. Talk to neighbors, old teachers, and the guy next to you in the ice-cream line. You never know whose uncle knows the manager of a ski resort or whose Portuguese friend needs a housesitter for the summer. A friend of mine was working at a bead store in her hometown when her boss announced that she was opening a store in Puerto Rico. Soon my friend was on her way to the Caribbean, where she was paid to be part of a challenging entrepreneurial and creative project in a (quasi-) foreign location. Keep your eyes and ears open, make and save piles of money, acquire all of the valuable skills you can, and never stop dreaming up ways to craft the perfect adventure. It's just around the corner!

CONCLUSION

THE POSSIBILITIES THAT FILL THIS BOOK SPEAK FOR THEMSELVES. You now know that there are enough fabulous experiences out there to keep you stimulated and very content until the day you die, let alone through your twenties. You're pumped, you're jazzed, you're giddy, you're ready to roll. But before you toss this little book aside and get on with your adventures, just bear with me until we settle this question of the looming real world.

Remember way back in the introduction when I laid out the most crucial pillars of post-college wisdom from young adventurers? The tenth one was "REDEFINE REAL." That should have been your first clue that this book wasn't about blowing off time before responsibility reached you with its nasty claws. If the message were just to put off the inevitable, then I would have enumerated a million ways to stay in academia with your nose in dusty books. But you won't find a grad school chapter here, and for good reason. This book is all about taking responsibility for your personal education and throwing yourself into the realest world there is.

ɦ 'You're going to CUBA to work in a nursing home? Couldn't you just do that here?' a friend's parent asked me on the eve of my departure to Havana. I couldn't help but feel a bit silly and wonder what peculiar experience I had signed myself up for.

My senior year in college, I applied for the Samuel Huntington Public Service Fellowship. Because I was up against nearly one hundred applicants from around the country, my proposal had to stand out. Luckily, I was dead set on a country that Americans don't usually visit and a cause young people hardly ever champion. I showed how my background in Spanish and eldercare made me the perfect passionate twenty-one-year-old to lend a hand to struggling Cuban nursing homes. And when the fellowship committee grilled me about how I would get permission from the U.S. government to live in Cuba, I promised them I would find a way. By some miracle, and in the face of skepticism from many Cuba experts, I did.

I could never have imagined how outlandish my daily reality in Cuba would become. I spoon-fed more plantain puree than I ever knew existed. I interviewed an eighty-two-year-old woman who had fought with Castro in the Sierra Maestra mountains and assumed I was a spy from the CIA. I hitchhiked rides in automobiles older than my parents (including a hearse that I flagged down on a country road) and learned to walk unflinchingly through a sea of hisses and air-kisses on the streets of Havana, which is much harder than it sounds.

Before I even left the island, my Cuba experience began aiding my future prospects—giving my graduate school applications an added oomph and convincing potential publishers that I wholeheartedly believed in my book's message. I become more convinced every day of my guiding mantra: it almost always serves you to do things a bit differently than most. You gain uncommon expertise, find a path more tailored to who you are, taste something truly unique, and set yourself apart for the rest of your life.

Sure I could have worked in a U.S. nursing home—there's one right around the corner from my childhood home. But I have the rest of my life to work in my own backyard, and just one shot at making today spectacular.

Carpe Diem. ɥɥ

What is more real than working with your hands, pushing your body against the elements, living in a slum halfway across the globe, sharing with people from countries you didn't know a thing about, or learning what it takes to make people feel satisfied? What is more real than that exposing yourself to realities, or placing yourself in the heart of the unfamiliar?

Before you start to carve out a living for yourself in a comfortable place, let your education run a few more years, in a different, more unique, more hands-on way. Give yourself a chance to make up your own mind about the world, in that short time between being taught and tasked by educators and employers. You have a small window of opportunity to focus solely on yourself—your interests, your development, your curiosities, your satisfaction. There are so many things out there to soak up. Fluency in Swahili is something that you may never use again once you settle back into your hometown in Minnesota, and your boss at the law firm might care less that you can communicate with locals in Kenya. But learning to think in a foreign language expands your mind beyond the base of words it is accustomed to drawing on; no other mental exercise compares. If you don't prioritize your development as a person and a world citizen, no one else will.

If you take a gutsy course of self-exploration after college (rather than a job at a faceless corporation that you have no particular interest or personal investment in) you will probably end up in a niche that is much more fitted to your passions and capacities. All cubicle jokes aside, there is nothing inherently wrong with a stable job. Rather the idea is to step up to bat in the employment field with a more confident sense of what you are committed to and where your strengths lie. The job market is so enormous, holding a million specialized nooks and crannies, each with obscure but fascinating positions. Most people who have interesting jobs got them by doing interesting things first. They weren't there in the office filing and answering phones the Monday after their college graduation.

Once during a long taxi ride in Havana, I got to talking with my young cab driver. He had been planning to immigrate to the U.S. for years, and was still waiting for the opportunity. I asked why he wanted to leave his country and he gave me the typical laundry list I had heard dozens of times: economic opportunity, more freedom, a better life for his family. But then he paused and tried to articulate a more unique sentiment: "To be . . . a little more of a person."

You just *know* when something's missing. It's nearly impossible to find it when you stay locked in the status quo and sign your life over to monotony. Don't let what you don't know about yourself scare you into a safe choice. Take off, throw convention to the wind, and find a way to survive by doing what makes you feel alive today. Life is too short to let other people set your agenda. Don't take cues from your peers unless you admire them. Redefine real as you see fit. Let it take you places you never imagined you'd go. Surprise everyone, and then yourself, too. Make the momentum of what you start now carry over into a life philosophy. Watch as your career prospects improve, your path becomes crystal clear, and your life is nothing less than a daily joy.

Drop me a post card from Timbuktu. While you're at it, visit *www.delayingtherealworld.com* and share your adventures with young people across the world.

ACKNOWLEDGMENTS:

Many thanks to the folks at SPS Studios who first gave this book a shot, especially Josh Lambert who was a terrific editor and offered his own ideas about charting an alternative course. A huge thank you to my personal team of editors—also known as the Kinder family—especially my parents who read the book countless times and my big sisters who contributed their own tales and lent all of their friends and acquaintances for comment. Molly, I could not have finished this from Cuba without your awesome efforts. Christopher, your tender support carried the book through to its completion! Thanks to Judith Riven, for being so kind as to give me and my book a chance, to Jennifer Kasius, for believing in *Delaying the Real World* and turning it into a new, stronger book, and to Jennifer Huntington and the Samuel Huntington Foundation, for giving me the chance to pursue my own enriching path. Endless gratitude to Karen Bidgood, Steven and Susan Schutz, Delbis Gomez, Ruchika Budhraja, Kate Kelly, Carol Weston, and the entire Running Press team. Lastly, special thanks, to all of the young adventurers who contributed stories and advice to this book. You are not only the reader's inspiration but the author's.